OUR WORK
IS BUT BEGUN

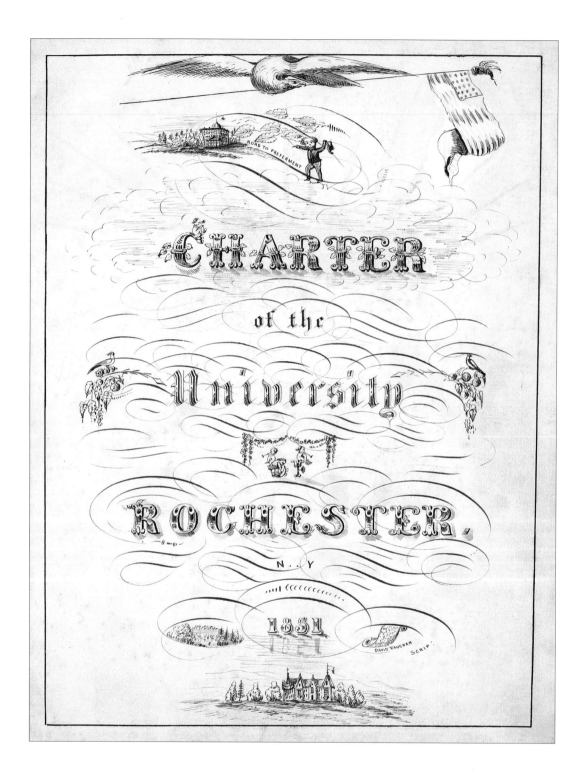

The original Charter of the University was granted in 1851 by the Regents of the University of the State of New York. It provided for the "establishment of an institution of the highest order for scientific and classical education."

OUR WORK IS BUT BEGUN

A History of the
University of Rochester
1850–2005

JANICE BULLARD PIETERSE

FOREWORD BY JOEL SELIGMAN
AFTERWORD BY PAUL BURGETT

MELIORA PRESS
An imprint of University of Rochester Press

First published 2014

Meliora Press is an imprint of the
University of Rochester Press
668 Mt. Hope Avenue, Rochester, NY 14620, USA
www.urpress.com
and Boydell & Brewer Limited
PO Box 9, Woodbridge, Suffolk IP12 3DF, UK
www.boydellandbrewer.com

hardcover ISBN-13: 978-1-58046-503-8
paperback ISBN-13: 978-1-58046-504-5

Library of Congress Cataloging-in-Publication Data

Pieterse, Janice Bullard.
    Our work is but begun : a history of the University of Rochester, 1850–2005 / Janice Bullard Pieterse ; foreword by Joel Seligman ; afterword by Paul Burgett.
        pages cm
        Includes bibliographical references and index.
        ISBN 978-1-58046-503-8 (hardcover : alk. paper)
        ISBN 978-1-58046-504-5 (pbk. : alk. paper)
        1. University of Rochester—History. I. Title.
LD4721.R533P54 2014
378.747'89—dc23

2014018812

This publication is printed on acid-free paper.
Printed in the United States of America.

Contents

This first version of the University seal—with hand pointing upward—
is carved on a bench located in the Eastman School of Music.
The school opened in 1921; the seal was redesigned in 1928 to include the
symbols of music and medicine.

Foreword

By Joel Seligman

JANICE PIETERSE'S NEW HISTORY OF THE UNIVERSITY OF ROCHESTER TRACES THE PROGRESS of the University from a small undergraduate program to a robust, nondenominational research university by the conclusion of Tom Jackson's presidency in 2005. This is a remarkable story of progress, evolution, and change, deeply influenced by the confluence of talented faculty, pivotal friends and donors, the vicissitudes of the city of Rochester, and the emergence of a fundamentally important new social institution, the research university.

The path to today's University of Rochester was not linear.

Martin Brewer Anderson, the University's first president, celebrated "The Ends and Means of a Liberal Education" in his 1854 inaugural address, implicitly agreeing with Cardinal Newman's assertion that "[k]nowledge is capable of being its own end"[1] and firmly rejecting vocational learning as "that which strictly belongs to the trade."[2] Anderson was a man of fervent principle who opposed an elective curriculum, dormitories for students, and university athletics.[3] For Anderson, "the foundation of this University was based on faith and prayer." This was a different world. Tuition in 1852–53 was $30 per year. The first graduating class had 10 students.

In its first 50 years under the leadership of Anderson and David J. Hill, Rochester succeeded as a university in name, but a college in fact. Housed for the first 11 years in the United States Hotel, the University was small, with an enrollment of 216 students in 1897; sectarian, long with an express require-

---

1 Newman quoted in Clark Kerr, *The Uses of the University,* 5th ed. (Cambridge, MA: Harvard University Press, 2001), 2. An earlier version of the first pages of this foreword was presented in my inaugural address in October 2005.

2 M. B. Anderson, *The End and Means of a Liberal Education: An Inaugural Address, July 11, 1854* (Rochester, NY: William N. Sage, 1854), 7.

3 Arthur J. May, *A History of the University of Rochester, 1850–1962* (Rochester, NY: University of Rochester, 1977), 31–32, 62–65, 68, 84.

Joel Seligman

ment that the president be a Baptist[4]; but accommodating to the fundamental reorientation then occurring in American higher education.

Harvard University's Charles Eliot popularized the elective system for undergraduates after he began there as president in 1869.[5] By 1891, the University of Rochester was steering a course between "the Scylla of conservatism and the Charybdis of reform."[6] In his last report as president, David Jayne Hill proudly informed the trustees that the University "offered all but two [of the] courses that President Eliot . . . reported as those most frequently chosen by undergraduates [at Harvard]."[7] Significantly, as early as his inaugural address, Hill emphasized "the growth of science [as necessitating] a great revolution in pedagogical methods. . . . Museums, laboratories, and apparatus are now indispensable to respectable collegiate instruction . . . It is now impossible to teach the natural sciences, even in their elements, by the use of text-books alone."[8]

These reforms were bounded. Among the most significant American educational innovations in the late 19th century was the founding of Johns Hopkins in 1876 as a graduate school that focused on research. Harvard soon emphasized graduate professional schools. In the late 19th century, the University of Rochester lacked the means to join these and other leading universities in the early development of graduate education.[9]

Then an almost miraculous series of events occurred. During the 35-year presidency of Rush Rhees, a small regional college was transformed into an authentic national university. Rhees provided the academic leadership for this transformation. But more than anyone else, George Eastman was responsible for today's University of Rochester.

In the first decades of the 20th century, new facilities for science and engineering were opened, largely funded by Eastman and Andrew Carnegie.[10] These buildings made possible our first engineering degrees in 1913[11] and an approximate doubling of the University's enrollment to 433 students in that same year.[12]

After World War I, Eastman's munificence increased. In 1918, Eastman posed to Rush Rhees the type of question that every university president

4 May, *History of the University of Rochester,* 26, 105.

5 Charles W. Russell, "Charles W. Eliot and Education," *Journal of Higher Education* 28, no. 8 (1957): 433.

6 May, *History of the University of Rochester,* 100, quoting Professor William Morey.

7 Ibid., 101.

8 David J. Hill, *The American College in Relation to Liberal Education: The Inaugural Address of President David J. Hill, LL.D., June 19, 1889* (Rochester, NY, 1889), 20, 23, 21.

9 Kerr, *Uses of the University,* 10.

10 May, *History of the University of Rochester,* 132–47.

11 Ibid., 145.

12 Ibid., 148.

yearns to hear: "Why don't you have a music school?"[13] Within months, Eastman committed himself to providing Rochester with two magnificent concert halls and a school of music "surpassed by no other in the world."[14] From the opening of the University of Rochester's Eastman School of Music in 1921[15], the basis was provided for what is widely regarded today as one of the finest music programs offered anywhere in the world.

Nearly simultaneously, Eastman provided decisive support for the founding of the University of Rochester's School of Medicine and Dentistry. In 1919, Eastman endowed what was then known as the Dental Dispensary and now the Eastman Institute for Oral Health.[16] The following year, after the personal advocacy of Abraham Flexner, author of the influential critique *Medical Education in the United States and Canada,*[17] Eastman committed himself to a pledge of $4 million that initially funded approximately one-half of the School of Medicine and Dentistry. Flexner, who then served as Secretary to the Rockefeller General Education Board, persuaded John D. Rockefeller Jr. to fund $5 million, with the Strong family providing the final $1 million. Eastman added another $2.5 million in 1923, wryly observing: "If I had known his baby was going to grow so fast I should probably have told Flexner to take it back at the beginning, but it was such a pretty baby that one does not want to give it up without a struggle to help support it."[18]

These gifts placed the University of Rochester in the vanguard of a revolution in medical education. The School of Medicine and Dentistry followed the model of William H. Welch, MD, of Johns Hopkins Medical School and Flexner's celebrated 1910 report. For admission, the school required an undergraduate degree to ensure that students were grounded in chemistry, biology, and physics. The medical school was linked both to a University and a teaching hospital and emphasized "learning by doing" with a full-time faculty that demonstrated a vigorous commitment to research led by the medical school's initial dean and future Nobel laureate George Whipple.[19]

Eastman also decisively facilitated the relocation of much of the University to the River Campus, which now aptly includes the iconic

---

13 Vincent Lenti, *For the Enrichment of Community Life: George Eastman and the Founding of the Eastman School of Music* (Rochester, NY: University of Rochester Press, 2004), 23.

14 Ibid., 36.

15 Ibid., 49–69.

16 May, *History of the University of Rochester,* 188.

17 Abraham Flexner, *Medical Education in the United States and Canada: A Report to the Carnegie Foundation for the Advancement of Teaching* (Boston: The Merrymount Press, 1910).

18 Eastman quoted in Kenneth Ludmerer, *Learning to Heal: The Development of American Medical Education* (New York: Basic Books, 1988), 272. See also May, *History of the University of Rochester,* 190; *The First Decade: 1926–1936, The University of Rochester School of Medicine and Dentistry and Strong Memorial Hospital* (1936).

19 May, *History of the University of Rochester,* 190–213.

Rush Rhees Library.[20] Among other consequences of the more capacious campus was a dramatic expansion of graduate education. In 1925, the University of Rochester awarded its first PhD degree.[21] Today approximately 44 percent of our students are graduate students.

Eastman's final gift to the University of Rochester was the largest single bequest made to an American university through the time of his death in 1932. The $51 million total of his bequest and other gifts provided the nucleus of the University of Rochester's endowment, which long after World War II was among the five largest in the country. Pieterse reports that these gifts would be equal to more than $800 million today.[22]

The complexity of our University accelerated after World War II. Four new schools emerged from existing departments by 1972.[23] The Warner Graduate School of Education and Human Development would provide a distinctive emphasis on interdisciplinary research[24]; the Hajim School of Engineering & Applied Sciences would include the first optics program in the country and later add a biomedical engineering program; the Simon Business School would set an international standard with Jensen and Meckling's pathbreaking work on agency costs[25]; and the School of Nursing would achieve national prominence for consolidating nursing clinical care, education, and research within its Unification Model.[26] In 1952, the Board of Trustees unanimously approved President de Kiewiet's plan to consolidate our men's and women's campuses into one college. In 1970, our Laboratory for Laser Energetics was established.

Allen Wallis pledged, "[t]o each his Farthest Star" at his 1963 inaugural, and under Wallis and his successor, Robert Sproull, the University of Rochester fortified its position as a Research One university, buoyed by expansive post–World War II federal funding.[27] Dennis O'Brien addressed the challenge of undergraduate education, proclaiming, "Let our signature be liberal education in a professional world,"[28] adding the distinctive Take Five undergraduate year and endorsing both metaphoric and physical bridges to the Rochester community. Tom Jackson's presidency will be remembered for the 1995

20 Ibid., 214–25.

21 Ibid., 230.

22 Richard Whitmire, "Benevolent George," *Rochester Times-Union,* October 10, 1981; see p. 48 below.

23 May, *History of the University of Rochester,* 323–26, 343.

24 Robert Kraus and Charles Phelps, eds., *Transforming Ideas: Selected Profiles in University of Rochester Research and Scholarship* (Rochester, NY: Meliora Press, 2000), chap. 6.

25 Michael Jensen and William Meckling, "Theory of the Firm: Managerial Behavior, Agency Costs, and Ownership Structure," *Journal of Financial Economics* 3, no. 4 (1976): 305.

26 Kraus and Phelps, *Transforming Ideas,* chap. 10.

27 See generally Hugh D. Graham and Nancy Diamond, *The Rise of American Research Universities: Elites and Challengers in the Postwar Era* (Baltimore: Johns Hopkins University Press, 1997).

28 Dennis O'Brien, Inaugural Address (October 1, 1984), 12.

Renaissance Plan, which, among other topics, articulated our model of decentralized administration; the 1996 Medical Center strategic plan; and the distinctive Rochester Curriculum of the College.

But the transformation of a small liberal arts college into a Research One university, replete with seven schools, a dental center, a Laser Lab, the Memorial Art Gallery, a leading academic health center, and several affiliated programs, fundamentally challenged the University's sense of collective identity. We were no longer "a single community . . . of masters and students,"[29] but a confederacy of separate communities, united by a common name, a common governing board, and a common location. As University of California president Clark Kerr stated in his exploration of "The Idea of a Multiversity":

> The multiversity is . . . not one community but several—the community of the undergraduate and the community of the graduate; the community of the humanist, the community of the social scientist, the community of the scientist, the communities of the professional schools; . . . the community of the administrators.[30]

To Kerr, the multiversity best could be characterized "as a series of individual faculty entrepreneurs held together by a common grievance over parking."[31]

I hold a more sanguine view. We are one University, powerfully bound by values that are responsible for this and other research universities being among the most significant social institutions in the world today.

We are first, and unabashedly, committed to the idea of academic excellence. We pride ourselves, regardless of school or department, on hiring the best teachers, scholars, and clinicians and limiting tenure to those who satisfy rigorous standards. Our students are admitted selectively, based on the comparative strength of their qualifications. We are, as former Harvard University president Derek Bok observed, distinguished by our sense of competition—"for faculty members, for students, for funds . . ."[32] This commitment to excellence has provided some of the finest scholarship, the finest teaching, the greatest health centers, and the most outstanding science the world has ever known.

As former Columbia University provost Jonathan Cole memorably wrote in *The Great American University* in 2009:

---

29 Kerr, *Uses of the University*, 1.

30 Ibid., 14.

31 Ibid., 15.

32 Derek Bok, *Higher Learning* (Cambridge, MA: Harvard University Press, 1986), 14.

[I]t is the thousands of scientists, scholars, and administrators who have been dedicated to their work on a daily basis that have truly put our universities at the top. Their ambition to excel and their fierce competitiveness to be "the best" have led American research universities to become the engine of our prosperity. The laser, magnetic resonance imaging, FM radio, the algorithm for Google searches, Global Positioning Systems, DNA fingerprinting, fetal monitoring, scientific cattle breeding, advanced methods of surveying public opinion . . . all had their origins in America's research universities, as did tens of thousands of other inventions, devices, medical miracles, and ideas that have transformed the world. In the future, virtually every new industry will depend on research conducted at America's universities. . . . The universities have evolved into creative machines unlike any other that we have known in our history—cranking out discoveries in a society increasingly dependent on knowledge as its source for its growth.

Long before it became fashionable, we encouraged collaboration and interdisciplinary study at the University of Rochester. The Rochester ideal long has championed a well-rounded education for all students, including those in a specific major or graduate degree specialty. After World War II, the University of Rochester School of Medicine and Dentistry initiated its own distinctive biopsychosocial model of medical education, linking science and the humanities.[33] In 1963, our Center for Visual Science linked scholars from optics, psychology, electrical engineering, brain research, and ophthalmology. More recently, our bioengineering, data science, and digital media programs have emphasized multidisciplinary collaboration.

Academic freedom is a second fundamental value of our University. Academic freedom, meaning the freedom of our faculty to research, publish, and teach without outside direction or restriction, is powerfully fortified by the institution of tenure. Subject to the adequate performance of their duties, our professors enjoy a freedom distinctly greater than that of business, government, or military employees. Academic freedom can be characterized as the ultimate social bet that individual merit is more likely to produce outstanding scholarship and teaching than thought directed by command and control.

Diversity is a third fundamental value of this University. Universities have learned that the exclusion of persons based on gender, race, nationality, religion, or sexual orientation, among other formulae, limited their ability to provide the most outstanding teaching, research,

---

33 Kraus and Phelps, *Transforming Ideas,* chap. 6.

and scholarship. Few memories are more cherished in the history of the University of Rochester than that of Susan B. Anthony persuading our Board of Trustees to admit women to the class that entered in 1900.[34] It is a measure of significant progress that today over half of all students enrolled in four-year American colleges and universities are women.[35]

A commitment to diversity, however, goes beyond an ending of typological exclusions. As the United States Supreme Court majority memorably wrote in Grutter v. Bollinger,[36] "student body diversity is a compelling state interest that can justify the use of race in university admissions"[37] because of such substantial benefits as promotion of cross-racial understanding, breaking down of stereotypes, empathy for persons of different races, the likelihood that diverse students "will contribute the most to the 'robust exchange of ideas'"[38] and, I would add, better preparation of all of our students for the intensely competitive multicultural world in which they will live and work.

Our goal, as Grutter stressed, is a university "that is both exceptionally academically qualified and broadly diverse."[39] This is a goal not limited to student admissions, but extends to each facet of our University.

There is a fourth fundamental value that has been recognized since the first presidential inaugural address.[40] We are committed to the greater Rochester community. We are proud to be an urban University; proud to be the major health care provider in this region; proud that our students, faculty, alumni, and staff are deeply involved in community service; proud of the role we perform as employers, consumers, and neighbors in a community and region we dearly love. We have become the largest employer in our immediate geographic area and the generator of an increasing number of new businesses.

We serve our community best by striving to be the most outstanding university that we can be. That is why universities are magnets for the economic progress that is the key to our increasingly knowledge-based society. We have also substantially contributed to the arts in a community celebrated for music, art, and dance. Our ties to Rochester are inextricable and continue to grow.

For our faculty, students, and alumni, Rochester is our home, but the world is our stage. Modern transportation and communications have

---

34 May, *History of the University of Rochester,* 113–21.

35 See, e.g., US Department of Education, National Center for Education Statistics, Integrated Postsecondary Education Data System (IPEDS), 2004.

36 Grutter v. Bollinger, 539 U.S. 306 (2003).

37 Ibid., 325.

38 Ibid., 329, 333.

39 Ibid., 333.

40 Anderson, *End and Means of a Liberal Education,* 63–64.

made ours an ever-shrinking world. Our faculty, students, and staff today come from more than 110 nations; the University has affiliated initiatives in 35 countries.[41] We are providing scholarship, research, and teaching designed to be of value across the globe. The University of Rochester will increasingly be part of an international community of higher education.

The significance of this evolving higher education community highlights the importance of our commitment to academic excellence, academic freedom, and diversity. For the University of Rochester and the American university generally, these are our comparative advantages. The leading research universities do not provide the least expensive education, nor the simplest, nor the most comfortable. We pride ourselves in involving our students and faculty in open and rigorous debate, original research and scholarship, and the challenge to work effectively in what will be a world of the intellect largely without borders. During the 21st century, academic knowledge, innovation, and highly trained professionals will be valued as never before.

One hundred sixty years ago, Martin Brewer Anderson concluded his inaugural address with the stirring peroration: "Our work is but begun."[42]

History is in part the study of consequences. What we have recently achieved or in the future will achieve can be related back to the determination and courage of our founders, who in 1850 began our University, to the commitment of pivotal friends, most notably George Eastman and consistently outstanding Boards of Trustees, to extraordinary faculty, students, staff, alumni, and administration.

Let me express my especial gratitude to Janice Bullard Pieterse for effectively capturing this saga and updating earlier historical accounts, including that of Arthur May. Janice has the unusual combination of reporting skills, historical sense, understanding of academe, and the ability to write lively prose with style and grace. She explored the University Archives, interrogated experts like Nancy Martin and Paul Burgett, and interviewed a number of key University actors, including the living former presidents. The result is a history that I have thoroughly enjoyed reading, and I hope that you will enjoy it, too.

---

41 University of Rochester; International Services Office; Office of Study Abroad; Office of the Dean, The College; Office of the Dean, School of Medicine and Dentistry; Office of the Dean, Eastman School of Music; Office of the Dean, School of Nursing; Office of the Dean, Simon Business School; Office of the Director, Eastman Dental Center.

42 Anderson, *End and Means of a Liberal Education,* 9.

ROCHESTER.

Engraving of the city of Rochester from the west, 1853. The United States Hotel, first home to the University of Rochester, is the four-story redbrick building near the bridge on the left side of Main Street, the prominent avenue at center.

Foundation

Martin Brewer Anderson, 1853–1888
David Jayne Hill, 1889–1896

THE COUNTRY WAS YOUNG, STILL STRETCHING WEST WHEN THE BAPTISTS OF NEW YORK State began in 1847 to consider establishing a university in Rochester. This city on the Erie Canal—known as the first westward boomtown—had swelled a hundred times, to 30,000 people, from what one astonished settler recalled as a "howling wilderness."[1] It was the largest flour-milling center in the world. With more than 30 churches, 4,000 homes, and 100 mills and factories,[2] a university seemed a fitting addition.

Churches were leading the way in a flurry of U.S. college building that reflected the optimistic expansion of the era, wrote historian Frederick Rudolph. Nearly 250 enduring schools sprouted between the Revolution and the Civil War. An effort by the Presbyterians to establish a college in Rochester had just fallen apart, to a certain extent because of objections from the community's leading Baptist, who worried the institution would be too sectarian. The Baptist denomination already had a new college in New York, Madison University, chartered as an outgrowth of its established theological seminary. But Madison— later renamed Colgate—was on poor financial footing, with uneven support from donors. Its picturesque hometown of Hamilton, in rural, central New York, was bypassed by new railroads and the Erie Canal by 30 miles. Professors complained of stagnation and isolation.

"You know how often I have had a depression of feeling, from the extreme loneliness and inactivity of our secluded place, especially when returning to it from the bustle and vivacity of the great cities and thor-

---

1 Ruth Rosenberg-Naparstek, "Rochester's Pioneer Builders: *Relinquishing* the Reins of Power," *Rochester History* 47, nos. 3–4 (1985): 3-4.

2 Blake McKelvey, *Rochester on the Genesee* (Syracuse, NY: Syracuse University Press, 1973), chaps. 2 and 3.

Meliora

Asahel Clark Kendrick, one of the University's first professors, is credited with suggesting *Meliora* as the University's motto. On May 15, 1851, the faculty voted "to recommend to the board the adoption of the word *meliora* as the motto for the seal of the University, the device to be a hand pointing forward and upward."

Meliora is a form of the Latin verb *meliorare*, meaning "better." It may be used to mean "better things," "ever better," or "for the pursuit of the better."

The term has been prominent on University seals, which have been revised twice since 1851. Homecoming became Meliora Weekend in 2000. In 2011, *Meliora* became the key inspirational message in the $1.2 billion capital campaign, *The Meliora Challenge: The Campaign for the University of Rochester.*

oughfares from which we are so effectually cut off,"[3] wrote Madison professor John Raymond after a clammy, bumpy, nine-hour stagecoach ride home in October 1847. Raymond, later Vassar College president, continued: "My only consolation was that there was some prospect of an effectual and permanent change. And most devoutly did I pray for the success of all measures tending thereunto."

Momentum built from a meeting a few weeks earlier in Rochester. Madison trustee and Albany civic leader John N. Wilder helped lead a meeting of the "Friends of Madison University" in the First Baptist Church on September 12, 1847. Wilder presented a resolution: Before considering investment in improvements to "dilapidated" buildings at Hamilton, the Board of Trustees at Madison should apply for state legislative approval to move to Rochester.

Wilder, one of Rochester's most fervent advocates, set out the argument: Madison would be better endowed in a city where members of the Baptist denomination could more easily see its progress and therefore be inclined to invest in its future; Rochester was the center of a large, wealthy agricultural district; the city was distinguished for its "favorable regard" for education; it was easily accessed from all points; and students and faculty would enjoy cultural advantages of a city, including lectures, libraries, and literary societies.

Madison trustees and the Baptist Education Society of New York were swayed, but the proposal did not sit well with Hamilton residents. Litigation over the university charter tying it to that community resulted in a permanent injunction against the move.

Rochester proponents pressed ahead. "I myself went with Messrs. Wilder and Sage . . . from store to store and from house to house, in city and country, soliciting subscriptions to the University,"[4] recalled Rochester newspaper editor and prominent Baptist Alvah Strong.

Wilder settled in Rochester, renting the mansion of the city's first mayor, where University supporters would gather. He took the lead on a new Board of Trustees, which obtained conditional approval from New York State to operate a university. The effort drew interdenominational support. Wilder's sister's husband, Presbyterian Everard Peck, a Rochester banker, became a strong proponent, as did Episcopalian Frederick Whittlesey, a prominent lawyer and Yale graduate.

The founders assembled a committee to develop Rochester's curriculum and set about finding suitable facilities. Former Madison

3   John Howard Raymond and Harriet Raymond Lloyd, eds., *Life and Letters of John Howard Raymond* (New York: Fords, Howard, & Hulbert, 1881), 161.

4   Jesse Leonard Rosenberger, *Rochester and Colgate: Historical Backgrounds of the Two Universities* (Chicago: University of Chicago Press, 1925), 111.

professors Asahel Kendrick, Thomas Conant, John Raymond, and longtime Rochester education advocate Chester Dewey worked with trustee Robert Kelly—a founder of the predecessor to the City University of New York—to develop the University curriculum. Kelly visited Brown and Harvard Universities. President Francis Wayland of Brown, a leading voice in Baptist education and controversial advocate of scientific electives—urged Wilder: "Try to establish an institution that will teach what people will pay for learning."[5]

The committee designed two tracks, one toward a traditional bachelor of arts centered on classical studies; the other, a radical path that would grant a bachelor of science letting students omit study in Greek or Latin. "It appears . . . there are weighty reasons for trying the experiment," the committee's Plan of Instruction report said. "The wants of the community are to be regarded."

This was a noteworthy decision. Debate on electives and scientific study formed a core conflict among American academics. "Involved in this struggle was a whole cluster of related issues, many of the highest significance," said John S. Brubacher and Willis Rudy in *Higher Education in Transition*. "Perhaps the central one was the following: Should the American college remain predominantly religious in orientation, training for Christian piety and a broad liberal culture or should it become essentially secular, serving the interests of utilitarianism, social efficiency, and scholarly research?"

The University declared itself committed to "high Christian education" in keeping with Victorian-era social norms while asserting itself nonsectarian and welcoming students from any denomination. The first students granted full scholarships in the University's outreach to Rochester city school students were Catholic, Presbyterian, and Jewish.

"It is the aim of the Faculty, in connection with the discipline of the intellect, to inculcate a pure morality, and the great truths and duties of evangelical Christianity," stated the 1852–53 catalog. Yearly tuition was $30. Room and board with Rochester families ran $2 to $2.50 a week.

The trustees, realizing funds did not permit new construction, rented a large, brick, former hotel on Buffalo Street, later Main Street. With fresh paint, carpet, new pine furniture, and planks set over the rutted front walk, the canal-side United States Hotel offered an "air of homelike neatness and elegance," by one account. Five professors, most from Madison, signed on at $1,200 a year. A treasurer and a janitor completed the staff.

---

5   Arthur J. May, "The Year of Decisions: 1850," in *A History of the University of Rochester: 1850–1962*, accessed January 9, 2014, http://www.lib.rochester.edu/index.cfm?PAGE=2347.

Most Quoted Alumnus

Francis Bellamy, author of the original Pledge of Allegiance, graduated from the University in 1876. After graduate study at the Rochester Theological Seminary, Bellamy served as a Baptist minister for 11 years and then became a writer at the *Youth's Companion* magazine. At the *Companion*, Bellamy helped organize a national public school celebration of the 400th anniversary of Columbus Day. Thousands of school children recited the first pledge in that celebration of 1892. Bellamy did not at first claim credit for his original text: "I pledge allegiance to my Flag and to the Republic for which it stands—one Nation indivisible—with Liberty and Justice for all."

"As the Pledge gained fame many were eager to claim credit for its authorship; however, the controversy focused primarily on James Upham and Francis Bellamy, who were editor and associate editor of the *Companion* at the time," a University archival record said. Francis's son, David Bellamy, produced voluminous documentation supporting his father's claim, which was upheld by the U.S. Flag Association in 1939, eight years after Francis Bellamy's death. The Library of Congress Legislative Reference Service in 1957 declared Bellamy the Pledge author. The phrasing of the Pledge has been revised over the years, including Congress's addition of the words "under God" in 1954.

Our First Home

The United States Hotel had been a hotel, de facto railroad depot, and temperance house by the time the new University acquired it. This image shows the building in the early 1920s when the ground floor included a barbershop, cleaning business, and a general store.

"Well, the thing is done," wrote Raymond after a simple opening ceremony November 5, 1850. "The university is no longer a thing of hope, a possibility and a promise, but a reality, substantial, visible, and alive. We open under cheering auspices, with a larger number of students than we had reason to expect."[6]

"We question whether a college has ever been started in our country with such facilities and advantages at the outset," praised Martin Brewer Anderson, editor of the Baptist newspaper the *New York Recorder*. Three years later Anderson would take his role as the University of Rochester's first president.

The earliest students told of arduous days. "In the first place, we are compelled to work too hard," 16-year-old Azro Dyer, a freshman in 1852, wrote to his father in Kentucky. Dyer awakened at 5:30 a.m. to study, went to chapel at 8:45, and attended classes through the morning. He studied later in the day and heard lectures at night.

"In my opinion, our time is crowded with too many studies—just to think—Greek Reader, two Greek Grammars, Algebra, analysis of the English language . . . Milton, Exercises in synonyms, history and

6   Raymond and Lloyd, *Life and Letters of John Howard Raymond*, 256.

Alpha Delta Phi Fraternity pin belonging to
George Bowerman, Class of 1892

EARLY FRATERNITIES

Thirteen brothers of Alpha Delta Phi met secretly for the first time in the janitor's quarters of the United States Hotel in September 1851. The students had transferred from Madison University, where many had defied Madison faculty rules and were inducted into the Alpha Delt chapter at nearby Hamilton College.

Rochester faculty also generally were disapproving of fraternal societies—thought to foster competitive cliques or rambunctious behavior—but Alpha Delt had key support in early acting president Asahel Kendrick, a professor of Greek who had been a classmate and close friend of Alpha Delta Phi founder Samuel Eells.

"This was enough," an ADP account said. "He knew that any brotherhood conceived and established by Brother Eells must be good."

"Prayers and odes, essays and debates were standard features of Alpha Delta Phi meetings, held in total secrecy, and it became customary for brothers who were scheduled for (orations) to speak their pieces in chapters . . . before public performances," wrote University historian Arthur May.

Delta Psi also debuted in 1851. Delta Kappa Epsilon was chartered five years later by the parent chapter at Yale. Delta Upsilon, known as the "equitable fraternity or anti-secret confederation," was founded in 1852.

Student journals shed light on the significance of fraternal friendships. Truman Backus, Class of 1864, wrote January 5, 1861, after the holiday break: "The old business, of study, was prosecuted to day. It is hard work to begin mental labor after a spell of

relaxation—took me three hours to get started—my right hand almost forgot its cunning after having been shaken by the *Brothers* this morning at the chapel—My interest, in AΔP, will never abate. Taylor, Potter and self skated an hour on the river this afternoon, is pleasant exercise but a fellow needs a cushion under him to catch the bumps he gets."

The fraternities provoked controversy at first. "Professors who had come from Hamilton, with the exception of Kendrick, regarded the 'Greeks' with hostility, but that mood softened rather quickly into a posture of harmony and mutual helpfulness," May wrote. "On behalf of the fraternities it was claimed that they encouraged high standards of character and academic achievement among the brothers."

Essays once a week," Dyer wrote. "Now there is nine lessons, and consequently some are neglected. The Old saying, 'If you have too many irons in the fire some will get burned,' is very true."

Charles A. Dewey, son of faculty member Chester Dewey and a member of the last graduating class—1861—from the old hotel, recalled: "At noon the three consecutive hours of recitation ended. The men, half asphyxiated, were glad to escape into the fresh air."[7]

Social opportunities were scant, Dewey said. Students formed literary, secret, and fraternal societies and took in public lectures.

William O. Stoddard—later secretary to President Lincoln—remembered exploits with college buddies that included dropping into a public séance of the Fox sisters and trying to swim rapids in the Genesee River.

"During all of my college days, I was a regular attendant at church, but we boys were in the habit of distributing our presence around among various houses of worship, according to circumstances,"[8] Stoddard said. "Perhaps some of the influential circumstances wore bonnets . . . and needed company to and from the meetinghouses."

The hotel was intended as a temporary home but lasted 11 years because of financial constraints. Charles Dewey said it seemed quite satisfactory for the young institution. "On the ground floor were the chapel, two recitation rooms, the chemical laboratory, the geological collection and, entered from the street, the halls of the Delphic and Pithonian Societies, where a goodly number of students, afterwards distinguished at the bar or in the pulpit, learned to debate. On the second and third floors were the small library and other recitation rooms. A few narrow apartments in the upper stories served as a dormitory. President Anderson did not approve of that form of gregariousness. He wished the students to be separated, finding homes in private families."[9]

Trustees turned to Anderson in the University's third year of operation. Wilder had been an early choice but declined due to new business affairs in Albany. Kelly, Wayland, and others also were considered. Albany statesman Ira Harris—later a friend to President Lincoln—acted as chancellor, mostly for formal events, but faculty members and William N. Sage, the treasurer for 40 years, ran the school day to day.

Anderson, a prominent voice among Baptists, supported the University as editor of the *Recorder*. He had taught Latin, Greek, and mathematics at his alma mater, Waterville College, which became Colby College. At six feet three and with rugged features to match a

---

7 Charles A. Dewey, "Recollections of Earlier Rochester," University of Rochester Library Bulletin 5 (1950).

8 Harold Holzer, *Lincoln's White House Secretary: The Adventurous Life of William O. Stoddard* (Carbondale, IL: Southern Illinois University Press, 2007), 131.

9 Dewey, "Recollections of Earlier Rochester."

Statistics

In July 1851, the University reported to the New York State Regents that it had started the year with 82 students. Seven were "honorably discharged," three left for causes unknown, and five dropped out. The average age of the 10 graduating students was 24.

In his *Outline History of the University of Rochester* in 1886, Professor Joseph H. Gilmore presented enrollment statistics reflecting steady growth until the Civil War, when young men joined the Union Army or left college under financial hardship.

Martin Brewer Anderson, 1862. "Not to become strong and able with such a beginning is to fail," Anderson said in his inaugural address July 11, 1854. "Our work is but begun."

stern disposition, Anderson earned comparison to the rocky coast of his home state of Maine. "When I, then a boy, saw him for the first time stride through our streets, I got the impression that he had come to conquer the town,"[10] recalled Augustus Hopkins Strong, president of the Rochester Theological Seminary. "In the vigor of his prime it was difficult to say whether he belonged to Rochester, or Rochester belonged to him."

Anderson hesitated, however, at the University's offer. The institution had not met its $100,000 endowment goal. And at 38, he believed himself an unseasoned inferior to the scholars there.

---

10 Asahel Clark Kendrick and Florence Kendrick Cooper, *Martin B. Anderson, LL. D.: A Biography* (Philadelphia: American Baptist Publication Society, 1895), 200.

Helen Wilkinson, 1893
Wilkinson, a nonmatriculated student, was the first
woman to officially attend classes at Rochester.

Women at the University

Several of the individuals who took a lead in the founding of the University of Rochester also tried to found a college for women. Professors Chester Dewey and John H. Raymond, trustees John N. Wilder and Azariah Boody, and lawyer Lewis Henry Morgan supported the 1852 effort to start the Rochester Female College or Barleywood Female University, wrote University historian May.

The campaign fell apart, apparently for lack of funding, and Boody gave his farmland intended for the women's college to the University of Rochester. But in the hometown of Susan B. Anthony, pressure built for equal opportunity.

Women were admitted to some University lectures in the 1870s, and some were enrolled as special students by 1881. By the mid-1880s a local women's group known as the Fortnightly Ignorance Club—which met regularly to pose and research questions on issues from Darwinism to hoop skirts—began pressing for coeducation at the University and raising money to fund it.

"Hardly had David Jayne Hill assumed the presidential office than several societies of Rochester ladies . . . intensified the demand for coeducation and requested that the University trustees indicate how much money would be required," May wrote. "Miss Susan B. Anthony, Mrs. Mary T. L. Gannett, wife of the Unitarian minister, and Mrs. Max Landsberg, wife of the rabbi at B'rith Kodesh, marshaled the forces of embattled feminism.

University faculty overwhelmingly supported admitting women, and trustees were said to be sympathetic, but alumni opposed the idea. Hill expressed approval of a coordinate women's college if funding were available. At a large reception in honor of suffragist Elizabeth Cady Stanton, Hill made a vague remark that drew national attention.

"The wife of President Hill of the University had just presented him with twins, a girl and a boy," wrote Stanton, "and he facetiously remarked [that] if the Creator could risk placing sexes in such near relations, he thought they might with safety walk on the same campus and pursue the same curriculum together."

In 1898, two years after Hill left for a career in U.S. diplomacy, Rochester trustees agreed to matriculate women students if $100,000 were raised to help underwrite the cost of more students. "Glory, Hallelujah!" Anthony proclaimed. "This is better news to me than victory over Spain. It is a peace-victory, achieved only by the death of prejudice and precedents."

A two-year, door-to-door fund-raising campaign raised $40,000. The trustees later lowered the requirement to $50,000. Susan B. Anthony famously pledged her life insurance policy, which later was returned, to meet the goal. In September 1900, 33 women registered for study.

Susan B. Anthony, 1895

When plans for the construction of a new campus at Prince Street were confirmed, the Class of 1858 inaugurated the custom of planting a class tree. The graduating students gave speeches, and each senior tossed a shovelful of dirt over the roots of an elm sapling, wrote historian Arthur May. The seniors then joined hands for a hymn. The tradition of planting a class tree continued into the 1890s.

"I am in much anxiety about the course I ought to take,"[11] he confided to a friend. "I am younger in years and as a scholar than any one in the college department . . . I can carry there no reputation either as a preacher or a scholar, beyond that of any ordinary man of my age. Nearly all the men there are ripe scholars and men of character in the State, while I, poor dog, have no roots except these few that have shot out in the last three years. I am distressed at this aspect of the case. The Faculty have said everything that it was proper for them to say, but I know that I shall go, if I go at all, on a sort of probation. There is great work to be done there . . . God help me."

Anderson accepted the position out of a sense of duty. He had been raised in a firmly Baptist household where education was valued highly. Universities served as an equalizing force in society, he thought, "giving to man a superiority over his accidents."

"Considerations of a personal nature alone would have led me at once to decline the proposal which your letter conveys,"[12] Anderson wrote to the trustees July 1, 1853, "but other motives which it seemed wrong for me to disregard have so influenced my mind that I have decided to accept the office which you have tendered me."

"The foundations of this university were laid in faith and prayer," he continued. "Its patrons had in view the glory of God and the highest well-being of man. So long as it shall continue true to its original design we may confidently expect the best wishes of the good and the favor of the Almighty."

Anderson was a classicist and generally disapproved of Wayland's "new education" at Brown University espousing utilitarian electives. Anderson valued original investigation but steered the University toward a traditional humanistic course. "A true man," he said in his inaugural address, "is the noblest product of earth; a nobler thing than a clergyman, a physician, an advocate, or a merchant. Let us shape our educational systems to make *men*, and upon this foundation we can superimpose the special learning which may prepare them for the special pursuits of practical and professional life."

He believed that denominational control of a college was essential but resisted excessive influence, including a church on campus, wanting students to feel free to worship at churches of their choice.

Students witnessing his frequent, unscripted chapel addresses were not likely to forget them. "The boys look on with awe," Frederick Gates—Class of 1877 and eventual advisor to John D. Rockefeller Jr.—wrote to his father. "I feel as I did on viewing Niagara Falls." The sermons centered on

11 Ibid., 119.

12 May, "Portrait of a President," in *History of the University of Rochester.*

CHAPTER 1

Requirements of the Bachelor of Arts and Bachelor of Science

With a nod to an unfolding national debate over the nature of American higher education, a committee of trustees and professors presented a significant deviation from traditional study for students at the new University of Rochester.

"The whole subject of education, in all its stages and departments, is undergoing an investigation, such as it has never before received," said the report to the trustees September 16, 1850—almost two months before the start of classes.

The Board approved the plan, which included a track that let students pursue a bachelor of science degree without studying Greek or Latin. Rochester would be one of the first American institutions of higher education to offer the degree.

"The plan above sketched will seem a bold one to many who have been accustomed to regard the established system as defining the limits within which a safe, sound and thorough education must be confined," the report on a plan of instruction said. "The feature which will strike them as a radical and dangerous innovation, is the permission to omit Latin and Greek in the regular undergraduate course

and admission to a degree without any knowledge of them."

Committee members agreed that extended study of the languages of ancient Greece and Rome exposed students to critical knowledge of vocabulary, philosophy, ancient civilization, and "examples of patriotism and heroic virtue." However, "A course of useful and sound education can certainly be arranged without them," the report said.

Freshmen and sophomores would study history, literature, mathematics, "natural philosophy" (science), and lan-

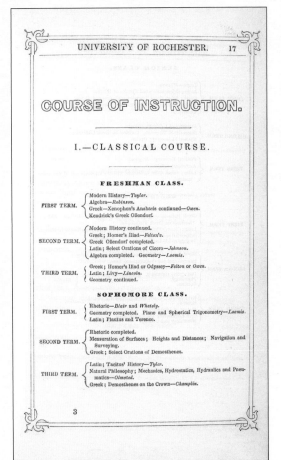

guages. Coursework diverged during the junior and senior years: All students would pursue extensive study in literature and philosophy, but students in the bachelor of arts track would, with the consent of faculty, choose additional courses from three subject areas—mathematics and mechanics; natural sciences, including chemistry; and Greek or Latin. Bachelor of science students could elect to study French or German and would pursue studies in both of the scientific departments.

Admission criteria differed for students in the two tracks. Students seeking a BA would need to pass exams in English, Latin, and Greek grammars; Caesar's commentaries; Virgil's *Aeneid;* Cicero's *Select Orations;* translating English to Latin; geography; and "all the rules of Arithmetic." Students pursuing a BS would need to pass tests in spelling and definition; reading, writing, geography, and English grammar and composition; American history; ancient history and geography; the U.S. Constitution; and arithmetic rules.

"No student shall be admitted to the Freshman Class who has not arrived at the age of fourteen years, nor to an advanced Class, unless at a corresponding age," the plan said.

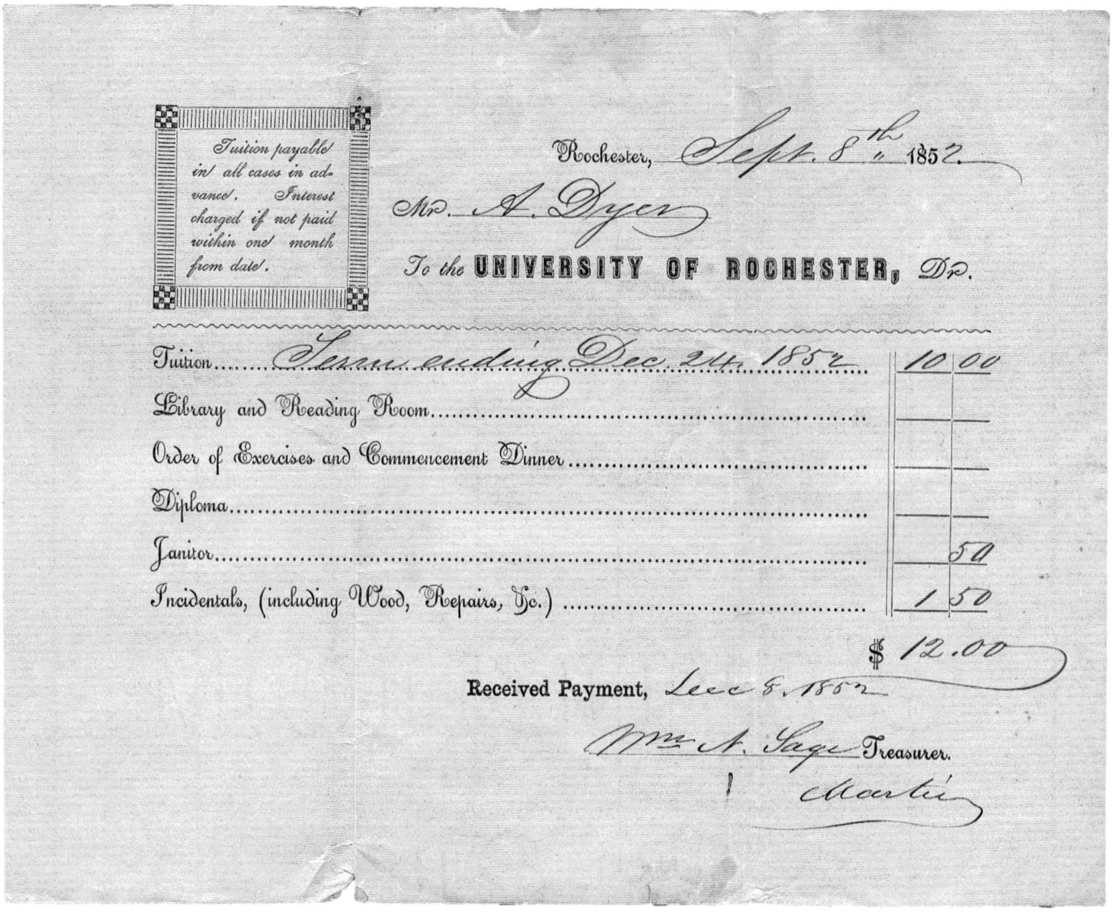

Rochester, Sept. 8th 1852.

Mr. A. Dyer

To the UNIVERSITY OF ROCHESTER, Dr.

Tuition payable in all cases in advance. Interest charged if not paid within one month from date.

Tuition........Term ending Dec. 24th 1852	10	00
Library and Reading Room........		
Order of Exercises and Commencement Dinner........		
Diploma........		
Janitor........		50
Incidentals, (including Wood, Repairs, &c.)........	1	50

$ 12.00

Received Payment, Dec 8. 1852

Wm. A. Sage Treasurer.

Martin

The Cost of an Education

Above, a receipt for the tuition bill of Azro Dyer, who entered the University in 1852. Right, an account of Dyer's expenses sent to his father: "Perhaps it would be better that you should always know the state of my pecuniary affairs. I submit the following Account current to your perusal."

Perhaps it would be better that you should always know the state of my pecuniary affairs, I submit the following Account current to your perusal.

Aug 27th/52 To amt received at Rumsey $120,00

Cr

Sept 1st	By total travelling expenses	$26,65
" 2	" Barber & Collar	35
" "	" Vest 175 Shirts 200	3,75
" 3	" Blacking	14
" "	" Bill at Hotel	2,00
" 4	" Collars	83
" 8	" 1 Greek Lexicon	4,50
" "	" 5 other School Books	5,12
" 9	" P.O. Stamps	50
" 22	" paid toward board	5,00
" 24	" Concert 25 Knife 40	65
" 27	" discount on 20$ Key money at 1½ percent	30
" "	" Paper & Stationary	51
" "	" Contributions	12
" 30	" Oil & Lamp	41
" "	" Cover for Book 13 Envelops 6	19
Oct 2	" Coat	9,00
" "	" Slippers	1,10
		$59,92
	Balance	$60,08

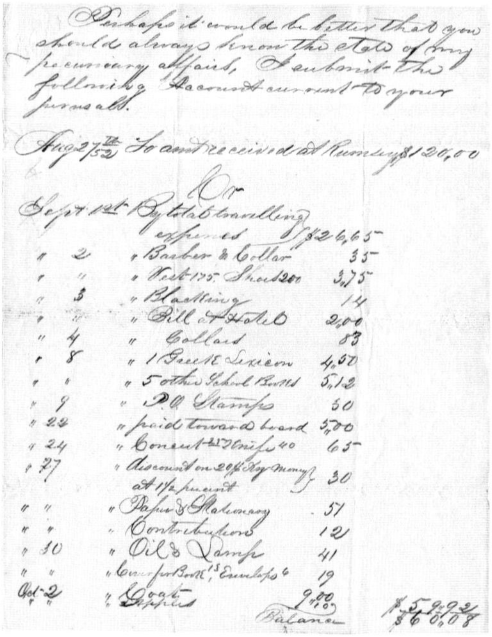

elements of good character, with Anderson's voice and body movements quickening to a fury. "Dr. Anderson gave a lecture in Chapel on punctual attendance on all duties of life," Francis Forbes entered in his diary. "The man that is always behind seldom makes his mark in the world."

Financial constraints vexed Anderson throughout his 35-year tenure. The first hit came in the national financial panic of 1857, prompting continued delay on hopes for a new campus. A trustee's donation of several acres of farmland and a $25,000 state grant—the only public money received during Anderson's tenure—enabled a celebrated move to Prince Street and the University's first campus building, Anderson Hall. Through the 1860s Anderson grappled with effects of the Civil War.

He was never supposed to handle University finances. The Board chair would have that responsibility, trustees assured him. But the role fell to Anderson for several reasons, including Wilder's death from a heart attack in 1858. Anderson told the Board the demands of academic leadership and his duties as campus patriarch left little opportunity for fundraising.

"I know that I am needed to raise money, but I am also needed at home,"[13] he said. "Every one of the young men sent to me is a special and most important trust. . . . No class passes through my hands which does not contain more or less young men who are on the eve of ruin from wayward natures, bad habits, or hereditary tendencies to evil. These men must be watched, borne with, and if possible saved to the world and to their families. This requires constant attention and untiring labor. . . . Those private and confidential reproofs, suggestions, and admonitions which, when judiciously made, do so much to form manners and character, must be attended to by the president."

Anderson would have liked to lead an institution such as the revolutionary, research-oriented Johns Hopkins University, founded in 1876, he confided to a friend. There was no great philanthropist yet inspired to enable such development at Rochester. Observers later noted Anderson's efforts probably focused too narrowly among Baptists.

The University's 20th-century transforming donor barely was paying attention. George Eastman sought only occasional technical help from chemistry professor Samuel Lattimore in the fledgling stage of his photography giant.

Still, by the time Anderson retired in 1888, the campus had three buildings and 172 students. His local standing had grown to the extent that community leaders debated whether a statue in his honor belonged on the University campus or in front of the city courthouse.

Charles Augustus Thompson

Charles Augustus Thompson, Class of 1891, was the first African-American graduate of the University. He had lived previously in Buffalo and in Memphis, Tenn. Thompson attended Buffalo State Normal School, later Buffalo State College, before enrolling at the University of Rochester, according to alumni records.

After earning his bachelor's degree at Rochester, Thompson studied theology for a year in Memphis and then served as principal of the Porter School there from 1892 to 1907. Also during his time in Memphis, Thompson was president of that city's John G. Whittier Historical Association and of the state teachers association.

Thompson proceeded with a variety of studies and professions. He attended the Howe Institute, later Lemoyne-Owen College, in Memphis, from 1906 to 1907. The Howe Institute, one of the earliest private educational facilities for African Americans in Memphis, provided practical education for students of all ages. Thompson next obtained a position as a clerk in government service in Washington, where he also studied at Howard Medical College and at Central Chiropractic College. From 1913 to 1915 Thompson served as pastor of Fairmount Heights Presbyterian Church in Washington and then embarked on a career in chiropractics. Thompson died in Washington in 1934.

The University's David T. Kearns Center for Leadership and Diversity in Arts, Sciences & Engineering holds a lecture series named in Thompson's honor.

---

13 Jesse Leonard Rosenberger, *Rochester: The Making of a University* (Rochester, NY: University of Rochester, 1927), 196.

Anderson wryly described the role of president for a friend: "The college president is expected to be a vigorous writer and public speaker. He must be able to address all sorts of audiences upon all sorts of subjects. He must be a financier able to extract money from the hoards of misers, and to hold his own with the trained denizens of Wall Street. He must be attractive in general society, a scholar among scholars; distinguished in some one or two departments of learning; gentle and kindly as a woman in his relations to the students, and still be able to quell a 'row' with the pluck and confidence of a New York Chief-of-Police. If he fails in any one of these elements of character, he is soon set down as unfit for his position. . . . In looking back over my career, I am simply astonished at having been able to bear up under my responsibilities as long as I have."[14]

With Anderson's strong endorsement, trustees next reached out to David Jayne Hill, who had led a transformation at Bucknell University. Hill's relatively short tenure at Rochester, 1889 to 1896, represented important change that set a new platform for his better-known successor.

Hill first asked the faculty to help develop curricular revisions that broadened course offerings from 46 to 95, weakening the emphasis Anderson had placed on the classics and giving students more freedom to choose electives.

The new president also supported athletic programs and facilities, describing them in his inaugural address as "a hundred time more effective against rowdyism and barbarism than proctors and informers." Intramural and intercollegiate football, baseball, and track took off. When Hill announced he would leave the University in 1896, alumni tried to sway him by kicking off a campaign to build a gymnasium. It was built in 1900. Hill soon embarked on a career in international diplomacy, serving as the U.S. assistant secretary of state from 1898 to 1903 and in later separate roles as minister to Switzerland, the Netherlands, and Germany.

Most significant were Hill's efforts to broaden support for the University, which meant changing perceptions of Baptist control. "To show that the University was not merely a stronghold of Baptist interests, he preached the baccalaureate sermon . . . in the Central Presbyterian Church instead of in the First Baptist Church . . . then followed this at the alumni dinner with a new plea for community support," wrote Hill's biographer, Aubrey Parkman. A national trend away from denominational education was "revealed with unusual clarity" at Rochester during the Hill years, Parkman said.

---

14 Joseph Ricker, *Personal Recollections: A Contribution to Baptist History and Biography* (Augusta, ME: Burleigh & Flynt, 1894), 307–8.

Asahel Kendrick

The University and Community

A number of professors rented rooms from "Miss Porter" while they looked for permanent housing. Maria Porter was a gracious hostess who entertained some of the most prestigious residents and visitors to the city—Frederick Douglass, Ralph Waldo Emerson, Horace Mann, and emancipationist Cassius Marcellus Clay, among others. Her home also served as a station on the Underground Railroad.

Professors John Raymond, Asahel Kendrick, and others engaged in lively debate over the table at Miss Porter's, noted Harriet Raymond Lloyd in a biography of her father.

Kendrick may have been the prototypical faculty member in community circles, according to city historian Blake McKelvey in a 1950 essay. A renowned Greek scholar, Kendrick became widely known as a preacher in local churches. He endeared himself to citizens with his breadth of knowledge, personal simplicity, and humor.

"The very insecurity of the college during its early years helped to merge its affairs into the life of Rochester," wrote McKelvey. "The commencement ceremonies and other public meetings were held at Corinthian Hall, the city's own cultural headquarters, or in one of the Baptist churches. Baptists and other Protestant churches made frequent use of faculty talents, both in their pulpits and their Sabbath schools. The choice boardinghouse where John H. Raymond and other professors dined was a favorite as well of talented young clerics and lawyers."

Raymond, who left Rochester in 1855 to become the first president of the Collegiate and Polytechnic Institute of Brooklyn—and later served as president of Vassar—remembered inspirational conversations at Miss Porter's, especially focused on the antislavery movement. Abolitionist and newspaper editor Frederick Douglass wrote to Raymond's daughter that her father had offered more advice and support in securing safe passage of fugitives on their way to Canada than anyone in the city.

"The city and the college have grown up together," said McKelvey, "each helping to sustain the other and to enlarge its vision."

David Jayne Hill

Hill resisted forcefully when leading Baptists made a public call for assurances of weighty representation by the denomination among faculty, staff, and governing officers.

"For the full board . . . he historically documented that the University's purpose as interpreted by its founders and by Dr. Anderson had always been educational, not ecclesiastical, and he called upon the trustees to reaffirm that purpose in order to remove all doubts about the institution's future policy," Parkman said. "The committee charged with considering his report then endorsed it, in language no one could misunderstand, with an emphatic declaration of the University's independence from ecclesiastical interference. The trustees approved both reports without a dissenting vote, though perhaps with one or two unwilling ones. There was never again any question as to what the intellectual stance of the University would be."

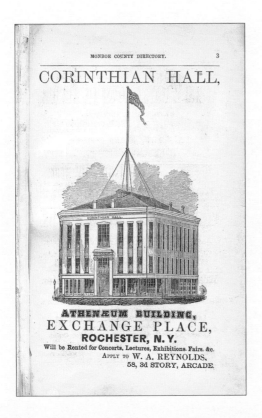

James Noble, the school's janitor and handyman from 1850 to 1868, preceded graduates in the commencement procession. With his wife, he functioned as a kind of resident advisor for students who boarded in the United States Hotel.

FIRST COMMENCEMENT

Thousands lined the streets July 9, 1851, to see a splendid procession. Schools and businesses closed for the first commencement of the University of Rochester. A brass band led the way from the United States Hotel to the city's majestic, two-year-old Corinthian Hall several blocks away, where the first 10 graduates would receive diplomas.

Marching behind the band were the University janitor; grammar school students and teachers; University freshmen, sophomores, and juniors; city and county officials; guests; founders of the University; local church leaders; and prominent judges. Next were the graduating seniors; faculty; members of the Board; chancellor Ira Harris and Board president John N. Wilder; and, last, the county sheriff.

"The *Rochester American* speaks of it as 'the largest and finest civic procession' that had ever been seen in the streets of that city," wrote *New York Recorder* editor and eventual University president Martin B. Anderson. "The Oxford cap, surplice, and fine person of the chancellor formed a special point of attraction. . . . The hall was crowded to its utmost capacity, containing, as near as we could judge, from eighteen hundred to two thousand persons. The fair forms and elegant costumes of the ladies, surrounding the center, which was entirely occupied by men, formed a unique and beautiful border, like a fringe of flowers around the walls of the building."

During the University's earliest years, graduation formalities lasted as long as four days, kicked off by a Sun-day evening sermon. Students read papers to compete for prestigious awards. One day was reserved for a morning sermon, a session of reports by the Board and treasurer, and an evening sermon.

In 1851, the commencement-eve sermon was delivered by prominent Congregationalist and social reformer Henry Ward Beecher, who spoke of "Character." The evening after grad-uation—which lasted hours—the chancellor played host to a "levee." The University spent $378.63 for use of Corinthian Hall, flowers, the marching band, a reading by poet Park Benjamin, Beecher's speech, and refreshments for parties.

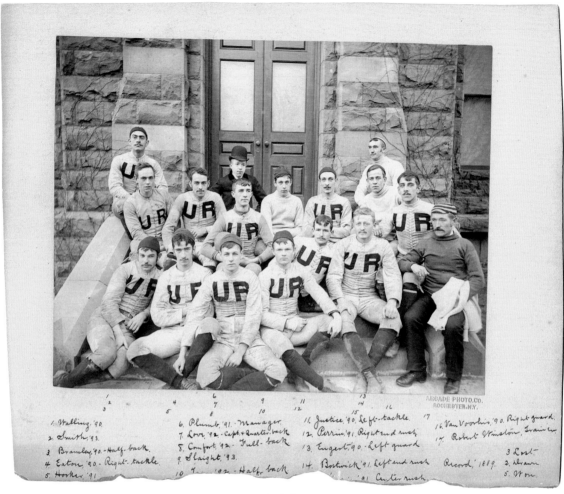

1. Walling '90.
2. Smith '93.
3. Bramley '90 - Half-back.
4. Eaton '90 - Right-tackle.
5. Hooker '91.

6. Plumb '91 - Manager.
7. Love '92 - Capt + Quarter-back.
8. Comfort '92 - Full-back.
9. Slaight '93.
10. — '92 - Half-back.

11. Justice '90 - Left-tackle.
12. Perrin '91 - Right end rush.
13. Engert '90 - Left guard.
14. Bostwick '91 - Left end rush.
— '91 - Center rush.

15. Van Voorhis '90 - Right guard.
17. Robert Winston - Trainer.

Record, 1889.

3 Lost
2 Drawn
5 Won.

1889 football team

A Sporting University

David Jayne Hill's presidency ushered a new realm of extracurricular activity. President Anderson had dismissed organized athletics as "relics of barbarism," but Hill considered sports an effective way to prevent boisterousness.

These still were early days in the development of American football, and the University student newspaper reported rough matches. Fans at Union College prodded players in the ribs with canes, while players took opportunities to kick Rochester players in the face, the *Campus* reported.

Rochester's first intercollegiate game in 1889 ended in dismal defeat by Cornell, 106-0. But the student-managed team shut out Syracuse 36-0 later that season. Rochester defeated Hobart 40-0 in the teams' first game, in 1892—the start of a lasting rivalry.

A field along University Avenue—later occupied by the Gleason Corporation manufacturing building—was cleared and a grandstand built.

"For avid undergraduate sportsmen football promptly became the most momentous item on the college athletic calendar," wrote May. A game with Hamilton College in 1896 attracted 5,000 spectators. "Not only did certain professors help the team along financially, but the faculty even excused absences from classes when players were competing on foreign fields. . . . Here was plain testimony that the 'all work and no play,' which President Anderson had consistently espoused, was undergoing modification."

Rochester defeated Plymouth State College, 1-0, in 1986 to win the first NCAA Division III Women's Soccer National Championship and joyously autographed the game ball. A year later the Yellowjackets did it again, defeating William Smith College, 1-0, at Fauver Stadium.

Much like baseball cards in bubble-gum packages, cigarette packages often included university-related premiums, like this one printed on silk (circa 1913).

The men's basketball program began in the 1901–02 season. The 1907–08 team, captained by George Ramaker, had a 7-6 record, the sport's first winning season at Rochester.

Ever since J. Howard Garnish '27 wrote a *Campus* editorial that ended with "Go to it, you Yellow Jackets! On to Rensselaer!" a yellow jacket, wasp, or bee of some sort has adorned many of the athletics uniforms.

The varsity basketball team of 1916–17 with coach Edwin Fauver in the back row center

April 10th 29

Rush Rhees Library is shown here under construction in 1929. Sketches for the building commenced at least eight years earlier. Library director Donald B. Gilchrist, who had overseen the Prince Street facility, welcomed expansion: "We are particularly fascinated with the prospect of having a properly planned building at Oak Hill, after occupying our present quarters for six years, squeezing a desk here, a thousand books there, getting tables a few inches closer together to make room for a few more readers."[1]

1   Catherine Hayes, "The History of the University of Rochester Libraries—120 Years," University of Rochester Library Bulletin 25, No. 3 (1970).

The new, $1.3 million library included space for a million volumes and was designed to enable additions without complete rebuilding. Among its distinctive features are a portico of six Doric pillars and a frieze across the front of the building that includes the carved names of philosophers, scientists, and writers. The 19-story, 186-foot tower has become the University's most recognizable symbol. Its upper portion is encircled by tiers of stone pillars illuminated by floodlights.

The main entrance, facing the Eastman quadrangle, features three sets of teakwood double doors inscribed with quotes:

"The doors of the past open to those who seek to know what has been the history of the stars, the earth, sunlight, life and man's long journey

The doors of the present open to those who seek to know what man can do to master his fate by science, sustain his spirit by art, and guide his life by wisdom

The doors of the future open to those who wonder what life may become when men are free in body and soul, loving all beauty, serving in many ways one God."

Transformation

Rush Rhees, 1900–1935

Rochester was in essence a small college, offering undergraduate education and a handful of master's degrees to its 200 students, when Benjamin Rush Rhees became president. Hill had set the groundwork for expanded educational directions and support beyond the Baptist community. Rhees, through a three-decade, growing bond with George Eastman, built a university—crowned by world-class schools of music and medicine. Rhees left the University in 1935 one of the richest and most-watched higher education institutions in the country.

The search to replace Hill did anything but foreshadow his successor's progress. The institution continued to struggle financially. The search took nearly four years, with faculty members stepping in as chief executive.

Trustees focused only on Baptists in the presidential search to avoid losing a $40,000 fund for salary donated with that stipulation in 1854. It was noted that Benjamin Ide Wheeler, a professor of Greek at Cornell University, turned down Rochester when the Board concluded it could not meet his requirement of raising $250,000. Wheeler became president of the University of California and in 1900 helped found the Association of American Universities, the standard-setter for U.S. research institutions. "He did not feel that any sense of duty called upon him to ally himself with a non-progressive institution," Board records noted.

Rhees, a scholar of the Bible teaching at Newton Theological Institution in Massachusetts, came to the University's attention by coincidence. John R. Slater, Roswell S. Burrows Professor of English at Rochester, who wrote a biography of Rhees, traced the connection to a social function attended by the wife of trustee Joseph T. Alling, Class of 1876. Rose Alling, visiting a friend, Lucy Waterbury, in Massachusetts, met Rhees at a gathering of villagers in Newton Centre. The next year, Waterbury, hearing that Rochester was looking for

Rush Rhees

a president, wrote to Mrs. Alling "that the young New Testament teacher was too good a man for his job and might be interested. Mrs. Alling told her husband, he told the committee, and so it all began."

Rhees, 39, had taught for eight years at Newton. He had earned a reputation as a progressive yet cautious biblical scholar. The son of a Baptist minister in Chicago, Rhees graduated from Amherst College in 1879, where he taught math for two years. He then earned a divinity degree at Hartford Theological Seminary and served for a time as pastor of the Middle Street Baptist Church in Portsmouth, N.Y. The day Rochester elected him president, Rhees married Harriet Seelye, the daughter of Smith College president L. Clark Seelye, a leading voice for traditional liberal education.

Described as quiet, deliberate, "somewhat stern but kindly," Rhees pursued projects only if he was certain they could be of highest quality. His leadership style meshed well with that of the similarly reserved Eastman Kodak founder Eastman, ultimately the University's largest benefactor. Slater wrote of a Newton colleague's reminiscence of Rhees: "He seemed to me like a well-adjusted, well-oiled machine, working to the exact second without hurry or fuss. I was puffing up the hill one day. Rhees said, 'Plenty of time.' He then told me that after much experience he had calculated that if he was at the tree at the corner of Chase Street by the time the bell rang in Colby Hall tower, his usual pace would land him at his classroom desk in ample time to be composed when the buzzer rang. If the bell rang before he reached the tree, he must put on steam, and that he disliked to do. I took it that this was an application of his mathematical training to affairs of daily life. He was quick in thought, speech, and action, but I have no recollection of any sign of nervous haste or 'rush' in my five years' association with him."

Rush Rhees's pocket watch

Rhees extracted from the Board a commitment it had not been able to make to Wheeler four years earlier: to raise $250,000 in endowment. This was modest against a backdrop of multimillion-dollar, historic university building in the United States. Business leaders such as John D. Rockefeller, Leland Stanford, and Ezra Cornell contributed toward new models of universities, often undergraduate schools paired with postgraduate research enterprises and professional schools. A new model of university president—as a visible recruiter and solicitor of donations—began to take shape as well.

The city of Rochester was just starting to recover from the effects of a deep national recession. Kodak, one of the few local companies to show real growth during the downturn, released its "Brownie" in 1900, which at $1 made the hobby of photography accessible for the first time. Soon the company broadened to employ 5,000 worldwide. Eastman's nascent philanthropic focus did not include the University. His reply when visitors sought donations toward admitting women in 1898 became local legend: "I am not interested in higher education."

In an inaugural in the new alumni gymnasium on October 11, 1900, Rhees highlighted Rochester's strength in liberal education. "Rochester has not developed, in its past history and in its present aim, those higher faculties which are essential to university work," he said. "It seeks with seriousness and frankness to do the work of an American college, and to meet the demands which the new century makes upon its schools of liberal culture. . . . It will be sufficient for our purpose, if we remember that a liberal education seeks first, to train a man in the

The Library in Sibley Hall, circa 1930–35

use of all of his intellectual powers; and secondly, to inform him, as widely as may be, concerning himself and his world."

The University would be open to opportunity, however. "Little by little the present will change into the better future," Rhees said. "Little by little this vision will be chastened, corrected, and disciplined by those larger views which will come with a larger experience; but always the aim before the college, in so far as it remains a college, will be to give to its students a culture genuinely liberal, by means of an education which is modern and economical.... We would give you here the opportunity for the most thorough modern education, which shall neither despise the past, nor be blindly tied to it; an education of the widest scope possible with our resources. As new demands arise and new resources are found, we pledge to you that we will meet the demands most eagerly, and use the resources with the broadest wisdom we can."

Guests at the inauguration included President Seth Low of Columbia University, who emphasized in his address the importance of community support: "Any city that hopes to be famous ... must crown its material successes with an intellectual life powerful both within its limits and beyond its borders." President William Rainey Harper of the University of Chicago, another Baptist university with high ambitions, was a second noteworthy guest. Chicago, funded with an initial $12 million gift from Rockefeller, exemplified notable changes in higher education of the era, especially in its national visibility and in pursuing advanced research.

Rockefeller and other leading philanthropists also influenced higher education during the early 20th century through the development of foundations. The Carnegie Foundation for the Advancement of Teaching's blistering critique of medical education in 1910 by Abraham Flexner led to development at Rochester a decade later. Standard Oil founder Rockefeller systemized his educational philanthropy with the General Education Board, which became a chief funder of Rochester's pathbreaking School of Medicine and Dentistry. "The major foundations tended to focus on the architecture of the nationwide system of higher education," said historian John R. Thelin. "The most far-reaching plans to reform the structure of American higher education percolated from the private sector of organized American philanthropy."

Eastman biographer Elizabeth Brayer described Eastman's early reluctance and Rhees's delicate approach. Eastman, who had quit his job as a bank clerk to pursue film and camera making, "had the self-made man's indifference toward formal education, believing that the most useful training came through trial and error and the rugged individual pitting himself or herself against experience," Brayer wrote. "Any

Kodak advertised frequently in the student yearbook. This 1891 full-page *Interpres* ad features the famous slogan "You press the button, we do the rest." Student photographs and films have become an important resource of the University Archives.

University of Rochester.   Eastman Laboratories (Physics and Biology).

notion of higher education as edifying the mind and imagination he found flighty and untrustworthy."

Brayer told the story of Eastman's first major gift, in 1904, when Rhees looked for a donation for a physics and biology building. President and Mrs. Rhees visited Eastman to tell him that $150,000 was needed to build it and equip the laboratory.

> Eastman offered $10,000. As the Rheeses were leaving, Eastman called them back. "You're disappointed, aren't you?" he asked. "What did you expect?" "I had hoped," Rhees replied, "that you might give the whole building." "Well, I'll think it over," said Eastman. The next morning a check for $60,000 to cover the cost of construction appeared on Rhees's desk, because, as Eastman told Walter Hubbell, "Dr. Rhees let me alone." Years later Eastman would boast, "Dr. Rhees never asked me for a cent." Rush Rhees's report of the incident to his trustees read: "Mr. Eastman, entirely on his own initiative, without any solicitation either direct or indirect on my part . . . increased his pledge to $60,000." In a defensive addendum that Rhees loved to quote after the Eastman sums had rolled into the many millions, the donor cautioned, "This is the last I shall do for the university."

An excerpt of a March 1904 letter from Rhees to Eastman, published by Slater, sheds light on the president's gracious care of the benefactor.

> Happy in your helpful interest, I set about securing the rest of the $150,000 to make your subscription valid, and had succeeded in bringing my total up to between $50,000 and

George Eastman, circa 1897–1900

These fraternity and honorary society keys belonged to Robert F. Metzdorf '33, '35 (Mas), '39 (PhD). Attached by a chain to his mother-of-pearl pocket-knife, they include his Phi Beta Kappa key and fobs of Alpha Phi, the Troubadours, Pro Concordia, the Mendicants, and Alpha Delta Phi and an alumni award from Theta Chi, presented to him in 1949.

$60,000, with several friends ready to lend a hand who had not named their sums. I did not see where my additional $100,000 was to come from, but believed I should get it by sufficiently persistent work. I believe you can appreciate what a relief it is to me to have that task more than cut in two by your unexpected but most welcome reconsideration of your subscription. Your addition of $50,000 much more than cuts in two my task, for it will be a challenge and encouragement to others. I shall not attempt to express my gratitude in words—rather would I assure you of constant study on my part to keep you well pleased with your generous investment in my enterprise.

As you will remember, you made your initial subscription on our form which provides that the subscription is binding only when $150,000 has been secured. Will you kindly tell me whether you wish me to delay active work on our building until I have completed the $150,000? You may be sure that every consideration alike of honor and of self-interest will impel me to complete that subscription. But I think you have made success certain. Should you not care to stand on the formal condition, I think we should find some advantage in pushing our plans and beginning construction at once, so that we may have our building enclosed at least before snow flies next season. If you should authorize me to go ahead at once, I think it would not reduce my chances of completing my subscription, and it might increase it. However, I most cordially recognize your right to regard the condition as binding, and shall happily abide by your preference in the matter. Knowing that you will reply to me quite promptly, I am

Very gratefully,
Rush Rhees

May I add that Mrs. Rhees shares fully in my own great happiness over your generous subscription?

A mutual appreciation grew. By 1912, when Rhees was courted for the presidency of his alma mater, Amherst College, Eastman pitched in $500,000 toward a $1 million endowment for University operating expenses to retain him. Eastman had sponsored a European tour by Rhees in 1909 to examine methods of technological education. In 1913, Rochester offered its first engineering degree. Their partnership strengthened in community endeavors during World War I.

MEMORIAL ART GALLERY. UNIVERSITY OF ROCHESTER GROUNDS.
ROCHESTER, N. Y.

Emily Sibley Watson and her son James G. Averell

The Hall of Casts, March 1917

The Memorial Art Gallery

The Memorial Art Gallery, dedicated October 8, 1913, was a gift of Emily Sibley Watson in memory of her son, James G. Averell, an architect who died of typhoid in his twenties.

Watson, the daughter of Hiram Sibley—a founder of Western Union—had been active in Rochester's art community and supported the museum as a cultural resource for the city. The dignified limestone building, designed by John A. Gade under the supervision of Claude Bragdon, resembled the Malatesta Temple in Rimini, Italy, which Averell had admired.

The Watson family supported an extension of the museum in 1926. By then the gallery had 1,500 members. The gallery, known as MAG, underwent other renovations and expansions—including the addition of a sculpture park in 2013 marking MAG's 100th anniversary. The museum "has firmly established itself as one of the country's leading community art museums owned by a national research univer-

sity," wrote curator Marjorie Searl in *Rochester Review* in 2012. The gallery's holdings expanded from its first acquisition of a lappet of lace to more than 12,000 works of art spanning cultures across the world and millennia.[2]

Emily Sibley Watson, who died in 1945 at age 90, was praised as one of Rochester's most generous citizens.

---

2 "Permanent Collection of the Memorial Art Gallery, Rochester," accessed March 10, 2014, http://mag.rochester.edu/collections/.

Edwin Fauver

A new era in University athletics entered with the appointment in 1916 of Edwin Fauver as director of physical education. Fauver, a physician, stood in contrast with a growing national trend identified by historian John R. Thelin of the "football coach and athletics director as public celebrities and campus czars." Fauver and his twin, Edgar, who held the same post at Wesleyan University, focused on promoting healthy lifestyles among students and shunned any hints of professionalism in collegiate sports. "The Fauver athletic code regarded intercollegiate sports as recreational outlets for bona fide students," said historian Arthur May. "It frowned upon recruitment of players and athletic scholarships. It restricted games to institutions with parallel ideals, insisted that men should be coached to observe the rules of the game . . . and banned drinking or gambling by players."

Fauver earned a highlight in Rhees's annual report of 1917. The new physical education director aimed to promote and develop the health and physical strength of the individual and make a "vital contribution to develop character and will power," the report said.

Alumni Gymnasium, Prince Street Campus, circa 1905

Eastman's interest coincided with increasing demand for scientific study and overall enrollment growth, two important themes in American higher education beginning in the latter 19th century. Law professor Judith Areen attributed a shift toward science and research in part to the influence of leading educators of that period at Johns Hopkins, Michigan, and Cornell. At the same time, more Americans began to see college as a path to greater earnings potential and social status.

From 1900 to 1915, Rochester enrollment jumped nearly 150 percent, to 495 students. Enrollment in its scientific track grew 13 percent in 1907 alone, while the number of students in the classical bachelor's degree track dropped 5 percent. The data prompted Rhees to reiterate Rochester's commitment to liberal education while reminding the Board of the institution's unusual scientific track in its original Plan of Instruction.

"It was remarkable as a broad consideration of the whole problem of college instruction—a problem which at that time was greatly agitating the educational world," Rhees told the Board. "It was particularly remarkable for the fact that it provided for a course of college work without Latin or Greek, to stand beside the time-honored classical course, for it not only substituted modern languages for Greek and Latin, but offered instruction in sciences which was very full for that time. The most remarkable thing about that early plan was that it not only provided a college course based on modern languages and science, but contemplated a provision of instruction in the applications of science to industry."

The president also noted that Eastman had voluntarily sent an additional $15,000 to cover extra expenses associated with the laboratory building. Andrew Carnegie had pledged $100,000 in matching funds toward an additional science building.

Music

WORLD WAR I PROVED A PIVOTAL PERIOD FOR EASTMAN IN HIS EMERgence as the community's most visible and galvanizing leader. The war also placed him and Rhees together in significant public endeavors. Eastman helped organize and became president of the Rochester Patriotic and Community Fund—forerunner to the United Way of Greater Rochester, a combined drive to raise money for war needs and a range of local charities. Rhees served as chairman of the organization's budget committee. Eastman also became president of a reorganized local chapter of the American Red Cross, among the state's most productive units. "His leadership in community affairs came to flower during World War I and the postwar period," said Brayer. "After the war he emerged as the city's dominant leader in practically every aspect of community life. His sense of social responsibility developed gradually and knew no bounds." Eastman has been credited with founding or an influential role in other important organizations: the Rochester-based Center for Governmental Research; a dental clinic that merged with the University's Medical Center; Rochester Philharmonic Orchestra; Hillside Children's Center; Rochester Friendly Home; Rochester Institute of Technology; and the Chamber of Commerce.

The war stressed the University. Enrollment and faculty ranks dropped precipitously—at one point 16 faculty members, or a third of

1917 Student Army Training Corps

IN DEFENCE OF THE UNION
DURING THE CIVIL WAR
1861 – 1865

ABOUT ONE HUNDRED
STUDENTS AND ALUMNI
OF THE UNIVERSITY OF ROCHESTER SERVED
AS VOLUNTEERS IN THE ARMY AND NAVY
THIS INSCRIPTION REPLACES A MARBLE
TABLET FORMERLY IN ANDERSON HALL
ON WHICH WERE RECORDED THE NAMES OF
TEN OF THESE ROCHESTER SOLDIERS WHO
GAVE THEIR LIVES TO PRESERVE THE UNION

JEREMIAH·C·DRAKE	CLASS OF 1852
SIDNEY·L·RICHARDSON	CLASS OF 1853
WILLIAM·L·BRISTOL	CLASS OF 1856
THEODORE·E·BAKER	CLASS OF 1857
SYLVANUS·S·WILCOX	CLASS OF 1860
CHARLES·H·SAVAGE	CLASS OF 1861
JOSEPH·WEBSTER	CLASS OF 1861
WILLIAM·C·HALL	CLASS OF 1863
WILLIAM·E·ORR	CLASS OF 1864
J·HARRY·POOL	CLASS OF 1865

VITA ENIM MORTUORUM
IN MEMORIA VIVORUM EST POSITA

IN DEFENCE OF THE NATION
DURING THE WORLD WAR
1917 – 1918

NEARLY NINE HUNDRED
GRADUATES FORMER
STUDENTS AND UNDERGRADUATES OF THIS
UNIVERSITY ENTERED MILITARY SERVICE
THIS TABLET ERECTED BY THE MOTHER OF
ROBERT·K·DENNISON RECORDS THE NAMES
OF ELEVEN OF THESE COLLEGE MEN WHO
LAID DOWN THEIR LIVES THAT THE CAUSE
OF LIBERTY AND HONOR MIGHT PREVAIL

HAROLD·C·KIMBALL	CLASS OF 1911
JOHN·H·LEHNEN	CLASS OF 1912
EVERETT·C·CASE	CLASS OF 1913
LAWRENCE·B·ATKINS	CLASS OF 1915
HARRY·O·FERGUSON	CLASS OF 1916
LEON·H·BUCKLER	CLASS OF 1917
CHARLES·H·EVANS	CLASS OF 1918
ROBERT·K·DENNISON	CLASS OF 1919
SAMUEL·R·MCNAIR	CLASS OF 1919
JULES·V·FISH	CLASS OF 1920
G·BARSTOW·FRALEY	CLASS OF 1920

DULCE ET DECORUM EST
PRO PATRIA MORI

This plaque honors the memory of
University of Rochester Alumni
who gave their lives in World War II
to preserve
the freedom and liberty
we enjoy today.

Alexander D. Allen '43	Robert L. Pritschel '42	Walter T. Menegazzi '43
Alan Y. Austin '43	Mason C. Gaffney '22	Joseph A. Morton '42
Albert H. Baker '42	Percival H. Granger '46	Robert A. Neumer '44
Bruce Beghold '47	Lyman Brinkman Hart '47	Donald T. O'Keefe '41
Walter E. Bond, Jr. '39	John Haruk '39	Franklin R. Parske '41
Philip William Carey '39	Allen J. Haupenthal '42	Robert H. Patchen '43
Harold Richard Carlson '46	David William Hayes, Jr. '43	Earl W. Rubens '35
Robert E. Claudius '46	John L. Hazen, Jr. '43	Paul Schmidt '45
Marvin Cooke	Paul Husted '44	Harold J. Schott, Jr. '46
Gordon E. Davis '45	Earl W. Krumwiede '46	Norbert Schulz '45
Robert S. Day '44	Gordon K. Lambert '32, '35(MD)	Roger D. Skinner '38
Robert George Dean '46	James C. Lawrence '43	Robert Speas '42
James Deming '44	James J. LeClare '37	Richard W. Stoll '43
Ronald W. Doll '36	Marvin E. Lee '42	Lee H. Streeter '44
Darwin K. Dunning '39	Bjorn S. Lindboe '45	Wilfred N. Tanenbaum '42
James E. Elliott '40	Armon H. Livermore '44	Gerald R. Thoman '42
Walter T. Enright '30	Arthur E. Loeser '23	Ralph E. Wersinger '35
Jacob Thomas Farris	Edward W. Maher '43	Vernon P. Winton
William H. Frick '44	Ellis Medvin '44	Robert H. Zwierschke '39

A gift from University of Rochester Veterans of World War II
Dedicated on October 25, 1996

Freedom Is Not Free

This plaque honors the memory of
University of Rochester alumni
who gave their lives in the defense
of freedom during the Korean War,
1950 – 1953.

George W. Dykema, Jr. '51
Charles S. Langtry '45
Spiro J. Peters '50
Lester L. Shade '47

A gift from University of Rochester veterans

Dedicated October 13, 2000 on the occasion of the University's Sesquicentennial

---

This plaque honors members of the University of Rochester community
who died serving their country during the Vietnam War.

Ralph Button '56
James R. Dennison '56
Robert N. Funk '67
Carl Hansen, Jr. '60
Gary D. Hopps '61
Thomas G. King '66
Joseph R. Klugg '65E
William Lanham '65
James E. Morse '68
Victor Ohanesian
Lester E. Oonk
Hendrick H. Pruyn '56
Rodney Reed '66
Edward L. Romig '63
Donald C. Thompson '62
Thomas J. Walter '62
Armour D. Wilcox III '68

Dedicated on October 12, 2001 by grateful alumni, students, and staff
during a weekend celebration of freedom.

Plaques hanging in Wilson Commons' Hirst Lounge
commemorate those Rochester alumni killed in battle
from the Civil War through the Vietnam War.

the teaching force, were in military service. By August 1918 nearly half of the undergraduate men were in military service. "Our laboratories and their personnel, our classrooms and teachers, our whole equipment of men and appliances were dedicated to service for the victory of the Army and Navy," Rhees reported. *The Watchman Examiner,* a national Baptist newspaper, described the June 1917 commencement at Rochester: "'Grim visaged war,' showed 'his awful front' at every turn, even here among the classic and peaceful shades of interlacing elms." The remains of junior-year student Charles Evans, among the first to leave for service, returned to Rochester during the 1917 graduation exercises.

Rhees told the Board that spring: "We have sought to impress on our students the importance of a steady head in all the excitement of this most serious time. While encouraging and assisting those to enlist who were eligible for special forms of service, we have urged all others to recognize that they can best serve their country by keeping steadily at their intellectual work, until the duty to enter some other form of service has become definitely clear. Only so can our country escape the loss of men trained for leadership in civic as well as in military life for the very important years which will follow the war."

Even during the war, Eastman began contemplating formation of a new school of music. This project came to consume him, Brayer wrote, the way his photography business had in the late 19th century. A music lover—some said addict—whose quartet-accompanied gatherings were a Rochester society highlight, Eastman grew intrigued with development of a University-affiliated music school through dialogues with the director of a struggling conservatory, the D.K.G. Institute of Musical Art, on Prince Street near the Rochester campus. A *Post-Express* newspaper article captured the first step of this project, reporting in May 1918 Eastman's purchase of the Institute of Musical Art on Prince Street and its contemplated link with the University. "Lovers of music in Rochester will welcome this promise of larger developments for musical education in the community," the *Post-Express* said.

Eastman School historian Vincent A. Lenti recounted an interview of Arthur See, a D.K.G. graduate who served as the D.K.G. director. See, interviewed by author Roger Butterfield '27 for a planned biography of Eastman, recalled: "Once the idea of a music school took root, [Eastman's] energy and imagination brought it to full bloom in no time. The genius that had built a worldwide industry out of a revolutionary plan played with full force over a new field. Almost at once GE [Eastman] saw the project in its entirety."

The University amended its charter to clarify that its educational authority would include both college and university programs, including

Dexter Perkins

Dexter Perkins joined the history department in 1915 and served as chairman from 1925 until his retirement in 1954. During World War I he served in the historical section of the Army in France, according to University historian Arthur May.

Perkins, a leading authority on the Monroe Doctrine and U.S. diplomatic history, was the official U.S. historian at the 1945 San Francisco Security Conference preceding the organization of the United Nations.

The civic-minded professor also served as historian for the City of Rochester from 1936 to 1948 and was the first president of the Rochester Association for the United Nations.

In 1912 Alf Klingenberg joined the faculty of the Rochester Conservatory of Music—shown here in 1912 at 81 South Fitzhugh Street—as head of the piano faculty. A year later, Klingenberg partnered with violinist and conductor Hermann Dossenbach to open their own music school at 47 Prince Street, which in turn would become the D.K.G. Institute of Musical Art until purchased by George Eastman for $28,000 in 1918.

graduate departments, professional, technical, and vocational schools. Eastman contributed $17 million for construction of the music school and an endowment. He supervised construction and faculty plans in detail, visiting the construction site almost daily. Prominent first faculty included German-trained pianist Max Landow, Norwegian composer Christian Sinding, Scottish pianist Frederick Lamond, and vocalist Lucy Lee Call.

"The scope of this undertaking was very broad," Lenti said. "The school was to function as a university department which would train candidates for the bachelor of music degree and, in addition, serve as a community school offering instruction to both adults and children. Furthermore, the theater was designed to provide a cultural exposure to the broadest possible segment of the community."

Movie poster production, 1923

The Eastman Theatre, where Eastman envisioned expanding community interest in classical music through combining performances with movies, featured a capacity of 3,300; a 10,000-pipe organ; and a two-and-a-half-ton, 20,000-piece chandelier. Its façade was engraved, on Rhees's recommendation, with "For the Enrichment of Community Life." An estimated 10,000 attended opening shows of *The Prisoner of Zenda*, accompanied by the Eastman Theatre Orchestra, the week of September 4, 1922, and 1.8 million attended events there that year.

In 1923, Eastman and Rhees sought ambitious new leadership for the fledgling school. Composer Howard Hanson, a Nebraska native and recent winner of the American Prix de Rome, met with Rhees and Eastman to discuss his educational philosophy. Eastman disclaimed

The main stage and lobby of the newly completed Eastman Theatre, 1922

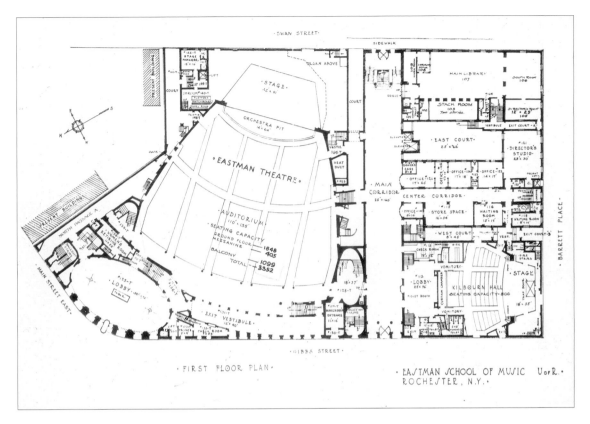

Eastman Theatre and Eastman School of Music architectural drawings

any knowledge of education or music—"but his questions were models of clarity and incisiveness,"[3] Hanson remembered. Just shy of age 28, Hanson articulated an appealing vision. He embarked on a 40-year tenure that solidified the Eastman School of Music as a world leader in balancing training for performance with scholarship.

Lenti summarized the school's unique stature:

> The Eastman School of Music is not the oldest music school in the United States, nor is it the largest. Nonetheless, it has had an enormous influence on music education in the United States. Creating a professional music school within the context of a university was a bold experiment at the time. American music education had traditionally followed the European model of training performers in conservatories and creating musical scholars in universities. The Eastman School would be a home to both performer and scholar, as well as being a home to both composer and educator. It would offer instruction to students whose interests were purely avocational, while also offering training to those preparing for

---

3   Howard Hanson, "Music Was a Spiritual Necessity," University of Rochester Library Bulletin 26 (1971).

Howard Hanson, 1925

a professional career in music. It would be a professional music school, but one committed to a broadly based education leading not to a professional diploma but to a baccalaureate degree. The Eastman School would be in the forefront of national efforts to establish and regulate the curriculum for the bachelor of music degree. It would be a leader in the training of musicians at the graduate level through the awarding of the master of music degree and through the creation of a new professional doctorate in music, which would be known as the musical arts degree.

Even more important, however, was the effort to establish the Eastman School as a truly American institution, dedicated to American ideals and to the encouragement and support of American music.

Medicine

By 1920, Rhees had established a reputation in higher education circles as an administrator who supported high-quality programs. That and Eastman's largesse caught the attention of Abraham Flexner, author of the 1910 critique, *Medical Education in the United States and Canada: A Report to the Carnegie Foundation for the Advancement of Teaching.* Appointed to Rockefeller's General Education Board (GEB) in 1913, Flexner was working with a handful of leading universities dispersed across the country to institute reforms, which most importantly emphasized full-time clinical faculty—versus community doctors teaching part time—and training in hospitals that were fully controlled by the universities.[4] Flexner had discovered wide variation in the quality of training at medical schools, many of which were owned by local doctors and run for a profit. He sought a model with significant new regulations, longer training of physicians based on scientific research, and increased state oversight. Frustrated with delays advancing his model with other New York schools, Flexner began to contemplate an entirely new medical school in Rochester.

Abraham Flexner

Brayer quoted an exchange recollected by Flexner with Wallace Buttrick, MD, president of the GEB, a former trustee at Rochester and classmate of Rhees. "I said to him quite casually, 'The University of Rochester is a modest but good institution, isn't it?' Buttrick agreed, calling Rhees a 'fine college head.' 'It has occurred to me,' Flexner continued, 'that if we could help plant a first-rate medical school there, perhaps New York City would wake up.'

'Why Rochester?' Buttrick wondered.

'Rochester has a clean slate; and besides there is Mr. Eastman.'"

Flexner soon received an invitation to join Eastman for breakfast. Rhees had refused to approach Eastman on Flexner's behalf but arranged for the interview. Brayer's account of their meeting:

> At the appointed breakfast, Flexner outlined his proposal in detail. Eastman listened so quietly that Flexner was uncertain what kind of impression he was making. When noon came, however, and Eastman pressed a button for lunch, Flexner began to think he was making progress. At 4 p.m. Eastman announced that he had to go to his office but invited Flexner and Rhees to dine with him.

---

4   Thomas Neville Bonner, *Iconoclast: Abraham Flexner and a Life in Learning* (Baltimore: Johns Hopkins University Press, 2002), 84–85.

George Hoyt Whipple, 1920

"I am interested in your project," Eastman said in the
sitting room after dinner, "but in these recent years I have
given away thirty-one million dollars. . . . I can only spare two
and a half million" (out of a needed $8 or $10 million). Flexner
left, but a few days later was summoned by telegram to return.
This time the offer was $3.5 million. Eastman wanted it settled
before he went to Japan.

Eastman then upped the offer to $5 million, including his Roch-
ester dental clinic valued at $1 million. The GEB provided $5 million
in matching funds. Eastman also persuaded Gertrude Strong Achilles
and Helen Strong Carter, the daughters of Henry Alvah Strong, his
former business partner, to donate $1 million toward a teaching hos-
pital. Members of the Strong family later made other contributions,
including funds for the Strong Auditorium on the River Campus.

The University simultaneously opened a nursing training center, as it worked to raise the status of nursing. "The affair will be so financed and staffed that there is no question but what the hospital will be one of the most distinguished in the world and second to none unless it be Johns Hopkins,"[5] Eastman wrote.

Rhees consulted Johns Hopkins pathologist William Henry Welch for suggestions on naming a dean for the medical center. Welch directed Rhees to George Hoyt Whipple, dean of the University of California School of Medicine and head of the newly established Hooper Foundation for Medical Research in San Francisco. Whipple, also fully engaged in research into anemia that later earned a Nobel Prize, declined. Rhees went to San Francisco to encourage him to reconsider.

Whipple did. He explained later:

> No appointments had been made. The school was to be a part of the university. There was no old medical school in Rochester to complicate the problem. The dean would have the support of President Rhees in constructing a modern school with its hospital and an adequate full-time staff, everything to measure up to the highest standards. . . .
>
> New schools of medicine are established rarely, and opportunities to take responsibility at the very start are unusual,

5   Elizabeth Brayer, *George Eastman: A Biography* (Rochester, NY: University of Rochester Press, 2006), 433.

Medical school faculty and staff, 1926

Form Follows Function

Eastman and Rhees were deeply interested in the architectural design, Whipple wrote in a 1950 history of the Medical Center. An architect had recommended a memorial design that would beautify the area. "Mr. Eastman insisted that adequate demonstrations of memorial types of building were spread about the country, that he was convinced that there was real need for a building with a minimum of external adornment to demonstrate maximum facilities and optimum service, containing all the best modern equipment," Whipple stated. "With Mr. Eastman's militant support, the buildings were planned and built of brick with reinforced concrete frame. . . . 'Function rather than façade' was a master word."

to say the least. The endowment seemed generous and adequate for construction and maintenance. Perhaps it is not wise to attempt a detailed analysis of all the factors involved in this proposal. At least it would be a test of leadership and would give a chance to build, from the ground, a new school with the very best young teachers and students and with the necessary laboratories for research in all departments. Co-operative teaching and research would be inevitable with a united hospital and school. All this carried visions and excited thrills.[6]

Whipple recruited heavily from Johns Hopkins for his department leaders, looking for rising talents there and in other top-quality institutions. Anatomy chair George W. Corner, MD, and chairs in bacteriology, obstetrics, and medicine came from Johns Hopkins. Others among the first leadership team included Walter R. Bloor, MD, professor of biochemistry at the University of California–Berkley, as professor and associate dean, and Nathaniel W. Faxon, MD, assistant director of Massachusetts General Hospital, as hospital director. The chairs shared with Whipple and Rhees in decisions on hiring, including choosing other department heads, and in operational matters. By the time the school opened in 1925 it had 65 faculty.

"University's Medical School to Rank with World Leaders," a headline in the Rochester *Times-Union* declared in January 1924, a year before the first 22 medical students entered. The city would become one of the great centers in the world of medical and surgical science, the article said.

6   May, "Shaping the Medical Center," in *History of the University of Rochester.*

UNIVERSITY OF ROCHESTER
MEDICAL SCHOOL & HOSPITAL
GORDON & KAELBER, ARCHS.
MCKIM, MEAD & WHITE, ASSOC. ARCHS.
J. F. ANCONA, CONS. ENGR.

Postcard showing the completed Strong Memorial Hospital and its original entrance on Crittenden Boulevard

The Strong Family

An oak panel over the fireplace in the original lobby of Strong Memorial Hospital memorializes Henry Alvah and Helen Griffin Strong, parents of donors Gertrude Strong Achilles and Helen Strong Carter: "May the kindliness and human sympathy which characterized their lives continue forever through the ministry of this hospital." Historian Arthur May noted appreciatively that Eastman's Spartan principles were not applied to the lobby. "Fine wood paneling, paintings on the walls, comfortable settees and chairs, and a fireplace bespoke welcome and cheerfulness as in a high-class club."

Dad! GIVE for me.

The concept of building for the future was embodied in the slogan "A Greater University for a Greater Rochester." This idealized rendering of a campus set beside the Genesee was used on a campaign brochure in 1924.

THE RIVER CAMPUS

PLANNING FOR THE MEDICAL CENTER PROMPTED STUDY OF HOW the campus would expand. The Eastman School of Music would rise near Prince Street, but administrators doubted the campus could accommodate the growth of the medical center—or enlargement that could follow. Rhees and the trustees considered several prospects, the president urging the Board to consider space for engineering programs, an institute of optics, or, farther into the future, professional schools of education, business, and law. Rochester industrialist and University supporter George W. Todd pressed for a new campus at Oak Hill, at that time a golf course on the bank of the Genesee River. Rhees envisioned a men's campus at Oak Hill, situated near property suitable for the medical center, while the Prince Street Campus became a separate college for women—preserving for University use its historic buildings and keeping the Memorial Art Gallery within an academic neighborhood.

Todd invited 50 or so influential Rochester citizens to his home on a July evening in 1923. Rhees set out options for University expansion ranging in cost from $5 million to $10 million—the Oak Hill plan. "Dead silence reigned," historian May wrote, "until George Eastman, according to one of the guests, dryly observed, 'I think we'd better run up the ten million flag and see what we get.'"

Later that month the University shared its plans with an estimated 1,000 in the main hall of the city's Chamber of Commerce. The $10 million goal was more than double ever pledged for a cause in Rochester, and the University sought to raise it in 10 days. The crowd roared—the campaign for a Greater University was on.

Eastman promised $2.5 million if the General Education Board would match it, leaving $5 million to be raised locally. "As this $10,000,000 is mainly to buy clothes for the baby it left on our doorstep I hope the G.E.B. will recognize the reasonableness of the suggestion," Eastman wrote to Rhees, referring to the medical center. "If I had known his baby was going to grow so fast I should probably have told Flexner to take it back home in the beginning but it is such a pretty baby that one does not want to give it up now without a struggle."[7]

When local businessman Daniel Clark declined to donate—telling Eastman, "The smart and successful business men we have known were not college men"—Eastman replied: "Fifteen or 20 years ago, I used to feel pretty much the way you do about college education. From the Kodak point of view I consider it a very highly desirable thing to

Postcard showing the clubhouse at the Oak Hill Country Club, where the River Campus stands today

---

7   Brayer, *George Eastman*, 439.

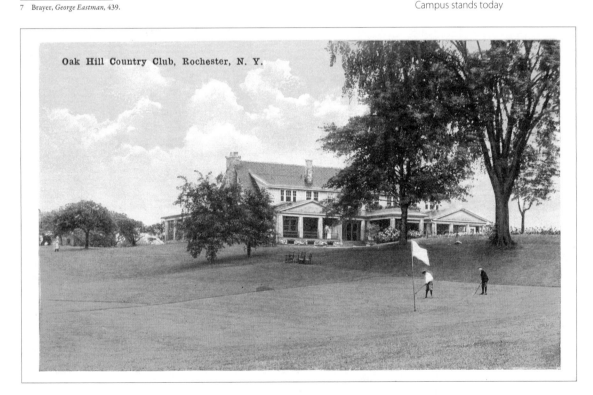

Oak Hill Country Club, Rochester, N. Y.

The Genesee

A College Song

Dedicated to
The University of Rochester
by
T. T. Swinburne

MUSICAL CHEER

Students enjoyed Rochester songs, many written by professors Kendrick P. Shedd and John R. Slater, the *Campus* reported. "For years the college students have sung much about their Alma Mater and somewhat about their city and the Genesee but now a new song chapter opens. A great impetus is being given to the city song idea." At song booths in the city's convention hall and Sibley, Lindsay & Curr department store, students sang tunes titled "Rochester Made Means Quality," "Put Me Down at Kodak Town" and "Lester, Lester, Take Me Back to Old Rochester." The chorus of "Jenny-See," by Slater and Shedd goes: "Her name is Jenny/her charms are many/she's fair as any e'er known to me;/with beauty beaming, with treasures streaming/of her I'm dreaming my Genesee."

have a good college here, not only to help train good men but also to make Rochester an attractive place for Kodak men to live and bring up their families. It seems to me that as a pure business proposition, you ought to give the university some help."

Messages blanketed the city, from billboards to postcards. Posters showing a father and son gazing at colorful drawings of a riverside campus proclaimed, "Dad! GIVE for me! A Greater University for a Greater Rochester." The alumni magazine carried updates—Rhees and others detailed the need for funds: $5 million would further endow the undergraduate school, enabling faculty growth and increased pay to maintain the standard set by early professors such as Asahel Kendrick in Greek, Samuel A. Lattimore in chemistry, Henry F. Burton in Latin, William C. Morey in history, and Herman L. Fairchild in geology. The endowment also would support the library and recruitment of students qualified for advanced instruction and research.

More than 70 percent of living graduates and almost all undergraduates pitched in, May said. An honor roll produced after the campaign listed 13,651 subscribers. Rhees happily announced success during a banquet at the Chamber on November 24, 1924. "The future service of the University to Rochester will be a constant testimony to your energy, ability, and unselfish devotion," he said.

A week later, Eastman, elated with the community response, went further—signing over $6 million in Kodak stock to the University. He also divided $6 million in stock among Massachusetts Institute of Technology and Hampton and Tuskegee Institutes, and $9 million to Kodak employees. Rochester's endowment, at $25.9 million, stood sixth in the nation behind Harvard ($47 million), Columbia, Yale, Chicago, and Stanford.

Excited alumni gathered at Oak Hill in the spring of 1924 for their first reunion at the site of the eventual campus. They enjoyed canoe races, baseball, and tug-o-war. "Altogether it was an epoch-making occasion, the initial dedication of our beautiful campus-to-be," wrote Hugh A. Smith, Class of 1907, in the *Rochester Alumni Review*. The day closed with the crowd singing "'The Genesee,' the first time in the history of the University, on the very banks of the old river. As the lights gleamed in reflection from the bosom of the Genesee itself, they sang Tom Swinburne's beloved verses as they were never sung before. It was a wonderful curtain to a wonderful day."

Construction began in 1927, with a design of brick and limestone, Greek Revival–style academic buildings framing a quadrangle, its centerpiece a 19-story library that, over Rhees's objections, would bear his name. An estimated 5,000 people attended celebrations marking the River Campus opening in October 1930.

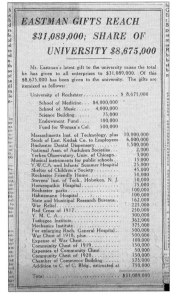

The Rochester *Democrat and Chronicle* itemized the beneficiaries of George Eastman's generosity through 1920.

A panorama of the construction of the academic quadrangle, 1928

Through the late 1920s, Eastman, his health failing, increasingly foreshadowed his final words. "When considering one philanthropy or another," wrote Brayer, "he would end with: 'I am convinced my work in that area is done.'... Once, in 1928, he wrote: 'Most of my stuff is finished. I am getting pretty well down to the dregs now and it is not feasible for me to take on anything new. I am just cleaning up.'" He asked clergy friends and doctors for their opinions on suicide. He had observed with dismay close friends debilitated by disease and senility. By late 1930 specialists at Strong Memorial Hospital and the Mayo Clinic diagnosed atherosclerosis of the spinal cord. Few who knew Eastman well were surprised—although both Whipple and Rhees wept—when they learned he had killed himself with a gunshot to the heart March 14, 1932. His parting words:

> To my friends
> My work is done—
> Why wait?
> GE

A few days before his death, Eastman revised his will. He designated a handful of personal bequests, then the bulk of his remaining estate, including his home, to the University of Rochester. The bequest was believed to be the highest to an institution of higher education to date. His gifts to the University, spanning 30 years, were estimated at more than $51 million, comparable to $800 million to $1 billion in 2013 dollars.

Rush Rhees enjoying a boat ride with his daughter-in-law, Helen, and his Irish setter, Peggy, 1928

Symbols of Authority

Originally a weapon, the mace has become a symbol of authority and dignity in academic ceremonies. Rochester's mace was introduced during the 1935 induction of Alan Valentine as president and has been used in academic processions ever since. Designed by Philipp Merz, who also is responsible for many of the architectural features of the early River Campus buildings, the mace is about four feet long and is crafted from mahogany and hand-wrought silver. The head of the mace features the seal of the University, and two silver bands are engraved with the names of the University's presidents. The dandelion, the floral symbol of the University, can be found in the decorative motif of the silverwork. The original mace is part of a pair of symbols created to mark academic ceremonies. The other is a smaller wooden baton, which also features dandelions and stars in its silverwork.

In 2011, an additional baton was commissioned to be used in the Simon School's Rochester-Bern Executive MBA Program graduation ceremony in Bern, Switzerland. Intended to complement the original mace and baton, the new baton is also carried in University and academic ceremonies. Designed by Scott D. Sober and silversmith Alexis Romeo, the new baton features sterling silver pommels, dandelions, and stars.

The mace is carried by the University grand marshal, who leads the processions alongside a marshal carrying the less imposing baton.

Arthur J. May with President de Kiewiet

George C. Curtiss, left, with baton; Edwin Fauver carrying mace

Grand Marshal Jesse T. Moore at the 2013 Commencement ceremony

President Alan Valentine during his inauguration in 1935 is presented with the University Charter by, left, University librarian Donald B. Gilchrist and Board chair Joseph T. Alling, Class of 1876.

A master engraver carving President O'Brien's name onto a silver band for the mace in 1984

In his 1931–32 annual report, President Rhees announced that the main quadrangle would bear Eastman's name, "setting the name of our great patron at the heart of the new development in which he took delight."

Modern Thought and Old Ideals

ALAN CHESTER VALENTINE, 1935–1950

GEORGE EASTMAN'S SURPRISE BEQUEST PUSHED THE YOUNG RESEARCH UNIVERSITY TO fifth place among the wealthiest in the country, with a nearly $50 million endowment. President Rhees set about expanding the institution's intellectual framework, especially in the sciences. As he had done with music and medicine, Rhees sought young professionals who showed rare promise.

Physicist Lee Alvin DuBridge, then teaching at Washington University in St. Louis, received a telegram from Rhees inviting him to talk about becoming chair of the physics department. Rhees had gathered names of prospects from Nobel-winning physicist Robert Millikan.

"I think I suggested that I stop in when I was going East to a meeting,"[1] DuBridge said, "but I got a wire back saying, 'No, that's too late, please come at once at our expense.' So I went directly to Rochester . . . just to talk with them about the position."

Rochester would appeal to vigorous researchers such as DuBridge. He did some background research and learned of the University's recent inheritance. Funds for salaries and research were then meager at Wash U, hard hit through the early years of the Great Depression. "So when I visited Rochester and talked to them, I found a very handsome salary increase, a position as professor with quite nice laboratories and promise of a quite adequate research budget," DuBridge said in an interview for California Institute of Technology, where he later served as president. "It was, for me personally, extremely attractive; an almost new physics building and very good equipment, obviously a moderately well-to-do university."

---

1 Judith R. Goodstein, "Lee A. DuBridge (Part II)," Oral History Project, California Institute of Technology Archives, Pasadena, 1981.

Lillian Benz '37 '44 (Mas) and
Minerva Scott '37

Faculty rosters lengthened with now-iconic names: optics specialist Brian O'Brien, embryologist Benjamin Willier, geneticist Curt Stern. Stern was among a wave of German scientists emigrating to American universities as Nazi power grew.

Rhees submitted his resignation in 1933. The Board had convinced him to stay when he tried to step down at age 70 three years earlier. He helped the trustees identify an extensive list of characteristics desirable in his successor. The next president would need to be practically perfectly healthy and have unusual amounts of energy. "Horse sense" and strength of character also were important. The next top administrator would need executive ability and a progressive mindset—"willing to make such changes as will provide a better and broader education, as expressed by 'not the first by whom the new is tried, nor yet the last to lay the old aside.'"

Just as Rhees had sought up-and-comers in most roles, he thought the Board should find someone whose reputation was still to be made: "In other words, someone who has the prospect of a brilliant future, rather than the reputation of an accomplished past."

After more than a year of searching, the committee narrowed its focus in late 1934 to a rising scholar and administrator at Yale University.

Alan Chester Valentine was 33 and master of Yale's residential Pierson College. He had led an acclaimed revamping of Yale admissions policies. Valentine was a Swarthmore graduate, Rhodes Scholar, U.S. Olympic rugby team victor—and movie-star handsome. He had taught history at Swarthmore and Yale.

Rochester trustees heard favorable comparison between Valentine and University of Chicago reformer Robert Maynard Hutchins. Hutchins and Harvard president James B. Conant were part of a new generation of university leaders who reinforced core academic values through the Depression and World War II, said historian Jonathan R. Cole, author of *The Great American University*. Presidents grappled with plummeting endowment income, extraordinary disruption of faculty and students—and pressure against academic freedom.

Prominent theologian the Rev. Orlo J. Price wrote to Rochester trustee Edward Miner from Florida: "The report I get is that he is an extraordinary young man from the point of view of his administrative ability and his educational ideals, to my mind the two important gifts for the new President to have. The contrast of Valentine and Hutchins . . . as to their leadership of men especially impressed me. Valentine moves more slowly but carries his crowd with him and leaves no 'soreheads' around when he is through; and over a period of years he will get further than Hutchins in making changes."

Alan Chester Valentine

Other remarks presented a picture of a mature and energetic academic: "Tremendous mental and physical capability, wise beyond his years." "Has high scholastic ideals." "A most attractive personality." The trustees were assured that despite Valentine's disinclination to talk about religious matters, he would value spiritual life at the Baptist-founded institution. Valentine was a Quaker.

He set conditions for the Board before accepting. Most important, he wanted to allocate funds for scholarships and fellowships to draw the very highest quality students to the College of Arts and Science, putting it on the same national plane as the prestigious schools of music and medicine. He would invest more in library collections. He probably would need to encourage retirement or departure for "dead wood" on the faculty. He would expect active support of the entire Board even if situations arose that would lead to severe criticism.

Lee Alvin DuBridge

"For 18 months the trustees of the University of Rochester have been dangling a rich prize before the eyes of U.S. educators," reported *Time* on January 14, 1935. "In a search for a successor to President Rush Rhees they examined the qualifications of no less than 101 candidates. Last week they voted to drape the presidential mantle over the husky shoulders of Alan Chester Valentine, 33-year-old Master of Yale's Pierson College."

A magnificent inaugural the next fall reflected expectations. Nearly 100 deans and presidents of top universities and colleges across the country marched with Valentine into the Eastman Theatre. Presidents of Swarthmore, Amherst, and Yale spoke. Valentine focused on undergraduate life, suggesting that American colleges needed to emphasize high scholastic values over the "ballyhoo" of athletics and extracurricular activities, toward an aim of graduates finishing with a mature point of view. The University must ensure that new leaders in society "use instinctively the scholarly approach and the scientific method."

His words inspired John C. Ransom, an 1879 graduate who had served as secretary to President Anderson. "While strictly in accord with modern thought," Ransom wrote to the *Rochester Review,* "his address rings true to the old ideals planted deep by the pioneers of our university."

Valentine took prompt steps to strengthen Rochester's name across the nation. Press clippings of his speeches on critical issues mounted in the newly formed University News office. The president created a scholarship program to draw exceptional students from a

Life in the Eastman House

The Valentine family experienced an almost royal existence in the 37-room Eastman House. George Eastman willed it to the University to be used as a residence for the president for 10 years, including a $2 million endowment to staff and maintain it.

Garrison N. Valentine, six years old when the family moved in, remembered consoling his four-year-old sister, Laurie, on the grand entry staircase. "We couldn't figure out how to get up to our rooms on the third floor." But the children reveled in exploring the mansion and grounds. When their parents hosted University functions, they peeped down to formal scenes from hall railings outside their bedroom.

The children enjoyed playing with their "mighty" father in the house and on the grounds. They would push an imaginary button on President Valentine, and he walked like a robot, through or over anything in his path.

That changed as of December 7, 1941. The Valentine family had gone for a long drive, a typical Sunday activity. Garrison Valentine remembered many long walks—sometimes 20 miles—with his father before the war. That day they walked near Geneseo. Back at home in the evening came the stunning radio report of the attack on Pearl Harbor. From the boy's perspective, free time for his father ended right then.

His mother, Lucia, was a gracious hostess, Garrison Valentine said. She had the family pause for tea every afternoon. Houseguests included renowned figures such as Heinrich Bruning, former German chancellor, and Hollywood luminary Ingrid Bergman.

Lucia Valentine came from a distinguished family: Her father, Charles Dyer Norton, had served as assistant secretary of the Treasury under President William Howard Taft. Her grandfather, Wendell Phillips Garrison, was editor of the *Nation*. Her great-grandfather was William Lloyd Garrison, famed abolitionist.

Lucia was active in the City of Rochester's planning board and the regional chapter of Planned Parenthood. She stepped in as an advisor to women students during the University staffing shortage of World War II.

Garrison remembered a surprise visit at the house by an official in a shining Army car. After the war ended, President Valentine told his son about the man—Gen. Leslie Groves. Valentine confided in the boy that he had regretted insisting that Groves tell him about the Manhattan Project. The president had been unable to sleep at night knowing the Americans were racing the Germans to create the horrific bomb. "I lived in fear," Valentine told the boy.

After World War II, President Valentine recommended discontinuation of the use of the house as a president's home; it later became the world-renowned George Eastman House International Museum of Photography and Film.

The *Campus* report on a tuition increase for 1940

wide geographic range, especially the growing Midwest. The Board of Trustees similarly diversified geographically and divided critical functions among new committees. Valentine began a quiet campaign for University membership in the esteemed Association of American Universities.

He was hampered to a certain extent, however, throughout his tenure. The University depended heavily on endowment income—in some years for 60 percent of operating expenses—and that income fell precipitously. Among periodic reports by the administration was a 1938 announcement that plans were on hold for faculty raises, River Campus cottages for professors, and gym improvements for the women's campus at Prince Street. Annual operating costs had increased 10 percent in the previous two years to $3.6 million. The University announced a $60 tuition hike for 1939 to $360, which was followed by a $40 increase a year later. The *Campus* reacted with one of its largest fonts: "University Jacks Tuition to $400." Private educational institutions and philanthropies throughout the country were facing a similar squeeze, the newspaper reported.

Valentine repeatedly told the Board that important progress hinged on donations. Fundraising was primarily a Board role, he believed. In delaying the 1938 projects, Valentine told trustees, "Until financial conditions better, we can only hope that several of these projects will appeal to individuals with the vision, generosity, and ability to help make them possible."

Some faculty were frustrated by what they perceived as excessive frugality by Rochester administrators—who clearly were intent on preserving endowment principal. Professors and deans were plucked away to become presidents of Wells College, Tufts University, Purdue University, and California Institute of Technology. A few leading scientists left, taking along their bright research assistants.

Rochester celebrated distinct recruiting successes, however. Chemistry chair W. Albert Noyes Jr., the leading physical chemist in the country, came from Brown University in 1938. Physicist Robert Marshak—later founder of the International Conference on High Energy Physics—joined the faculty in 1939. John Romano, MD, who revolutionized medical education with a new emphasis on the social aspects of patient care, joined the School of Medicine and Dentistry in 1946.

Valentine placed the University at national center stage in many instances. A Rochester conference on "New Frontiers in American Life" in the spring of 1940 featured top executives from leading corporations, including General Electric, E. I. du Pont de Nemours, General

Brian O'Brien, director of the Institute of Optics, uses a high-speed camera
that he helped design and build. The camera made exposures in
one millionth of a second.

Dudley DeGroot

Dudley DeGroot and the Football Revival

Alan Valentine, president of the University—and a 1924 U.S. Olympic Rugby teammate of DeGroot—appointed Dudley S. DeGroot varsity football coach after the 1939 season ended 0-7. At that point, Rochester had tallied six years of losing seasons, including a winless 1937.

Valentine recruited DeGroot from San Jose State University, where DeGroot tallied a 59-18-0 record in seven years. DeGroot, with a doctorate in education and Phi Beta Kappa key, quickly earned widespread awe. By one account, the University treasurer offered to classify his salary as an investment rather than an expense.

DeGroot urged Rochester alumni to promote the University among promising high school athletes. He won approval for practices through the winter and spring—training that helped students meet extra physical education requirements during the war years. He wrote to players during the summer with tips on nutrition and conditioning.

"For the first time since 1934, six dreary years ago, the varsity football team in 1940 has overbalanced games lost by games won, and alumni fans and downtown partisans, emaciated from a diet long deficient in touchdown vitamins, will have something to talk about and chortle over for many months to come," said the *Rochester Alumni-Alumnae Review* in October 1940. Among other victories, the *Review* cheerfully reported a 40-6 win over "the heavier Union team that had rolled over the 1939 Yellowjackets and scarred them with 46 points to Rochester's zero score."

In 1942, James Secrest '45, '48M (MD) joined brother Richard '43 (co-captain) on the varsity team. James ran a spectacular 1,002 yards and scored 22 touchdowns in that one season in this remarkable period in Rochester football history.

The NFL's Washington, D.C., team recruited DeGroot from Rochester after the 1943 season. His years in Rochester remain a highlight in the program's history. "Dud" DeGroot racked up 23 wins against 6 losses at Rochester.

ROCHESTER vs. HAMILTON
Saturday, October 26, 1940

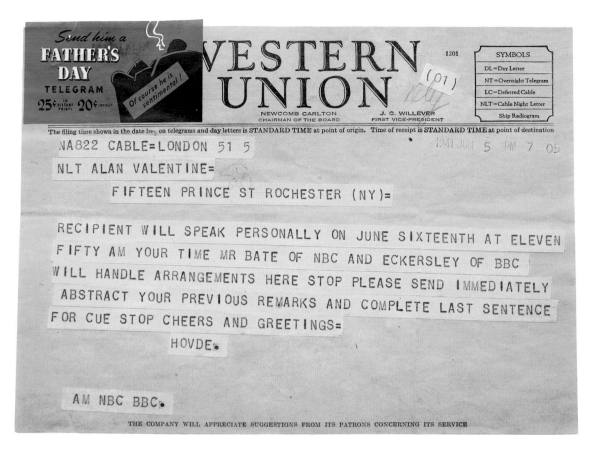

WESTERN UNION

Send him a
FATHER'S DAY TELEGRAM
25¢ TO DISTANT POINTS 20¢ LOCALLY
Of course he is sentimental!

1201

SYMBOLS
DL=Day Letter
NT=Overnight Telegram
LC=Deferred Cable
NLT=Cable Night Letter
Ship Radiogram

NEWCOMB CARLTON
CHAIRMAN OF THE BOARD

J. C. WILLEVER
FIRST VICE-PRESIDENT

The filing time shown in the date line on telegrams and day letters is STANDARD TIME at point of origin. Time of receipt is STANDARD TIME at point of destination

NA822 CABLE=LONDON 51 5   1941 JUN 5 PM 7 05

NLT ALAN VALENTINE=

FIFTEEN PRINCE ST ROCHESTER (NY)=

RECIPIENT WILL SPEAK PERSONALLY ON JUNE SIXTEENTH AT ELEVEN
FIFTY AM YOUR TIME MR BATE OF NBC AND ECKERSLEY OF BBC
WILL HANDLE ARRANGEMENTS HERE STOP PLEASE SEND IMMEDIATELY
ABSTRACT YOUR PREVIOUS REMARKS AND COMPLETE LAST SENTENCE
FOR CUE STOP CHEERS AND GREETINGS=

HOVDE.

AM NBC BBC.

THE COMPANY WILL APPRECIATE SUGGESTIONS FROM ITS PATRONS CONCERNING ITS SERVICE

After months of planning, negotiation, and preparation, Frederick Hovde's telegram to President Valentine confirmed the plan for Winston Churchill to address 1941's commencement via transatlantic radio broadcast.

Motors, the railroad, steel and banking industries, and philanthropic foundations. "Job Horizons as Wide as Those of Old in Geography, Say Industrialists in Forum," the *New York Times* headlined its lengthy treatment.

The president threw himself into national politics as international affairs increasingly hinted at U.S. involvement in war. While many university presidents preached neutrality to their students, few were as "militantly neutral" as Valentine, reported *TIME*. He left the University for two months to help lead Democrats in the 1940 campaign for Republican Wendell Willkie.

The University experienced an honor in June 1941, playing host to British prime minister Winston Churchill's first radio speech to an American audience. Valentine's top assistant, Frederick Hovde, recruited by the FDR administration in early 1941 for a high-level role in London coordinating British and American scientific advances for defense, was a central figure in arranging the Churchill exchange.

Churchill accepted Valentine's invitation for an honorary degree broadcast by BBC and NBC during commencement. The prime minister used his brief platform to reach out to the American public, which at that time was divided over the level of engagement appropriate for the United States as Hitler moved across Europe.

If there had been unity as in World War I, Austria, Czechoslovakia, Poland, France, Yugoslavia, and Greece would not then be under Nazi influence, Churchill suggested.

"The nations were pulled down one by one while the others gaped and chattered," he declared. "One by one, each in his turn, they let themselves be caught. One after another they were felled by brutal violence or poisoned from within by subtle intrigue.

"And now the old lion with her lion cubs at her side stands alone against hunters who are armed with deadly weapons and impelled by desperate and destructive rage. . . . Time is short. Every month that passes adds to the length and to the perils of the journey that will have to be made.

"United we stand. Divided we fall. Divided, the dark ages return. United, we can save and guide the world."

A 10-minute standing ovation stretched as long as Churchill's poetic appeal.

Hovde, later president of Purdue University, wrote to Valentine from London: "It was a real thrill for me to be at No. 10 Downing Street that afternoon. I met the doughty old warrior, who looked marvelously fit, and accepted his thanks to you and the Board for his degree. . . . We had all the breaks on transmission and reception—it was literally perfect."

University administrators had been trying to assess the effect on students and faculty were the United States to enter the war. Meanwhile, a committee of faculty leaders met to discuss prospects for Rochester in defense-related research. Like other universities, Rochester had contributed several faculty members by June 1941 for allied projects in a global conflict that many believed would be won by science.

The University's next milestone came in November. Rochester was invited to join the elite Association of American Universities, making it the 34th to join the group then largely responsible for ensuring the quality of American graduate education. Valentine quickly assumed leadership roles and became AAU president in 1945.

On December 7, 1941, Japanese warplanes bombed Pearl Harbor. On December 8, the United States declared war on Japan and then against Germany on December 11, after Hitler's declaration against the United States.

Valentine proclaimed previous political differences "past history" and traveled to Washington to consult with military and education leaders. What would the war mean? How would other schools manage? He returned from an enormous conference of the Association of American Colleges, where higher education officials from 1,000 insti-

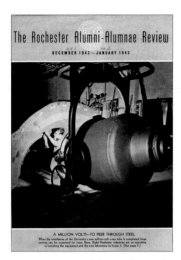

The Rochester Alumni-Alumnae Review

DECEMBER 1942—JANUARY 1943

A MILLION VOLTS—TO PEER THROUGH STEEL

Review trumpeted the installation of the University's million-volt x-ray tube.

tutions debated ramifications and policies, pledging together to give full cooperation to the nation's commander-in-chief in the war effort.

In January, Valentine crafted a message to anxious undergraduate students, who were returning from their winter break.

The University adopted an accelerated schedule, squeezing four years of coursework into three, Valentine said. "Soft and polite" sports, such as golf and tennis, were out; young men would play rugged games such as football and boxing to prepare for combat. He suggested they curtail their social lives.

"Most of us do not yet realize the great extent and the fundamental nature of the changes that must be made in our individual lives and in our college life and program, to meet the demands that will inevitably be put on us," Valentine said.

"The best thing you can do now is to get to those classes and work your heads off," he said. "Don't take any time off to be sorry for yourselves, or for anyone else."

The spirit of his words could apply in a broad sense to the University and others like it. Campuses faced enormous pressure in ensuing years with decimated enrollments and teaching ranks; Rochester scraped by mainly due to securing a large Navy contract for officer training. But new potential rose: Academic research contributions to crucial defense projects caught the nation's attention.

Going forward, the federal government would depend on civilian scientists for much of the basic and applied research relevant to its many interests, said historian Roger L. Geiger. Policy scholar John R. Thelin wrote that the success of massive, classified endeavors—primarily DuBridge's radar initiative and the Manhattan Project to develop the atomic bomb, in which Rochester also figured—provided the rationale for future partnerships. Even professors in relatively obscure subjects experienced sudden demand.

"Deep within the departments and electives of the American university there were faculty who could read, write, and teach Japanese, Italian, and Russian," Thelin wrote. "Professors of geography and history promptly provided government agencies with briefings on culture, terrain and politics as well as customs and languages for a host of understudied regions and countries. A biologist who had won little recognition on campus for his research on tropical diseases could become a national hero by contributing his expertise to the war effort."

Rochester faculty led the way in many disciplines. By the fall of 1942, 45 Medical Center scientists were engaged in defense projects, while a dozen faculty members from the college took full-time leave for government posts.

President Alan Valentine bestowed an honorary degree from the University of Rochester on George Washington Carver at Tuskegee Institute in 1941.

George Washington Carver

On June 17, 1941, President Alan Valentine began the long journey—by plane, train, and automobile—to Tuskegee Institute in Alabama, where he conferred another historic honorary degree.

Valentine began corresponding with George Washington Carver, renowned agricultural researcher, early that year. It was clear immediately that Carver, in his late 70s and in poor health, could not travel to Rochester for the June 16 commencement ceremonies. The Rochester committee determining recipients for honorary degrees made the unprecedented recommendation that Valentine arrange to see Carver at Tuskegee, where Carver had worked since becoming agriculture director in 1896.

"The committee . . . feels that it would like to see you receive this honor from the university, which will in turn be honoring itself by the award of a degree to you," Valentine wrote.

Valentine wholeheartedly adopted the Carver proposal, first raised in a letter from athletics director Edwin Fauver the previous fall. Valentine

noted in his citation to Carver his own family connections to William Lloyd Garrison, a prominent abolitionist who served as editor of the radical abolitionist newspaper, the *Liberator*.

"That Rochester should honor you is particularly appropriate, for many years ago that city was a haven of refuge for your people on their way to freedom. And that I should be the proud bearer of their greeting gives me special satisfaction, for I am a Quaker and my children are direct descendants of William Lloyd Garrison."

Carver, born to slave parents, educated himself growing up, particularly in the behavior of plant life. Passionate about art and music as well, he studied piano and painting at Simpson College. Encouraged by his art teacher, Carver became the first African American to enroll at Iowa State University, where he studied agriculture. After graduating from Iowa State, Carver taught at Tuskegee Institute, where he gained an international reputation for his discoveries, most notably in

the creation of hundreds of products from peanuts and sweet potatoes. His discoveries contributed substantially to the southern economy in providing alternatives to cotton.

Rochester's was only the second honorary degree Carver received during his life, but he had received numerous honors, including the Roosevelt Medal for Contributions to Southern Agriculture.

Said Valentine: "Because you have opened new doors of opportunity to those Americans who happen to be Negroes; because you have once again demonstrated that in human ability there is no color line; because you have helped thousands of men acquire new confidence and self-respect, the Trustees of the University of Rochester, by secret and unanimous ballot, have voted to confer upon you one of the highest honorary degrees at their disposal, and by another special action have authorized me to confer this degree in a manner never attempted before in the ninety-one years of the University."

Sports were an important part of the Navy V-12 College Training Program during World War II. In this photograph from the June 20, 1945, issue of the Rochester *Democrat and Chronicle* Thomas Wearing, dean of the Colgate-Rochester Divinity School and Rotary Club president, presents Rotary Club awards to members of the last V-12 class. From left to right are Marian Tucker, James McHugh '50, George Vercity, Wearing, Robert Cannon '45, Edward Kern '47, and Robert C. Harvey '46.

"Rochester has responded, to an inspiring degree, to America's mobilization of scientific skill," the University alumni magazine said.

Lee DuBridge was the first to leave. Physics chair and dean of the college faculty, DuBridge headed for Cambridge, Mass., in November 1940 to put together what became a 4,000-person, wide-ranging research effort into radar at Massachusetts Institute of Technology.

DuBridge had drawn national attention at Rochester in the mid-1930s for plans to build a five-million-volt accelerator—the largest existing then—to make artificial radium. DuBridge initiated the University of Rochester's faculty committee on defense in 1940, consulting his close associate, Vannevar Bush—FDR's top science advisor during the war and later credited with the creation of the National Science Foundation.

Noyes, Rochester's chemistry chair, also left before Pearl Harbor. Noyes led a range of chemical studies at 30 American universities. Institute of Optics director Brian O'Brien began coordinating research projects for military agencies well before the United States entered the war, trying to avoid the shortages of optical devices experienced in World War I. In 1942, he juggled military contracts for night-vision and other mechanisms worth $491,000, or $7 million in 2013 dollars. The University took pride in its assessment that O'Brien held more research contracts than any single scientist in the country.

Medical Center physiologist Wallace Fenn shifted from his path-breaking studies in muscle function to help the military better understand breathing. Working with a large, old beer tank rigged to test oxygen and air pressure levels, Fenn provided critical information in the development of pressurizing masks for pilots. Fenn's colleague Edward Adolph made comparable discoveries in hydration for soldiers in desert warfare.

Stafford Warren, Rochester's top radiologist and a pioneer in nuclear medicine credited with developing the mammogram, was recruited to lead worker safety efforts associated with the Manhattan Project, the government's covert project to make nuclear bombs ahead of the Germans. Warren had secured funding at Rochester for a million-volt X-ray machine, first intended to scan castings of war materials produced by local companies to ensure flaws could be detected before they were shipped off for combat. He had earned international recognition for innovations in fever therapy and studies on the use of radiation to treat cancer. His department became an important center for government research in radiation for decades.

Geologist Quentin Singewald prospected for strategic war minerals in South America. Geologist and dean of the college J. Edward Hoffmeister directed charting projects for the Army Map Service. Economists Frank J. Smith and William Dunkman worked as consultants for the federal Office of Price Administration. Sociologist Raymond V. Bowers was senior statistician for the Army general who

Kathrine Koller

Kathrine Koller began her 25-year tenure in the English department in 1942. A Guggenheim Fellow, she became the first woman to chair a major discipline at the University, in 1946. Koller was named an honorary member of the Rochester Alumnae Association in 1952. The citation noted her research on the English Renaissance, her teaching, and her leadership—including drawing top educators and writers to the University in 1948 to discuss cultural trends in literature.

Engineering lab, circa 1944. Kneeling on the left is Dean Parker '45 with Richard Mack '45 standing behind him. Kneeling on the right is Richard F. Eisenberg '45, '48 (Mas). Eisenberg joined the mechanical engineering faculty upon graduation and moved to the chemical engineering faculty in 1959, specializing in metallurgy. He retired in 1983. Since 1994, the Eisenberg summer internship program that he initiated has provided real-life experience for undergraduate chemical engineering students.

Leonard Raymond, left, and Raymond Schneider '48, '52M (MD)

AIR RAID INSTRUCTIONS

When You Hear ✕✕✕✕✕✕ **Air Raid Is Probable**
(Blue Signal)
(One Minute Blast From Heating Plant Siren, and From City Sirens.

All campus lights will go out from master switch, except Dewey, Physics and Library. Go to shelters at once. Wardens will take charge, and all personnel will report to stations.

When You Hear ✕✕✕✕✕ **Planes Are Overhead**
(Red Signal)
Intermittent Blasts From Heating Plant, Chime Rings, City Sirens Warble

Remaining lights go out from master Switch. Everyone must remain in shelters.

When Lights Go On Again Raid Is Over
(All Clear)
Street Lights and Campus Lights Go On - City Sirens Give Intermittent Blasts

Leave shelters and go about your business; be ready for a resumption of alert.

Remain Calm, Obey Instructions of Air Raid Personnel. Walk to Shelters - Don't Run.

Shelter For This Building:
First and Second Floor Corridors

Dorothy Jean Quigley '47

Judy Rebasz '45 and Eunice Lisson '45

Women in the War Years

Dorothy Quigley, 18, made news across the country—for landing a job as a butcher.

The Rochester *Democrat and Chronicle* published a feature on Quigley, a freshman in the College for Women, when Star Market hired her for a job traditionally filled only by men. The Associated Press picked up the story, and it soon appeared in cities from Newark to Denver.

Across a spectrum of trades, women came into previously unthinkable demand during the war.

A Kodak official headlined a luncheon on the Prince Street Campus in the fall of 1942. Kenneth Ogden of the Kodak Hawk-Eye Works—then making optical products for the military—would outline opportunities, the women's *Tower Times* reported.

"Some 20,000 more workers will be required to meet the demands of Rochester industries before the end of the year and at least 50 percent will have to be women," the article said.

Women were needed to fill spots left by men entering military service and to help industries grow to meet war production demands. Women were gaining roles as factory supervisors, as employment and public relations officers, architects, engineers, meteorologists, and budget administrators.

The University developed curriculum for women interested in adding a "war minor"—study in practical scientific fields suited to industry. The extra courses in the decidedly liberal arts college centered on mathematics, chemistry, physics, engineering, economics, and business administration.

The "near equality" of the sexes through the industrial needs of two world wars presented a profound revolution in American lives, University President Valentine said in an address to the College for Women.

"Women will have to face questions when the war is over," Valentine said. "Can she surrender easily her economic independence? If marriage is combined with the career, can both be fulfilled with emotional, psychological, and spiritual satisfaction?"

Women's continued interest in education and work outside the home after the war came as news. "Experts expect the trend to continue," a wire-service article in the *Campus* said in November 1945. "Many major problems have arisen with the development of the new trend. One is the housing problem, but perhaps the most significant from a student's point of view is the influence of the women on extracurricular activities. During the war years women have in a large part taken over the student newspapers, headed the undergraduate societies, become class officers, and in general dominated campus events. Undoubtedly this condition will be altered to some extent with the return of the men, but the women indicate that they intend to remain a force in these outside activities."

In 1945, the School of Medicine and Dentistry admitted 13 women, its largest class of women ever. "As a result of their war endeavors, more women have become greatly interested in medicine and other fields of science, and the indications are that they are going to take an increasingly important part in them," said George P. Berry, MD, head of the department of bacteriology.

Nobel Winner

A high point of the war years came with the news that senior research associate Henrik Dam had won the Nobel Prize in Physiology or Medicine for discovery of vitamin K. Dam shared the award with Edward A. Doisy of the St. Louis University School of Medicine, who developed methods for its use.

Dam joined the University of Rochester Medical Center in 1942 after emigrating when the Nazis occupied his homeland of Denmark. He stayed at Rochester until 1945, then joined the Rockefeller Institute for Medical Research before returning to Polytechnic Institute, Copenhagen, in 1946.

Discovery of the vitamin's role in blood coagulation won acclaim, especially for its benefits in helping to prevent bleeding in newborn babies. The vitamin was named "K" for the Danish "koagulation."

"The possession of a single Nobel Prize winner is a distinction few universities or cities in the world can boast; to have Nobel Prizes awarded to two members of the faculty of a single school in a single small university is an almost unparalleled recognition," President Valentine said.

ran Selective Service. Romance languages specialists Sterling Callisen and George Raser worked for the Office of Naval Intelligence, while English professor John Pendleton consulted for Army Intelligence. Librarian John R. Russell led the American Library Association's committee on aid to devastated libraries in Europe and Asia.

Medical research teams studied infectious diseases, gas gangrene, shock, silicosis, burns, and tooth decay. John Murlin was chair of FDR's committee on food and nutrition.

"I cannot even give you a clue as to the names of some of our war research projects," Valentine told a gathering of the Rochester Ad Club in October 1942.

Enrollment went topsy-turvy. With every edition through the war, the *Review* carried more and more pages of fine print listing students or graduates and their military roles. Ultimately, full pages listed casualties. One heartrending report included:

> Pfc. Walter T. Enright, '30
> Reported missing in action in North African theatre, November 26, 1943. Later reported deceased. Was a cryptographer in the AAF Unit.

> Ens. Ralph E. Wersinger, '35
> Formerly serving on board U.S.S. SC-1279, was killed in line of duty, October 1943.

> Cpl. Ronald W. Doll, '36
> Killed in action in Laon, France, on September 23, 1944. Was a member of an Army Air Forces ground crew.

An important contract with the Navy helped sustain the University. The Navy selected Rochester and a handful of universities for its V-12 program, designed to educate officers with an emphasis on science and engineering. Roughly 800 Navy students studied at the University on various rotations; Rochester estimated 1,500 had been on campus by war's end. A strong Navy relationship remained for many years after the war—resulting in part with the 1946 construction of Harkness Hall, for naval science and training, and a new, 250-million-volt cyclotron for research in nuclear physics in 1949.

Women at the Prince Street Campus formed volunteer groups to salvage metal, sell war stamps, and make bandages. They found unprecedented demand for their services in factories and scientific research jobs as Rochester industries ramped up production of war materials.

A survey in the fall of 1944 suggested one in five women students had summer factory jobs earning up to $650. The University began offering River Campus engineering courses for women needed in industry.

DuBridge, physics chair through the war, communicated frequently with Valentine from the lab at MIT, which he headed until early 1946. He was a vital confidante and advisor. As early as April 1942, he urged Valentine to prioritize investment in science—or at least, if cuts had to be made, to cut scientific programs less than others.

The University was fortunate to have major war-related research on its campus, through the Institute of Optics and the Manhattan Project, DuBridge pointed out. Many universities saw all their top scientists leave for other labs during the war.

The Manhattan Project division at Rochester focused on the health effects of exposure to radiation. An annex on Elmwood Avenue that had housed Warren's X-ray machine was expanded twice to house the growing project, where scientists tested blood samples from workers at bomb-making sites and performed separate research on radioactive dust. By 1945, roughly 300 people were working in the guarded brick buildings.

Valentine created an office to coordinate research and began plans for investment in expansion of science facilities, including physics.

After the bombings of Hiroshima and Nagasaki, the University planned a somber and reflective response to Victory over Japan Day. There would be classes as usual, chapel services, and chimes from the Rush Rhees Library tower. Valentine discouraged students from boisterous celebrations.

The end of the war left many with a sense of bewilderment. DuBridge came back to Rochester and soon realized that after six years at the "Rad Lab," he not only had fallen behind in physics research but also couldn't remember basic facts to teach undergraduates. Noyes recalled a sinking feeling: "I had thought almost exclusively about military matters for four to five years. Would I make the necessary readjustment to peacetime activities?"[2]

Valentine was a changed man, DuBridge said. "He had very uncharacteristic—I thought very uncharacteristic—bursts of temper towards the end of the war." When Caltech convinced DuBridge to become president two months after his return to Rochester, Valentine fired off an "outrageously angry" letter to the chair of the Caltech Board, DuBridge said.[3]

Universities scrambled for faculty. Administrators also coped with expanded need for facilities for veterans, many returning or starting college under generous G.I. Bill benefits. Total enrollment at Rochester hit 6,400 in 1946, a 23 percent increase from 1940, and swelled to 9,444 by 1950. The Federal Public Housing Authority funded makeshift dorms for 145 veterans on the River Campus while local developers built apartments south of the Medical Center. The University rented classrooms and lounges from the city school district.

Valentine began a development effort, compiling files of salary and investment data on dozens of potential donors. Armin Bender, his

---

2   Albert W. Noyes, *A Victorian in the Twentieth Century* (Austin: University of Texas, 1976), 275.

3   Goodstein, "Lee A. DuBridge (Part II)."

first publicity director, served briefly as an assistant on the project. The president also corresponded with national science advisor Vannevar Bush—including reporting to him about futile efforts to build AAU support for Bush's proposed National Science Foundation to support academic research. Valentine alerted Whipple to examples of institutions supporting the notion of federal funding of research—a source of discomfort for Whipple and many in the national medical community.

Valentine detailed proposals for potential donors, including a 10-page, single-spaced letter urging Hollywood producer David O. Selznick—a participant in Rochester's 1940 highly publicized "New Frontiers in American Life" conference featuring top executives from leading corporations—to contribute $500,000 toward new research facilities for physics and biology.

The president's national passions took him to the Republican nominating convention for Thomas E. Dewey in 1948, where he received an invitation to The Hague to oversee the Marshall Plan for economic stabilization in the Netherlands. Rochester trustees granted a leave of absence for the 1948–49 academic year.

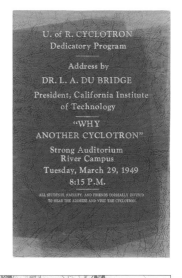

He kept a hand in some matters, including pressing at high U.S. government levels to clear the name of a University junior physicist caught up in the Red Scare of the late 1940s and early '50s. Valentine's handling of the case of Bernard Peters earned praise for the University in its stance for academic freedom—in contrast with some institutions that summarily dismissed scientists under suspicion.

Peters, hired for Rochester's growing physics department in September 1946, was one of many scientists involved in the Manhattan Project who came under scrutiny after testimony by J. Robert Oppen-

Clockwise from top: cyclotron dedication program; cyclotron under construction, 1947; physics professor Sidney Barnes and physicist J. Robert Oppenheimer with the University of Rochester cyclotron

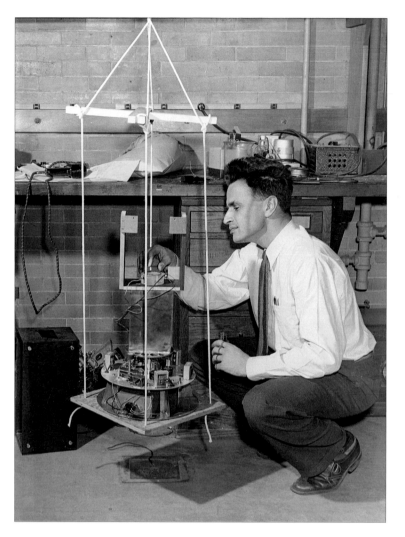

Physicist Bernard Peters's research led to important discoveries in primary cosmic rays. The University defended Peters during the Red Scare.

heimer before the House Un-American Activities Committee. Oppenheimer reportedly told the committee that Peters, a native of Germany who emigrated in the mid-1930s after serving time in a Nazi prison camp, had joined the German National Communist Party. Peters acknowledged communist associations but denied any involvement in communist causes.

Peters, traveling to a conference in Europe on behalf of the Office of Naval Research in August 1948, was strip-searched and had his Navy credentials revoked without explanation as he boarded a train to Paris. A host of University officials—including University lawyers, physics chair George B. Collins, and Valentine—appealed to numerous officials in ensuing months. University records do not show any indication of Navy or State Department officials ever specifying allegations against Peters, and he never was charged.

Lou Alexander

Richard Baroody

John Baynes

Robert Erikson

Glenn W. Quaint Jr.

BASKETBALL GLORY

Rochester celebrated a perfect basketball season in the winter of 1942. Coach Lou Alexander's squad defeated Princeton, Yale, Michigan State, Vermont, Colgate, Cornell, Harvard, and Ohio State.

Star performers were Richard Baroody '44, who later served a 35-year career with the East Rochester public schools; John Baynes '47, who coached basketball and football in Rochester-area schools until 1981; Robert Erikson '42, who served as director of merchandising for Disneyland; and Glenn W. Quaint Jr. '42, whose engineering career took him to Goodyear Aerospace, where he served as project manager on military and NASA hardware test programs.

Eastman School Stars
Doriot Anthony Dwyer, above, and Dorothy Ziegler were among an impressive roster of Eastman graduates of the early 1940s. Dwyer '43, a distant cousin of Susan B. Anthony, was named principal flute of the Boston Symphony in 1952. Ziegler, of the same class, was named principal trombone of the St. Louis Symphony in 1944. Other Eastman graduates of the early 1940s included Prix de Rome winners Ulysses S. Kay and Jack Beeson; Pulitzer-winning composer and pianist John M. LaMontaine; William L. Bergsma, director of the University of Washington School of Music; Peter Mennin, president of the Juilliard School of Music; vocalist Mac R. Morgan; legendary concert baritone and actor William C. Warfield; and leaders of Radio City Music Hall, the School of Fine and Applied Arts at Boston University, the Oberlin Conservatory of Music, and the Louisiana State University School of Music.

Valentine wrote at length on the issue in his annual report to the Board at the end of the 1948–49 academic year.

It is the first article in the creed of the scholar, the scientist, the teacher that he is sincerely in pursuit of truth, and that he is acquainted with the methods by which truth should be sought—accuracy, careful distinction between fact and opinion, and between his professional knowledge and his personal convictions, and no conscious distortion or perversion of the material with which he deals. This, or any university, has the right to insist that those who work here, in every field and at every level, whatever their personal, political, religious or other convictions, shall subscribe to and act within this established article of the scholar-scientist credo. Those who put some other loyalty above loyalty to truth and its pursuit or who would distort facts to forward their own special dogma are inconsistent with its ideals and have no place here. In such matters we can judge only by the results, and must give thought to the results of the teacher who thinks he means well but betrays his profession as well as to him who betrays it deliberately. We know of no one in our university staff who is not entitled to the full privileges of academic freedom. If any should come to be in doubt, we would need convincing proof before we would qualify one iota our devotion to academic freedom. If such proof emerged after fair and thorough consideration in which the man in question had been given full opportunity to be heard, I should favor his prompt separation from the University staff.

But my position should arouse no alarm in the minds of members of our staff whose consciences are clear. The record of this university in defense of academic freedom is a fine one. We shall continue to maintain that record and defend to the utmost the right of free expression by all members of our academic staff, who are loyal to the standards of their profession and loyal to the basic concepts of freedom and justice as we can collectively best assess them. For honest men differ among themselves and those differences are the essence of thought and progress. Without such differences there could be no university, which should encourage the ferment of thought expressed in terms, and in a manner, reasonably consistent with the standards and dignity of the academic profession and environment.

Later that year, Valentine, though expressing deep admiration for the ideals of academic leadership, submitted his resignation. He had no definite plans but a growing sense, he said, that he did not want to devote his life to higher education. He served a brief stint in 1951 as President Truman's director of the U.S. Economic Stabilization Agency. He later wrote a memoir as well as biographies of British political figures, including Lord North, prime minister during the American Revolution.

DuBridge wrote to the president of "considerable shock" on reading a report of his resignation in the *Los Angeles Times*. Valentine replied quickly: "It was my opinion that any contribution I could make to this University could be made in the first 10 years, after which point the law of diminishing returns would set in, certainly for the University and possibly for me." He could not leave during the war and immediate postwar period, he added. "My relations with trustees, faculties, and students could not be happier, and in that respect I have been lucky all along. But I do think that the beginning of Rochester's second century, next fall, is an appropriate time to start off with new leadership, new ideals, new enthusiasm, and in general a fresh clean deal."

University history professor Glyndon G. Van Deusen summed up the Valentine administration after the former president died in 1980. Van Deusen credited Valentine with important policies, such as leaves of absence for productive scholars, which enhanced teaching quality. Valentine led the University through the chaos of World War II. Negatives were his occasional temper and his tacit acceptance—by maintaining a separate campus for women—of unequal opportunities for the sexes.

"Of course there were faults and failures; there always are," Van Deusen wrote, "but the final judgment must be that, after 15 years marked by the havoc of war, Alan Valentine left behind him a vigorous and improved University."

The need for wartime conservation of resources may have inspired this 1942 photograph of Valentine, who would have been accustomed to bicycle riding from his days at Oxford.

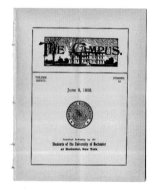

CAMPUS TIMES

The first student newspaper, the *University Record*, debuted in 1873. The monthly publication was designed "to supply a want long felt . . . by furnishing a reliable organ through which the College may speak," reported the city's *Union & Advertiser*, according to historian Arthur May.

The paper became the *Rochester Campus* in 1876. Coverage included activities of alumni, acquisitions by the library, and pieces by professors or the president.

"The tone and content of the U. of R. paper, called simply the *Campus* from 1883, depended upon the talents and whims of the current staff and standards ranged from the dignified to the plebian," May wrote.

Women created their own newspaper, *Cloister Window*, in 1925. In addition to campus matters it provided commentary on new books, updates on alumnae, and news from other women's colleges. The

paper was renamed the *Tower Times* in 1832, a tribute to the elegant tower of Cutler Union.

The men's and women's papers merged with the move of women to the River Campus in 1955. Before and after the merger, the papers traditionally put out April Fools' editions. The 1956 prank headlines included "UR Admits 10,000 Frosh" and "Garage Planned in Quad."

The *Cloister Window* and the *Tower Times* served the College of Women from 1925–55.

Humorous issues, especially on April Fools' Day, have been a long-standing tradition.

Until the merger of the colleges for men and women in the fall of 1955, academic processions reflected the coordinate nature of the University. The Eastman School of Music and the School of Medicine and Dentistry were both coeducational from their founding.

A Dynamic Attitude

CORNELIS W. DE KIEWIET, 1951–1961

ORNELIS WILLEM DE KIEWIET ARRIVED FAST—TRUSTEES ACKNOWLEDGED A "SOME-what irregular" procedure in their rush to hire him in the fall of 1950. This would prove a fitting start for the fifth president of the University of Rochester.

Nine months into his first year, de Kiewiet convinced the Board of Trustees to approve the merger of the colleges for men and women on the River Campus. Later, new professional schools were formed in business, education, and engineering. De Kiewiet also began innovative programs in international studies. He created a host of administrative offices to manage the increasingly complex research and educational enterprise. And by 1961, when he retired, de Kiewiet had succeeded in some measure in his perpetual effort to change public thinking about supporting higher education: rather than charity, this was a social and economic necessity.

In 1950, as trustees looked for a successor to Alan Valentine to lead Rochester into its second century, the University had weathered a series of enormous stresses. As a true university it was relatively young. In the three decades since the founding of the esteemed schools of music and medicine—as well as the stately River Campus—University finances, enrollment, and faculty had been buffeted by inflation, the Great Depression, and World War II.

In a sense, the University now faced its first opportunity to plan and define itself—in an era of significant American social change. And it would prepare for unprecedented growth in higher education nationally. College and university enrollments swelled more than 200 percent from 1949 to 1969, much of that growth coming with changing demographics and increased availability of financial aid. Meanwhile, state and federal investment in academic research swelled, particularly when the 1957 Soviet launch of

Cornelis W. de Kiewiet

Sputnik heightened concerns about U.S. defense. At the University of Rochester, projects sponsored by outside agencies became a critical component of ever-growing operations, providing 23 percent of the University's $26 million budget by 1959.

The presidential search committee collected reports from deans and officers as it assessed Rochester's leadership needs. Among the more serious issues presented: succession plans—or lack of—at the Eastman School of Music and the Medical Center. Both schools had risen meteorically to premier world ranks, the Eastman School under the groundbreaking guidance of director Howard Hanson, approaching his 30th anniversary; and the medical school under founding dean George Whipple, who, in his 70s, showed little obvious intent to retire. "It is an unsound condition when so much of a school's success depends upon the presence of a single individual," provost Donald Gilbert told the committee.

Also, the institution had an "uneven" character to it, treasurer Raymond Thompson observed. While Valentine had set out to place the College of Arts and Science on the same plane of quality as the schools of music and medicine, that had fallen short. Some programs, especially in scientific fields, were heavily funded, leaving little to invest in others. History professor Dexter Perkins "should not have to 'pass the hat' for his graduate history fellowship program," Thompson said.

Faculty salaries remained low—lower than prewar levels when adjusted for inflation, estimated at 70 percent from 1939 to 1949. Both the River Campus and the Prince Street Campus needed significant capital investments, especially for the women's library and gymnasium.

In addition, the University would need to examine its expectations of a president. Provost Gilbert told the search committee: "In the modern university the functions of this office have become too manifold to be exercised effectively by a single individual." The president was expected to be the institution's academic leader, community leader, involved in national activities, and carry principal responsibility for the growth of University financial resources. An enlarged administrative structure was required, Gilbert said.

By August 1950, search committee members had discussed nearly 150 individuals, looked closely at 70, and interviewed a handful. Trustees Charles Wilcox and Raymond Ball drove to Ithaca to talk with de Kiewiet, then acting president at Cornell University. Wilcox recalled immediate, strong enthusiasm: Ball wanted to extend an offer that day.

At Cornell, where he had stepped in as president after the sudden resignation of Ezra Day, de Kiewiet was credited with turning around serious budget problems. Accounts of him described uncommon gusto and a great scholarly and executive mind. If anything, de Kiewiet could run too hard and fast with an idea, a Cornell administrator cautioned the Rochester trustees. De Kiewiet was not always diplomatic, and he was not popular with the Cornell faculty. Wilcox remembered hearing, "He was a Dutchman and . . . the trustees would have to ride herd on him carefully."

De Kiewiet, a native of the Netherlands, spent most of his early life in South Africa, where his father worked as a railroad construction supervisor. The continent held an important place in de Kiewiet's intellectual passions throughout his life and factored into a notable push for international awareness during his administrative career. De Kiewiet earned his bachelor's and master's degrees at the University of Witwatersrand in Johannesburg and a PhD in history from the University of London. He accepted an assistant professorship in history at the University of Iowa in 1929, the year he published his first of many

Howard Hanson, 1963

George Whipple, 1956

The City

The Rochester community evolved in its own ways through the 1950s. The economy boomed with success of its industrial base, notably Kodak, where net earnings doubled from 1947 to 1957 despite annual investments of up to $57 million in new or improved plants.

A new eastern expressway connected the city with the New York State Thruway, while private-automobile use swelled—a factor in suburban population growth. Ten towns surrounding the city experienced combined growth of 100,000 through the decade.

Other life patterns changed. Within six months of the June 1949 inauguration of Rochester's first local television station, WHAM, the number of TV sets in homes skyrocketed from 2,000 to 12,000, wrote former city historian Blake McKelvey in *Rochester on the Genesee: The Growth of a City*. Eastman School of Music director Howard Hanson welcomed the challenge presented by the new media, McKelvey added. "He eagerly exploited the advantages of radio and television and in 1957 conducted thirteen television programs on the theme, 'Music as a Language.'"

The full impact of Rochester's transformation from an industrial center into a well-rounded metropolis became evident in the late 1950s, McKelvey said. "It was only as the outward migration of some of its plants as well as of numerous inhabitants swelled to major proportions, and the outward reach of its institutions created new and broader ties during the late 1950s, that Rochester began to acquire the character of a regional as well as a technological center. Almost without realizing it, the city's population had become metropolitan in character."

eminent studies, *British Colonial Policy and the South African Republics, 1848–1872.*

De Kiewiet joined the Cornell faculty as professor of modern history in 1941 and promptly earned leadership roles. During the war years he oversaw language-training programs for the military. He became dean of Cornell's College of Arts and Sciences in 1945 and provost in 1948. He was in line for the presidency of Cornell when Wilcox and Ball visited.

De Kiewiet shared their eagerness. "The first time that I saw the U of R and its people, I liked the whole spirit and tempo so much that I knew that was the place that I wanted to be," he recalled. When the Rochester search committee learned the Cornell board would convene October 20, 1950, to name a president, it took the unprecedented step of making an offer before Rochester's full Board could convene for final approval on November 4. "Your committee . . . trusts that the Board of Trustees will recognize the urgency of action that arose," Chair Albert Kaiser, MD, explained in a report.

Installed as president the following June, de Kiewiet spoke of the need for ongoing growth in a university. "A university is never fully mature," he said. "It must grow and change, else it languishes and loses its place." This conviction, he said, applied to the three main activities a university supports: to pursue knowledge wherever it may lead; to cooperate in the technological process that advances business and industry; and, most important, to relate both knowledge and technology "to man's quest for dignity, peace, justice, the good of life—all the qualities and aspirations which make man a spiritual as well as a physical being."

As the 1951–52 academic year opened, de Kiewiet announced the creation of the University's first office of development, headed by former provost Gilbert. It was the first in roughly a dozen major new administrative posts, and it would support efforts on many fronts.

De Kiewiet shared candid thoughts in retirement that shed light on his decisions through this transformative period. He participated in an oral-history interview with a University public relations officer in 1971. In the early 1980s, he submitted a poignant draft of an essay for a planned, but never published, University of Rochester Library Bulletin on presidential recollections.

Reflecting on his early impressions of the University, de Kiewiet described an "absence of any sense of wholeness, from which the University suffered grievously." The women's Prince Street Campus was five miles away from the men's campus. The administration operated from a residential block there. The Eastman School was downtown in a neighborhood suffering some decay. The medical school, though near

D. A. HENDERSON

Donald Ainslie Henderson, or "D. A.," credited his Rochester medical education with strategies that helped him lead the way to the worldwide eradication of smallpox.

Henderson, a native of Lakewood, Ohio, earned his medical degree at Rochester in 1954 after graduating from Oberlin College. He served his internship and residency at Mary Imogene Bassett Hospital in Cooperstown, N.Y., and then earned a master's in public health at the Johns Hopkins University. Between his internship and residency Henderson worked in the Epidemic Intelligence Service of what is now the Centers for Disease Control and Prevention.

From 1966 to 1977, Henderson directed the World Health Organization's campaign against smallpox. "D. A. Henderson was the Eisenhower of the group of scientists and doctors and nurses and linguists and medical technicians and soldiers and academics who eradicated smallpox," wrote John Ellis in *Business Insider*. With any reported outbreak, a team flew into the region, tracked down people infected with the disease, and immunized anyone in the area.

In a 2009 interview with *Rochester Medicine*, after the release of Henderson's book, *Smallpox—The Death of a Disease*, he described the influence of Rochester. First, Henderson said, he became interested in epidemiology in the course of a project to win the George Corner Prize. Henderson wrote a paper on the spread of cholera in upstate New York in 1832, work that would play a role in being selected for the CDC's Epidemic Intelligence Service. Also, the instruction of John Romano, MD, and George Engel, MD, on interviewing patients influenced Henderson's approach to other situations.

Henderson served as dean of what became the Johns Hopkins School of Public Health, advisor to President George H. W. Bush, and as a senior advisor to the federal government on defense against possible biological attacks by terrorists after September 11, 2001.

His awards include the Presidential Medal of Freedom—the nation's highest civilian honor, the National Medal of Science, and the National Academy of Sciences' Public Welfare Medal. In 2005, Henderson was awarded the Hutchison Medal, the highest honor given to an alumnus by the University of Rochester.

President Rush Rhees posing with the women of the class of 1910 at the base of the statue of Martin Brewer Anderson. Annette Gardner Munro is seated in the second row. Munro was hired as dean of women students in 1910. With the establishment of the coordinate colleges for men and women in 1913, she would serve as dean of the College for Women until she retired in 1930.

the River Campus, also seemed disconnected. "The closest that I feel entitled to come was that each [institution] was conceived and considered in its own right," de Kiewiet remembered. He worked throughout his 10-year term to form a cohesive University "silhouette."

De Kiewiet immediately questioned the logic of a separate women's campus, which, with some buildings nearing 100 years old, would need $4 million in updates. Faculty and students wasted time, the president believed, traveling between the campuses for various courses or facility use. Further, the arrangement implied inequality for women. De Kiewiet sounded out his idea—transferring women to the River Campus—with Board chair M. Herbert Eisenhart.

This notion, though sometimes raised in prior years, had never been considered seriously. There were strong traditions and attitudes. The venerated Rush Rhees, president when benefactor George Eastman led contributions toward development of the River Campus, believed in coordinate education for men and women. Rhees also had wanted to preserve the University's first campus, opened in 1861. Alumni and alumnae held strong sentiments for their respective colleges, and there was considerable opposition to coeducation among River Campus men who believed the presence of women would cause a drop in academic quality.

De Kiewiet recalled, 30 years later, the powerful impact of his private talk with Eisenhart in the chair's home.

"Mr. Eisenhart was a man of great politeness and attention. He heard me patiently for two full hours. Then he arose to put a glass of whisky in my hand. Then he said with real kindness: 'I am happy to

12 ROCHESTER TIMES-UNION Sat., Oct. 1, 1955

SPREADING ITS WINGS in a mammoth arc is the new women's residence hall of the University of Rochester, newly completed on the coeducational River Campus.

Coeds Change Campus Character

Once All-Male Domain
Now Coeducational

Six hundred and twenty "Helen Evelive Wilkinsons" began moving into the once all-male domain of the University of Rochester's River Campus this week.

They're the female portion of the 1,820-member student body which will begin mixed classes Monday on the newly-combined campus.

The new coeducational program is a far cry from the policy in effect when Miss Wilkinson took her seat at the chapel lecture on Sept. 21, 1893—sole woman among 70 entering freshmen.

Miss Wilkinson defied tradition and stubborn trustees to

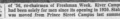
IN THE SHADOW of the statue of Martin B. Anderson, first UR president, stand Beneth Brigham, Endicott, Class of '56, and David S. Benedict, Glens Falls, Class

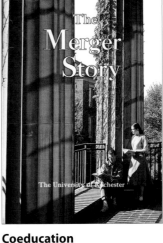
The University of Rochester

Coeducation

A 1954 booklet for alumni explains the merger of the men's and women's campuses. Photographs in the brochure, along with other promotional materials of the era, were taken by Ansel Adams, famous for his black and white images of the American West. George Eastman House curator Beaumont Newhall, a friend of Adams, recommended the photographer to the University. Adams stayed roughly three months: "Your University turned out to be about ten times as large and interesting as I had expected," he told *Rochester Review*. At left is a *Times Union* article describing the merging of the two campuses.

HELEN E. WILKINSON

become the first woman to take regular courses at the university and—in so doing—gain the distinction of first coed.

THIS YEAR'S CROP of freshmen girls—235 strong—was the first group to become entrenched on the joint campus. The coeds arrived Wednesday with 335 male freshmen.

They were greeted by several new facilities, including a new women's residence hall, all part of a 7 million dollar construction program.

The six-story women's residence hall with glassed-in rooftop solarium cost 6 million dollars. Opened this week, it overlooks the Genesee River and university athletic field.

A men's dining center will be opened next week. Later in the fall a women's gymnasium

and swimming pool are scheduled to be completed.

THE PROGRAM effecting the merger of the two campuses also is resulting in extensive remodeling to provide additional classroom, laboratory and office space and more dormitory space for men.

The old service building is being remodeled for the University School and a new fraternity house—Kappa Nu—has been added.

The merger of the campuses for a coeducational program is described by Dr. J. Edward Hoffmeister, dean of the College of Arts and Science, as the beginning of "a new era on the banks of the Genesee."

THE ENROLLMENT of freshmen girls represents an increase of 42 per cent over the 165 girls who were enrolled last year.

The male half of the freshmen enrollment is an increase of 35 per cent over last year and the largest number regularly admitted to the college for a four-year program.

The entering freshmen come from 30 states and five foreign countries in addition to Puerto Rico. One hundred and fifty are from Rochester or Monroe County.

MEN STUDENTS were first separated from women undergraduates in 1930 with the opening of the River Campus. This left the Prince Street Campus for the women students who had been enrolling in steadily increasing numbers after the pioneering efforts of Miss Wilkinson.

The university's first coed never received her degree. In 1895 her studies were interrupted by illness and two years later she died.

But in the interval of 62 years since her enrollment hundreds of other women have realized her ambition at the university.

of '56, co-chairmen of Freshman Week. River Campus had been solely for men since its opening in 1930. Statue was moved from Prince Street Campus last summer.

NEW DINING FACILITIES in the women's residence hall are admired by Carol Smith (left), Summit, N.J., | Class of '57, and Barbara Ellen Thomas, Lake Placid, one of the 570 freshmen entering this year.

GETTING SETTLED in their room in new women's residence hall are Ann Dalrymple (left), Warren, Pa., Class of '56, and Jodi Lewis, Ashville, N.Y., Class of '58.

Times-Union Photos by Jim Osborne

have listened to you, and I would like to give you some advice. Outside this room, never mention again the idea of bringing the men's and women's college together.' I finished my drink speechlessly, and felt like a marathon runner who falls over at the beginning of the race. On my way home, I remembered what I had said, and the enormity of what had been said. I recalled standing on the verandah of the administration building, and seeing nothing around me. My resolution was like a physical sensation. I would go on and talk, or would go away."

That November, the president told the Board's executive committee he intended to study "the financial and academic justification" of maintaining separate colleges for men and women. The next month, he reported to the full Board on the cost of improvements to the women's campus—and the national trend toward coeducation. By January 30, 1952, de Kiewiet could report that after consultations with faculty, students, and Rochester graduates, he believed a college merger would have support.

Student opinions were mixed. "I feel it would lower our school's standing," Arthur Bernhang '55 wrote to the *Campus*. "At present we do not lack social contacts with women, and if they were in our classes it would be distracting." Bob Gordon '52 raised a counterpoint: "[It is] necessary financially as the women's campus is definitely falling behind and needs major improvements. Co-education would be nice and I don't feel it would have any bad effect on marks. We'd also get rid of the inter-campus transportation problem."

On April 26, 1952, the Board of Trustees unanimously approved that the two colleges "be consolidated at the earliest possible moment." A cost comparison had been compelling: the women's college would need $4 million in facility improvements and $10 million to endow program expansion; estimated merger costs were $8.6 million. Said Board member James E. Gleason, a Rochester manufacturer, "Women are taking an increasingly important part in the industrial and professional life of the Nation. This move is in the spirit of the times."

"ROCHESTER ADOPTS ONE-COLLEGE PLAN," the *New York Times* announced April 30. The news became bigger: That fall, the University kicked off a $10.7 million capital campaign, with $4 million planned for construction of women's dorms; upgrades to the student union (Todd Union); and new buildings for the administration and University School, the community-education division. The remaining $6.7 million would support faculty recruits and salary increases, scholarships, and student services. Donations ultimately lagged by at least $2 million—a symptom of Rochester's ongoing struggle with perceptions of its wealth as the principal heir to industrialist Eastman.

De Kiewiet preferred the term "integration" to "merger." In his annual report for 1951–52, he explained, "Rochester is seeking an integration of many parts into a structure that will retain the elements of its present form but welded into a new shape that will be stronger, more active, more effective in the educational life of the community and nation."

Rochester committees examined a range of matters in the years leading to the merger—admissions, accounting, curriculum, dining, student services, and preservation of meaningful artifacts from the historic Prince Street site. Most important, the merger would present an opportunity for the University to reexamine its role. "The merger gives us an opportunity to begin with a clean slate, to develop anything we desire and determine," officials wrote in a grant application for self-study in October 1952.

De Kiewiet envisioned an entirely different kind of institution. He referred to a new "center of gravity" for the University. Higher education already was forever changed—in part due to sheer growth in the number

Deans Margaret L. Habein and J. Edward Hoffmeister with professor Arthur S. Gale at ceremony breaking ground at the site of the women's dormitory, September 1953. Student at left is Ruth Anne Williams '54.

Vera Micheles Dean

Vera Micheles Dean led the Non-Western Civilization program from 1954 to 1961. When she arrived at Rochester, Dean, fluent in seven languages, had held a leading role in the Foreign Policy Association, a nonpartisan educational group, and taught at Barnard, Harvard, Wellesley, and the Institute d'Etudes Politiques in Paris. She also had served as an advisor to the American delegation at the founding of the United Nations in 1945. Dean told the *Rochester Review*, "Today, when the United States is assuming new responsibilities in Asia, the Middle East, and Africa, it has become a matter of life and death for American citizens to know and understand the traditions, political and economic conditions, and aspirations for the future of the peoples living in these areas."

of students postwar; in part due to changes in research influenced by the Manhattan Project and other wartime endeavors. Referring to a popular concept then of Rochester as being on par with prominent undergraduate colleges such as Amherst, the president recalled, "I came with a different point of view as to where the most effective center of gravity of the American university system might be or should be, and that clearly was upwards a distinct notch in the direction of more professional education, more graduate education, more research, more of a relationship to the whole phenomenon so much stressed by the Manhattan Project of scientific and intellectual investigation and research." He also wanted the University to benefit from a close relationship with the prestigious—but decidedly independent—schools of medicine and music.

Distinguished scholars were hired: Vera Micheles Dean in international studies; pioneering political scientist Richard Fenno, the Don Alonzo Watson Professor of History and Political Science; and economist Lionel McKenzie, the Marie C. Wilson and Joseph C. Wilson Professor of Economics. The University drew worldwide acclaim for physics professor Robert Marshak's annual organization of the Interna-

The River Campus as it appeared in early 1954. The women's residence halls are well under way at lower right. Initially, the wings of the building would be named in honor of Susan B. Anthony, Mary T. L. Gannett, Elizabeth Weed Hollister, and Lewis Henry Morgan; the dining center was named in honor of Edwina Danforth. In 1974 the building as a whole would be dedicated in honor of Susan B. Anthony, and the Anthony wing renamed in honor of Frederick Taylor Gates, Class of 1877.

tional Conference on High Energy Physics, commonly known as the "Rochester Conference."

There would be difficulties. Some faculty complained of "second-class" treatment compared with research scholars. De Kiewiet's efforts to exert stronger influence in music and medicine met resistance. Hanson, according to Eastman School historian Vincent Lenti, criticized: "The new president's policy . . . called for a strong centralization of authority in the university administration, the final authority resting with the president and filtering down to the deans through a series of vice-presidents, provosts, and other university officers. Coupled with this was his insistence that the central core of the university should be the College of Arts and Sciences. Under this policy the College of Arts and Sciences became, itself, the university, the rest of us being adjuncts of the main body. Fortunately for us, the Eastman School was located in downtown Rochester, four miles from the River Campus, and our physical separation kept us from being entirely drowned in the Genesee."

De Kiewiet's style may have estranged some. Soon after arriving at Rochester, he sent letters to national medical educators requesting names of a potential dean to replace Whipple—before realizing Whipple had not yet decided to retire. On another occasion, de Kiewiet apologized to trustees for publicly announcing key administrative appointments before sharing the information with the Board. In a letter to Whipple's successor, Donald G. Anderson, de Kiewiet seemed to explain his sense of urgency: "A president has three years for innovation, three years for consolidation, and three years for loss of reputation."

At least two deans resigned over differences with the president, and a Middle States accrediting committee raised a concern about lack of communication between the University administration and Medical Center leadership. "President de Kiewiet soon became a controversial figure at the University of Rochester," longtime chemistry chair W. Albert Noyes Jr., the Charles Frederick Houghton Professor of Chemistry, wrote in a memoir. Noyes served as graduate studies dean and, temporarily, dean of the College. "But I can honestly say that I have never served under a university president with a better . . . understanding of the essentials of a good university."[1]

Noyes helped gain faculty support for de Kiewiet's second organizational feat: to create the professional schools of education, busi-

---

1   Noyes, *Victorian in the Twentieth Century,* 358.

President de Kiewiet posing with his staff at the new administration building, 1958. Forty years later, the building was named in honor of W. Allen Wallis.

Photochemistry pioneer W. Albert Noyes Jr. over the course of his career researched topics related to the photochemistry and photophysics of ketones and simple aromatic compounds and the photochemistry of polymers using vacuum ultraviolet (VUV) reactions.

Edmund A. Hajim

Edmund A. Hajim '58, eventual chairman of the Board of Trustees and a transformational donor, made his first real home at the University.

Raised from age three by a single father who was an officer in the U.S. Merchant Marine, Hajim spent time in foster homes and in orphanages from a young age, he told an interviewer for *Rochester Review*. Assisted by a Navy ROTC scholarship, Hajim enrolled at Rochester and threw himself into academic and extracurricular life. Mechanical engineering professor Oscar Minor became his mentor; lifelong friends Dick Wedemeyer '58 and Al "Jesse" James '58 invited him to their homes for holidays. Hajim held leadership roles in student government; his fraternity, Theta Chi; and numerous other organizations. He helped found the school's first humor magazine,

UGH—an acronym for undergraduate humor, and played freshman basketball and baseball, and intramural football, basketball, and softball.

After receiving his bachelor's degree in chemical engineering, Hajim earned an MBA with distinction at Harvard Business School. His career path took him from securities analyst at Capital Group in California to senior positions with some of the nation's top companies in the financial industry, and in 1997 as chairman and chief executive of Furman Selz, he sold the company to ING Group. He also ran his own investment firm, MLH Capital, and subsequently became president of Diker Management, a company managing hedge funds.

Soon after graduating from Rochester, Hajim became involved in class reunions. In 1988, he joined the Board

and took a leading role in reorganizing investments for the University endowment. Hajim assisted in the presidential search leading to the selection of Joel Seligman in 2005. In 2008, when he became chairman of the Board, Hajim committed $30 million to the University, and the following year the School of Engineering & Applied Sciences was named in his honor.

Alluding to University benefactor Eastman, Hajim said he too sees education as a key to improving the future for all members of society. "Higher education is the cornerstone of economic strength in our increasingly interconnected world," he said. "It will be even more important in the decades ahead, and our nation's foremost research universities will lead the way."

ness, and engineering in 1958. The president saw these disciplines as anomalies in the College of Arts and Science that probably were not adequately supported in that liberal arts context. Demand was high for professional courses; part-time enrollment for employed adults in the community education division—known as University School—increased from 2,800 in 1954–55 to 4,300 in 1957–58.

A faculty committee examined options for two years before recommending the plan to develop the new schools. Rochester's industrial leaders had pressed for engineering expertise. More broadly, knowledge was expanding and subdividing in specialties, and the United States had become a world center for training, de Kiewiet told the Board.

"U. of R. Raises Its Sights," an editorial headline in Rochester's *Democrat and Chronicle* declared after the University's announcement of its new divisions. "The reorganization, in time, will change the profile of the university, physically, as higher enrollments, more facilities dictate expansion," the article said. "The inner change will be felt even more because it is indicative of the U. of R.'s resolution to meet the new, titanic challenges of higher education."

A fall 1954 get-together in the Todd Union cafeteria

COAT AND TIE IN TODD

Despite plenty of opposition, the Student Senate in the fall of 1951 passed a requirement for men to dress formally for dinner. Concerns were rising over "sloppy" sweatshirts and dungarees, the *Campus,* an advocate of the measure, explained.

As the Senate's proposal came under scrutiny, full pages of letters filled the editorial section of the *Campus*—many vehemently opposed. They complained of uncomfortable dress clothes, extra wear and cleaning expenses for costly shirts, and the hassle of changing for dinner. "The idea of being more presentable at the dinner table is good, but a person unwillingly subjected to this new proposal can appear much more appalling in a dirty tie and wrinkled jacket than one who is conscious of a trend toward neatness and accordingly is dressed in slacks and a sport shirt," wrote one student.

The newspaper supported the move vigorously. It acknowledged that the rule, which would apply only in the dining room in Todd Union but not in the cafeteria, might inconvenience some, such as graduate students in science or the undergraduate students who worked in labs through the afternoon. But more appealing attire could lead to better social circumstances and project a sophisticated image of the College, the newspaper said.

"It is the opinion of this newspaper that the few minutes required to dress for dinner and the small amount of extra wear on clothes that might result from this requirement are a small price to pay for the benefits it will bring to the college," the newspaper said. "Dinner may become more than a race to absorb some nourishment and rush back to work; it may develop into a period of relaxation and mingling with friends and classmates." The measure passed 15–0.

John W. Graham Jr., vice president of the Cooper Union, was recruited as dean of the College of Engineering and Applied Science. Previously he rose from instructor of civil engineering to dean of students at Carnegie Institute of Technology, later part of Carnegie-Mellon University. By 1963, Rochester's engineering school faculty doubled to more than 30, and sponsored research grew from $20,000 a year to $375,000. Doctoral programs were begun in mechanical and electrical engineering—chemical engineering already had offered a PhD. In 1960, the engineering college, working with the Medical Center, added one of the first biomedical engineering degrees in the country.

John Brophy, a professor specializing in organizational theory and administration at Cornell University, was appointed dean of the School of Business Administration, now the Simon Business School. During Brophy's five-year tenure, full- and part-time MBA programs were established. Later, Dean Charles Plosser, the Fred H. Gowen Professor of Business Administration and the John M. Olin Professor in Government, credited Brophy with setting the foundation for one of the country's leading business schools.

William A. Fullagar, the Earl B. Taylor Professor of Education Emeritus, served as founding dean of what became the Margaret Warner Graduate School of Education and Human Development. Under his leadership from its inception in 1958 until 1968, faculty increased more than fivefold, to 37. Enhanced graduate programs, including doctoral degrees, drew 141 full-time students and 482 part-time students in 1968.

The president would report at the end of the 1958–59 year, the first of operations for the new schools: "It is not customary for an institu-

John W. Graham Jr.

When this 1951 photograph appeared in the winter 1977 issue of the *Rochester Review* for identification, alumni rose to the challenge. The production was *Harem Scarem*, written by students Ray Rueby '51 and Gene Surasky '51. It was performed by members of the Quilting Club, the men's theater group. From left to right are Peter Peirce '52, Ray Rueby Jr. '51 (portraying Sultan Ibn Hadd), Frank Santini '51, Bruce Cloughly '52, Bill Beveridge '51, and Charles Wilson '53.

tion of higher education to create in one year three new, major educational units. Yet it seemed after mature and protracted reflection on the part of all concerned that the University in terms of the purposes it had set for itself in the anticipated dynamic period of the 1960s should complete the reorganization of its academic structure in one move and thus be as adequately prepared as possible for the demands which it was clear would be placed upon it." *Harper's Magazine* in 1959 identified the University among several whose distinction was greater than recognized, de Kiewiet told the Board.

University historian Arthur May described the creation of the three professional schools as "the most significant development in the University complex since the opening of the Medical Center more than three decades before." The separate units would enhance training for local industries and be in a better position to attract growth capital, May said.

A *Rochester Review* report marking the schools' 50th anniversary noted de Kiewiet wanted the units to have more autonomy to pursue their academic development and programs. Also, putting the divisions on a new professional and graduate level would better position them to attract faculty and students. "The moves also bolstered Rochester's position as a research university made up of academic units devoted to particular fields," the *Review* said.

A new sphere of demands began to surface. Students became more critical of University administration. Student newspapers of the 1950s show the beginning of familiar complaints about tuition, parking, and dining. Tuition more than doubled from 1951 to 1961, to $1,275. As automobile use increased—it doubled in the Rochester metropolitan area from 1946 to 1956, to 200,000—the University revised its parking poli-

The Sphinxes

During construction of Sibley Hall on the Prince Street Campus in the 1870s, donor Hiram Sibley sent two statues of sphinxes from Italy. They were placed in front of the building to "keep watch and ward," said historian Arthur May. After the women's and men's campuses merged at the River Campus the sphinxes were moved to the west side of Morey Hall. Below, Carol Cronk '58 (top photo) and Diane Weber '58 posed with the sphinxes at their original location.

cies and imposed fines of $40 or more for violations. When the University instituted a compulsory board plan in 1959, letters streamed to the *Campus-Times,* the newspaper formed after the merger of the men's and women's campuses. "Meals are obligatory now for the simple reason that if this were not the case, few would be foolish enough to pay for them," wrote A. Lapidus '60. "There are few people who, if faced with a choice between lime [Jell-O] and cottage cheese on lettuce with Russian dressing, and a good steak dinner for under a dollar in one of the restaurants which surround the campus, would not choose the latter. The fact is that the food bought by the University is bad and the preparation is worse."

Students became more active around deep social concerns, most evident when racial tensions grew in the South. At least 50 students picketed the downtown Rochester Woolworth's in March 1960 to protest the retail chain's policy of lunch-counter segregation in the South. "The act signals a revival of consciousness in a generation," stated a *Campus-Times* editorial. "Those students and few faculty members who silently and anonymously walked back and forth in front of Woolworth's for two hours last night in freezing cold, those people generated their own warmth." About the same time, student members of the NAACP demanded University pressure for removal of a clause in the charter of national fraternity Sigma Chi prohibiting membership of nonwhites.

By the end of the decade, it was time to look again at development. De Kiewiet drew up plans for the next phase of University growth—new dorms for men; a wing for physics, optics, and math; a science lecture hall and other academic buildings; and a chapel. The Medical Center, undergoing its own reorganization under the leadership of dean Donald G. Anderson, was enhanced by an expanded library, new buildings for the Atomic Energy Project, animal studies, and hospital facilities. The College aimed for enrollment growth of 25 percent, to 2,500. With 4,100 employees—including nearly 500 full-time faculty members—the University ranked sixth largest among Rochester employers.

"The nation's need for educated manpower is rising sharply and will continue to rise," de Kiewiet said. "The explosion of new knowledge in our time is unparalleled in world history. International crises on every hand require creative solutions to new and age-old problems."

"A university must have and show a dynamic attitude to its own future," de Kiewiet said.

But de Kiewiet was becoming restless. His correspondence with Board members showed frustration, especially on financial issues and control of the music and medical schools. He saw an ally in newly elected chair Joseph C. Wilson, founder of Xerox. Wilson would be a significant figure through the 1960s.

The March 11, 1960, *Campus-Times* showed opposition among students in Rochester to segregation in the South.

Ruth Merrill

Ruth Atherton Merrill, the first woman to direct a college student union, was in charge of Cutler Union on the Prince Street Campus from 1933 to 1954. She was named dean of women in 1954 as the University prepared to merge the women's and men's colleges at the River Campus and remained in that role until 1960, when she became the first director of volunteers at Strong Memorial Hospital. Merrill was known for an extraordinary rapport with students. When Wilson Commons opened in 1976, the student activities center was designated the Ruth Merrill Student Organization Center in her honor.

Above, Merrill posed in Anthony Lounge with the Marsiens, the women's honor society for seniors. Above, Merrill (third from right) and Professor Margaret Denny (center) posed in Anthony Lounge with the Marsiens, the women's honor society for seniors. The Marsiens from the Class of 1958 were Chrystal Murray, Suzanne Kwan, Mary Woolverton, Susan Hook, Nancy Kelts, Deanne Molinari, Todne Lohndal, Mary Lind, Ann Baldwin, Joyce Timmerman, Christine Hersey, and Mary Waite (not pictured).

In the summer of 1959, de Kiewiet raised privately with Wilson the prospect of moving the Eastman School to the River Campus. "I am aware that this sort of thinking may light fires from horizon to horizon," de Kiewiet said. "I am aware also that it may turn out to be completely unrealistic, but I am also aware, and this is important, that the total financial picture of the Eastman School of Music is going to call for some very radical handling." Evidently stunned, Wilson replied, "The idea . . . was so new to me that I will refrain from doing more now than to say that I will think about it thoroughly."

Within months, de Kiewiet would write of worsening malaise. "The combination of a tug of war between the executive and finance committees and of the lack of any clarity of responsibility in the Board of Managers of the Eastman School of Music have made me feel that my sense of unhappiness can only increase." Six months later, on news that his daughter was terminally ill, de Kiewiet requested a leave of absence. He resigned in the summer of 1961.

Historian Richard Glotzer credited de Kiewiet with helping shape the research university as it is known today. "At Cornell and Rochester, de Kiewiet recognized the urgent need for change in post-war universities," Glotzer wrote in an analysis published in *American History Journal*. "He understood that the jerry rigged arrangements hurriedly grafted onto pre-war university structures were ill-suited to sustain an ongoing explosion of knowledge and technology."

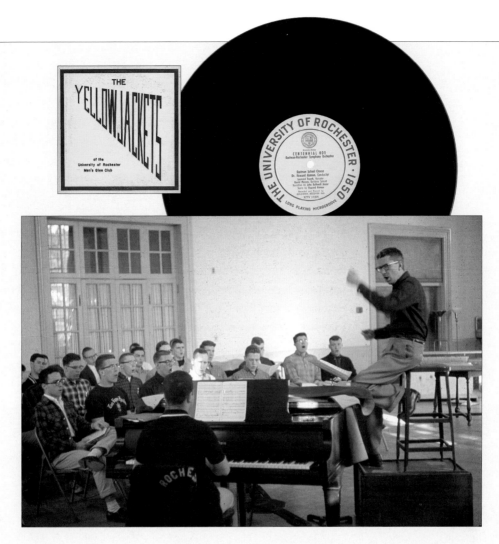

THE YELLOWJACKETS

Rochester's popular a cappella group has its roots in the Men's Glee Club of the 1950s. A *Campus-Times* article on November 22, 1957, introduced the singers as the "UR equivalent of the Whiffenpoofs" of Yale University.

The group was organized with singers selected from the Men's Glee Club. "Candidates' qualifications include outstanding vocal talent and ability to put a song over well," the student newspaper said. Roughly a dozen of the club's first 20 members performed for local Rotary clubs, parent-teacher associations, the YWCA, and other audiences, including, of course, those at the University.

The YellowJackets credit University music director Ward Woodbury Jr. '54E (PhD) with their formation. The group's singing and style have changed a number of times over the years: performers originally performed in blue blazers with red and black ties, then switched to yellow coats in 1958. The club said on its website: "The YellowJackets wasted no time making their mark on history and the group recorded its first record, a 78 rpm vinyl disc, in 1959." In 1981, the singers went a cappella, transitioning from accompanied music.

Eventually an independent, self-sustaining organization, the Yellow-Jackets' worldwide appearances have included *The Tonight Show,* the White House, and—in front of 75,000 fans—Ralph Wilson Stadium for the Buffalo Bills. Members of the club's alumni group often have joined in for songs during Meliora Weekend. In 2011, the YellowJackets succeeded in seven of ten episodes in NBC-TV's series *The Sing-Off,* a three-season program featuring top a cappella groups from across the nation.

The women's a capella group Vocal Point was founded in 1969. In 1998 two additional groups formed: the Midnight Ramblers and After Hours.

De Kiewiet was a force on the state and national level. In New York, de Kiewiet led a council of private colleges and universities to consult with legislators forming the state university system. He served as president of the Association of American Universities and of the American Council of Learned Societies, where he defended universities under scrutiny during the McCarthy era and articulated the importance of funding higher education as its services grew. De Kiewiet also served a variety of national roles as the U.S. government and grant-making organizations looked for ways to understand developing nations, including South Africa, and to support their educational institutions.

The president sent farewells to several trustees. He wrote to Eisenhart: "There is, of course, sadness in leaving an institution where we both worked with a sense of purpose that lay beyond ourselves even though perhaps sometimes my own hand reached too far. It always takes time for perspectives that have been rudely broken to re-establish themselves but I take comfort in the conviction that this decade has been useful."

He closed a letter to trustee Sol Linowitz, Wilson's business partner: "All men must be measured finally by the direction and the distance of their gaze. I am content to be measured by this test."

The October–November 1961 *Review* contained a 10-year report, "One University in a Changing World," and noted that during the decade of President de Kiewiet's tenure the University saw "the greatest growth and development in any decade of its history."

Early Computing

The University established its Computing Center in 1955 and bought its first computer, a Burroughs E 101, the following year. Just months later it acquired a more powerful, much larger IBM 650.

The University had tried to win a grant from the Atomic Energy Commission to establish a computing center in 1950 and had studied the matter since, research vice president LaRoy Thompson reported to the executive committee of the Board of Trustees in January 1956. This was 10 years after the introduction of the world's first computer, developed during World War II for calculations relating to the hydrogen bomb, and the University was contracting out for use of other data centers.

A computing tool had become necessary for teaching and research in mathematics, industrial management, optics, physics, and chemistry. "On a national level these machines have been developed more rapidly than personnel have been trained to operate them," Thompson said, explaining that IBM was interested in a Rochester center that could train individuals in the community to use the devices.

In the University's first year offering a data processing class to the Rochester community, 127 enrolled, Board records showed. Just a few years later, in 1961, the University acquired the IBM 7070, the company's first transistorized stored-program computer.

Freshmen!

Ye slick, sleek, city fellers, ye combed-back, smoothe lounge-lizzards, you corn-cracking, punkin busters, and up-country apple knockers who go to make up the Class of 1930–,

You come!

You are the luckiest gang on earth! Dean Gale's eyesight is getting bad or you would never have SNEAKED into this place.

NOW LISTEN!

If you want to stick around here and live, you must appreciate your own lowliness and follow very carefully the orders of the greatest class that ever entered the U. of R.—the glorious '29.

We see to it!

Death with torture follows these misdeeds:
Smoke on the campus—burned at the stake.
Speak to or look at a girl on the campus—flayed alive.
Step on the grass—six feet under the sod.
Enter front or rear door of Anderson—out on your ear.
Mount right hand stairs of Anderson—thrown down the left.
Wear knickers—and lose your pants.
Cut physical education—suffer Doc's pills and iodine.
Short Cut to library—padded cell.

And We   Conquer
The
Immortal
29

FRESHMAN PRIDE

For about as long as there have been freshmen there have been ways—official and unofficial—to acquaint them with University life. Among the more memorable unofficial traditions were Flag Rush and freshmen rules. Class of 1876 graduate Joseph T. Alling, later a member of the Board of Trustees, said the freshmen-sophomore "cane rushes" of his day evolved into Flag Rush, a battle for a flag on top of a greased pole, which continued until 1964. President Anderson, Alling remembered, would "seize two grappling students, separate them, and then plunge again into the fray." Into the 1970s freshmen received class beanies and were expected to wear them during the first semester except while dining or in class. The Frosh Bible listed expectations, which in 1952 included staying off the Eastman and fraternity quadrangles, being able to recite any University song or cheer when requested by an upperclassman, and sitting in the freshman cheering section at home football games.

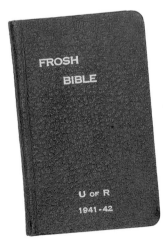

The Class of 2005 signing the pages of the freshman roll, which are then bound and stored in the University Archives. This Convocation tradition began in 1992.

Martin Mulundika '67

Freshman registration in
Rush Rhees Library, 1972

Seniors, from left to right, Sally Goddard, Cherry Thomson, June Fundin, Todne Lohndal,
Mary Lind, and Chrystal Murray don their freshman beanies in September 1957.

Edward Kaplan '58 masquerades
as a freshman.

Tug-of-war: members
of the freshman class of
1956 exulted after pulling
the sophomore class of
1955 into the Genesee
River, September 1952.

Ground was broken in October 1967 on the Interfaith Chapel, one of many construction projects of the 1960s. President de Kiewiet first advocated for a chapel on the campus in the early 1950s as part of an expanded religious program. It came to fruition with the generosity of Gilbert and Virginia McCurdy. Neither attended the University, but the family supported the University and other organizations in Rochester. Gilbert McCurdy served as a trustee from 1971 to 1993. He was the grandson of the founder of the family's downtown department store and was instrumental in developing Midtown Plaza, which at the time was among the first downtown enclosed shopping malls in the country. A plaque in the chapel states, "Given to the University of Rochester to foster and encourage the awareness and knowledge of God and the eternal truths of his ordered universe."

Expansion

W. Allen Wallis, 1962–1970

With the departure of de Kiewiet, Board chairman Joseph C. Wilson took the lead in the search for a president. Most of the process was entrusted to a faculty committee that narrowed candidates from a list of 200, crossed the country to interview prospects, and expressed preference for the final selection. Candidates learned of an institution preparing for strategic growth, especially in graduate programs. The College continued to assimilate the 1955 merger of the men's and women's campuses. New professional schools in engineering, education, and business were ready to be shaped. Music and medicine retained leading ranks worldwide, and the University's endowment placed it 10th wealthiest in the nation. The institution stood on the cusp of a remarkable era of growth.

The University could boast of a host city of notable vitality and technological promise. Xerox was hiring by the thousands and investing 10 percent of gross revenues in research, according to city historian Blake McKelvey. By 1964, Kodak disbursed $167 million in annual wage dividends—more than $1 billion in 2013 dollars. The metropolitan area grew more than any in the Northeast, to 883,000, during the decade. Important developments in education were under way. Monroe Community College would open in 1962 with 750 students and plans to expand nearly tenfold; Rochester Institute of Technology was buying 1,300 suburban acres for a new campus. New York planned to double its state university facilities in the decade to meet enrollment forecasts of a 38-percent increase.

The faculty committee drafted a statement describing the University's potential: "An adventurous expansion and improvement of the faculties, a marked expansion of research and graduate work in many fields, a building expansion program, and a campaign (now under way) to raise the endowment by $50 mil-

W. Allen Wallis

lion all give promise that this University will deservedly be recognized within 10 years as one of America's outstanding institutions."

Wilson Allen Wallis had built the University of Chicago's graduate school of business from 25 to 70 faculty members and was credited with forging its reputation as a leader in graduate studies with an emphasis on scientific knowledge. Wallis recalled later that he did not know much about Rochester when search committee members came to see him in the spring of 1962. He was immediately impressed, though, with the caliber of John Romano, MD, chair of the faculty advisory committee and of the medical school's Department of Psychiatry and internationally recognized for reforms in medical education.

The conversation was casual, intelligent, and friendly, and by the time the Rochester visitors left, both they and Wallis were intrigued. Wallis, 49, appeared clear minded and engaging and conveyed "a clear idea about what a university is all about in terms of the quality of faculty scholarship," Romano reported to the Board's search committee.

Members of the faculty committee and trustees sought opinions from contacts in higher education. An admirer described Wallis as "a man of reason and of purpose and determination" who made every effort to be fully informed before making decisions. Romano noted from one source, "At times Wallis may seem forbidding to others, particularly the romantics and phonies in a university faculty because Wallis can see through them." From others: "taciturn," "partisan," "authoritarian." Events of the tumultuous late 1960s prompted the same array of opinions at Rochester.

Wallis was a nationally recognized economist with a focus on statistics. He believed in minimal government intervention and free markets. When Rochester came to call, Wallis recently had served as special assistant to U.S. President Dwight D. Eisenhower, collaborating with Vice President Richard Nixon on policies for price stability and economic growth. Wallis remained connected in high-level Republican circles throughout his career—advising Presidents Richard Nixon, Gerald Ford, and Ronald Reagan—while describing himself as independent or even apolitical.

Wallis formed a strong partnership with Wilson, the founder of Xerox. They shared high aspirations for the University. Accepting Board leadership in September 1959, Wilson had sought to ensure every trustee shared his commitment. "I intend personally to devote every resource that I can muster to achieve greater excellence for this institution, and . . . must feel free to ask the same kind of contribution

Ike on Campus
President Dwight D. Eisenhower at W. Allen Wallis's inauguration, when he received an honorary degree, said of Wallis: "He always met the one test that I insist must be undergone by anyone close to me—that he has a little bit of that quality that we don't know how to define, but we understand, called 'ordinary common horse sense.' I am quite sure that you are going to feel the beneficent influence of that quality during the years that he will lead this great university."

from every one of you.... This is a kind of watershed in the University's history."

Wilson devoted his skills as a leader and entrepreneur to support Wallis and the University through one of its most significant periods of growth—and growing pains. This dovetailed with Wilson's influence on his home city. Two days before the September 1959 meeting, Wilson's business had introduced a photocopier that revolutionized office processes. Xerox grew to be one of Rochester's largest employers and helped define the city as a center for imaging technology and manufacturing.

The University, Wilson believed, played a vital role in community life, including the obvious contribution it made toward a talented workforce. "For those of us whose economic future depends upon the attractiveness of this community to the best intellects, the university's well-being is essential," Wilson remarked as he made one of several substantial gifts that ultimately totaled $40 million, or $230 million in 2013 dollars. His family continued to support the University after Wilson's death. His legacy would approach George Eastman's, as much because of the energy, wisdom, and compassion he gave as his financial contributions.

Wilson noted in announcing the selection of Wallis as Rochester's next president in the summer of 1962 that Wallis was a director of the National Bureau of Economic Research, a trustee of the National Opinion Research Center, and chair of the editorial board of the *Encyclopedia of Social Sciences.* A University of Minnesota graduate, Wallis had been a fellow at the University of Chicago and taught at Yale and Stanford universities. During World War II, he was director of research

From left, Gary Hartman '61, Stuart Miller '61, and Ned Topping '61 on the third floor of the Psi Upsilon ("Psi U") Fraternity chapter house, circa 1959

of the statistics center for the Office of Scientific Research and Development. Colleagues said he typically put in a 70-hour workweek.

Wilson and the trustees liked Wallis's background in building organizations, starting with the Statistical Research Group he pulled together at Columbia during World War II. The statisticians, economists, and mathematicians worked on problems including efficient testing of naval artillery shells; two staff members later received the Nobel Prize. At Chicago, "He went at the business of building the faculty in the most charming, persuasive and ruthless way, with an expert eye for a good man wherever the man might be," Chicago President George W. Beadle said at Wallis's inauguration. "He industriously stalked the campuses of the country; no one since Eleanor Roosevelt turned up in as many unexpected places."

The Wallis era at Rochester—he was president until 1970, then chancellor until 1978—marked a turning point in the University's maturity as a modern research university. Wallis's vision combined with Wilson's Board leadership catalyzed significant growth on all fronts. Graduate enrollment doubled, undergraduate enrollment rose 45 percent, and the University's annual budget climbed sixfold, to $200 million. Campus facilities expanded by 50 percent, to three million square feet. Doctoral degrees nearly tripled.

The University engaged the architectural consulting firm Sasaki, Dawson, DeMay Associates to help plan the growth of the campus. A pedestrian bridge to Brooks Avenue was proposed along with careful consideration of spaces and the integration of the new science buildings with both the Medical Center and River Campus. Student input played a large role in developing a master plan.

Research areas multiplied—in a range of disciplines stretching from the space sciences to the function of the human nervous system. The school of business built the framework for its distinct stature. Sponsored studies swelled as much as 20 percent a year, placing Rochester among the leading private colleges and universities for federally funded investigations.

New struggles emerged, from relatively small matters of allocating expenses for interdepartmental projects to profound questions of the University's identity and purpose. This was the era when the "multiversity" was realized—an increasingly complex institution as it continued to grow from disparate roots in English classical arts colleges and German scientific research universities. President Emeritus Clark Kerr of the University of California at Berkeley called the multiversity "a city of infinite variety" where a student faced a staggering range of choices. "In this range of choices he encounters the opportunities and the dilemmas of freedom."[1]

Wallis's tenure at Rochester spanned a turbulent period for American society and its burgeoning universities. Students and faculty fought for a greater voice in governance, a trend through the civil rights movement and the Vietnam War that ultimately reshaped student life. Rochester avoided the serious disruption that shut down some campuses but suffered a divide between faculty and administration.

Data always influenced Wallis's decisions. He could trace his interest in economic puzzles to around age six, when he learned about weighted averages through discovering why Ghirardelli chocolate with

---

1   Clark Kerr, *The Uses of the University* (Cambridge, MA: Harvard University Press, 1982), 32.

Sing Along with Mitch

Mitch Miller made his television debut in 1961. Miller, a 1932 graduate of the Eastman School of Music, followed a varied career path as a classical oboist and record-company executive before launching the program that made his name a household word. *Sing Along With Mitch,* an adaptation of his post-war album series, became a renowned program featuring a bouncing ball following lyrics along the bottom of the television screen.

Miller, born in 1911 in Rochester to working-class, immigrant parents, performed with the Rochester Philharmonic Orchestra at the start of a career that spanned seven decades. When he died in July 2010, the *New York Times*

credited Miller with helping define American popular music in the "pre-rock" era, carefully matching performers with music and "choosing often unorthodox but almost always catchy instrumental accompaniment." As an executive with Columbia Records, Miller shaped the careers of Tony Bennett, Rosemary Clooney, Johnny Mathis, and others. Disdainful of rock music, he was said to have rejected opportunities to work with the likes of Elvis Presley and Buddy Holly.

"He had an extraordinary intuition for the essence of music, a nose for talent, and a breadth of musical experience that spanned classical to pop," Douglas Lowry, the Joan and

Martin Messinger Dean of the Eastman School of Music, said at the time of Miller's death.

Miller was perhaps most publicly recognized for his 1961 to 1966 NBC sing-along show, featuring Miller and a male chorale. In later years, he continued the tradition, leading crowds in song at his appearances.

Miller visited Rochester in 2004 for a ceremony to rename Eastman Place the Miller Center in honor of his parents, Abram Calmen and Hinda Rosenblum Miller. The Miller Center houses the Sibley Music Library, University administrative offices, and several businesses.

The Boulders

The first boulder turned up in 1967. As construction crews excavated for a major expansion of Rush Rhees Library, they encountered a 10-ton rock that had been formed by a warm, shallow sea that covered the Rochester area 400 million years ago.

Trustee and alumnus Robert Metzdorf thought it might be worth preserving on campus, and President Wallis agreed. A crane deposited the rock in front of Susan B. Anthony Halls. Wallis considered placing a plaque on the rock to honor Metzdorf, who in 1939 earned the University's first doctoral degree in English, served as an assistant librarian, and achieved national distinction as a bibliographer and appraiser of rare books and manuscripts. However, Wallis was said to have decided against it out of concern it would be vandalized.

The second boulder turned up during excavation of the basement of the University Health Service Building in 2007. The 1967 boulder—"Metzdorf Mount"—had been moved temporarily for that construction. The two were then placed in the grassy circle in front of the residence hall and often are painted by students to reflect current events.

added sugar cost less than the brand's plain chocolate. (The plain chocolate version had a higher percentage of cocoa—more expensive than sugar.) Chicago colleague James H. Lorie liked telling a story about his first encounter with Wallis, on a slow elevator in a Hyde Park building where they both lived. "It takes a long time for the door to close, doesn't it," Lorie said. "Yes," Wallis responded immediately, "19 seconds."

Fresh at Rochester in 1962, Wallis began collecting data. He asked all academic department heads to determine the smallest size their groups could be and still aim to be "absolutely first rate." He wanted the chairs to calculate this number based on the important fields and subfields of their disciplines, each faculty member spending half his time on research, and faculty dividing teaching time between undergraduates and graduates. Departments then could gauge how many students they would accommodate.

In his inaugural address in the spring of 1963, Wallis specified that growth "means improvement in quality, not just in more easily measured things like numbers of students, faculty, or dollars." He initiated a faculty senate to help draft a long-range plan.

A host of analyses produced a $77 million growth plan that kicked off in 1964. Wallis articulated six adjectives to distinguish Rochester: small, coherent, advanced, diverse, independent, and noted. He and Wilson would work hand-in-hand on the vision and the means to support it.

Wallis's first important recruit to Rochester was College dean Kenneth E. Clark. Clark, a psychologist credited with major contributions to his field throughout his career, joined the University in the spring of 1963 from the University of Colorado at Boulder, where he had been dean of the College of Arts and Sciences. Clark led growth in graduate programs, particularly in chemistry, English, philosophy, and the social sciences, and he oversaw popular innovations in undergraduate study. In Clark's first year, the College added three doctoral programs—in social anthropology, general linguistics, and political science—as well as a joint doctoral degree option with the Medical Center's Center for Brain Research.

Additional advanced programs in the College soon would include foreign literature, electrical engineering, psychology, and astronomy. Doctoral degrees rose by 72 percent in the dean's first five years, with the number of graduate students growing from 515 to 679, and undergraduate enrollment expanding from 2,038 to 2,725 during that time. New offerings at the undergraduate level included freshmen preceptorials—small classes offering hands-on learning with distinguished professors—and a procedure for students to initiate new course offerings, as well as expansion into language studies such as Chinese and Russian.

Clark also demonstrated understanding and care for students during unrest in the late 1960s, in part by interpreting their frustration for Rochester alumni, who generally had little tolerance for protests. Clark steered the College until 1980 while also serving leading roles in a broad array of associations, including the President's National Medal of Science Committee.

Business dean William H. Meckling arrived in 1964 and began framing Rochester's economics-based approach to management education, revising curriculum and recruiting prominent faculty. Luminaries included monetary economist Karl Brunner, Fred H. Gowen Professor; banking and public policy specialist George Benston, LaClare Professor of Finance and Business Administration; economist Michael Jensen, later LaClare Professor of Finance and Business Administration; and accounting expert Ross Watts, the Frontier Communications/Rochester Telephone Professor. Meckling and Jensen's 1976 paper on agency theory became a classic in business, economics, and legal scholarship.

William H. Meckling

Leading scholarly journals in accounting and economics, financial economics, and monetary economics were founded. Meckling began a doctoral program a year after joining Rochester, and by 1970 the school would be renamed the Graduate School of Management to reflect its sole focus on graduate work. MBA enrollment swelled from 24 in 1964 to 200 in 1969, while full-time faculty nearly doubled, from 19 to 35.

Wallis also would appoint new leaders for the University's two leading professional schools. Respected conductor Walter Hendl, who had studied under maestro Fritz Reiner and served as associate conductor of the Chicago Symphony Orchestra, was named director of the Eastman School of Music when Howard Hanson retired in 1964 after 40 years. Hendl was credited with initiating Eastman's FM radio concerts and sending the Eastman Wind Ensemble and Jazz Ensemble on worldwide tours. J. Lowell Orbison, MD, George Hoyt Whipple Professor Emeritus, led the Medical Center from 1967 to 1979; during that period enrollment grew almost 30 percent as a new education wing was completed, the first cancer center was developed, and Strong Memorial Hospital was expanded.

In a key gathering in the spring of 1964, Wallis explained to trustees that Rochester would grow within a general concept of permanence and change. Board Chair Wilson called the meeting not for particular action by the trustees but for a "wide appreciation of the challenge before them," historian McKelvey wrote in a biography of Wilson. "Aggressive planning and generous provisions for growth were his favorite tactics," McKelvey said. Wilson secured agreement from Xerox executives to pledge continuing and increasing corporate support that

would total $6.4 million over the next five years, one of many steps that would lead to his reputation as a model for corporate responsibility.

The intangibles of 1850—spirit, quality, and goals—would influence the tangibles of 1964's vision for the decade ahead, Wallis told the Board in that session. He called for a 50 percent increase in enrollment and a 30 percent increase in faculty, which would encompass communities of scholars in every discipline. Graduate study would be a priority, the president said, noting that more students earned master's degrees in 1962 than bachelor's in 1920.

Among the most distinguished innovations to unfold were a scientifically based program in political science under William H. Riker, PhD, the Marie C. Wilson and Joseph C. Wilson Professor of Political Science, and a neurology training program at the Medical Center headed by Robert Joynt, MD, the Edward A. and Alma Vollertsen Rykenboer Chair in Neurophysiology. The growth would necessitate major additions: a large addition to Rush Rhees Library, a new building for life sciences, a new University commons, a chemistry building, expansion of the Medical Center, and renovation of the Eastman School of Music. A Nuclear Structure Research Laboratory that housed one of the country's first two Tandem Van de Graaf accelerators also was built.

CHAPTER 5

A $38 million campaign kicked off in 1964 exceeded its goal by almost $6 million by 1969. The University would have a construction-zone feel for years with projects including the Interfaith Chapel, a new fraternity building on the Quad, expansion of the central heating plant, a new Graduate Living Center, University Park apartments, and renovation of two wings of Strong Memorial Hospital.

Wallis's 1968 annual report to the Board provided the status of 16 construction projects totaling $142 million. Wallis had received advice from influential sources in architecture and landscape design, first consulting with Pietro Belluschi, dean of architecture at Massachusetts Institute of Technology (and architect for Rochester's Temple B'rith Kodesh) and then with influential landscape architect Hideo Sasaki, chair of landscape architecture at Harvard University. Sasaki recommended locations for buildings for the next five decades to preserve the natural beauty of the campus.

Academic programs grew in comparable fashion. The medical school created departments in genetics, medicine, anesthesiology, clinical dentistry, and orthopedics in addition to neurology. In the College, anthropology and sociology were divided into separate departments, and new study areas sprouted in literature, linguistics, and foreign cultures. Faculty were recruited for the expanded offerings: in 1964 alone, the College faculty increased 11 percent, to 235. The University at the time ranked 13th nationally in salaries for professors. Wallis would tell a Rochester *Times-Union* interviewer: "I doubt if we get anyone by salary alone. We just fix it that salary is no obstacle."

Other leading faculty included Pulitzer Prize–winning poet Anthony Hecht; economist Walter Oi, the Elmer B. Milliman Distinguished Professor in Economics, whose research contributed heavily

Poet Anthony Hecht spent most of his career teaching at Rochester. Soon after his 1967 arrival, Hecht was awarded the Pulitzer Prize for *The Hard Hours*. He was appointed poetry consultant at the Library of Congress in 1982.

Goler House, shown here under construction, was dedicated in 1972. The housing for Medical Center staff was then the largest apartment building in Rochester. Its name honors George Washington Goler, health officer of the City of Rochester during the time the Medical Center was built to include a new municipal hospital.

Patrick Barry House

A significant symbol of Rochester's era as the "Flower City" became part of the University landscape when descendants of horticulturalist and entrepreneur Patrick Barry donated his Italianate villa in 1962. The rose-red brick home, built in 1855 on Mt. Hope Avenue, has been used as a residence for provosts—the University's top academic officer below the president—and as a gathering place since the 1970s.

Barry and George Ellwanger established the Ellwanger & Barry Nursery soon after Barry moved to Rochester from Long Island in 1840. By 1850—the year the University opened in a former hotel downtown—the nursery was believed to be the largest in the world, providing fruit and shade trees for estates in Europe and Asia. The 650-acre nursery helped define Rochester, previously nicknamed the "Flour City" due to its milling activity, as the "Flower City." By 1856, more fruit trees had been raised in Monroe County than in the rest of the country, according to city documents.

As the United States population expanded westward in the late 1800s, more specialized nurseries began to compete. Ellwanger & Barry phased out the business and closed in 1918, transitioning to a real estate company that operated until 1963.

The 16-room home, designated as a historic landmark in 1970, served as a residence for President Robert Sproull. Provost Brian Thompson and his family lived there from 1984 to 1999, and extensive perennial gardens on the property were named in memory of the provost's wife, Joyce Thompson, who designed and planted them. The Thompsons endowed the gardens to ensure their maintenance.

An extensive renovation was completed in 2008 under the direction of Provost Ralph Kuncl and his wife, Nancy. The building had been closed for practically nine years. Renovations were designed to highlight distinctive features, such as beautifully grained hardwood floors and painted plaster reliefs on the 13-foot ceilings. The mansion also features eight carved marble fireplaces and numerous collections of portraits, furniture, and tableware of the Barry family.

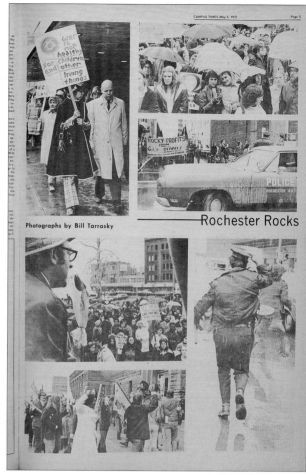

Campus Times pages from April 24, May 5, May 12, and May 15, 1972, reported the extent of student activism.

to ending the military draft; historian Christopher Lasch, the Don Alonzo Watson Professor of History and Political Science; and Norman O. Brown, professor of classics, whose *Life Against Death* "became one of the most hotly discussed intellectual works of the early 1960s," wrote Jan LaMartina Waxman in *Beside the Genesee.*

Toward the end of the 1960s, Wallis turned much of his attention to managing campus unrest. Concerns centered largely on social issues that led to questions about the University's role in public affairs and the appropriate voice for faculty and students in academic governance.

The *Campus-Times* highlighted student-sponsored speakers such as civil rights activist Julian Bond and LSD advocate Timothy Leary. Students and faculty members marched in Selma, Ala., to support desegregation and voting rights for African Americans and protested Vietnam in the nation's capital. Wallis came under fire as a member of Kodak's board when a community group—formed after race riots

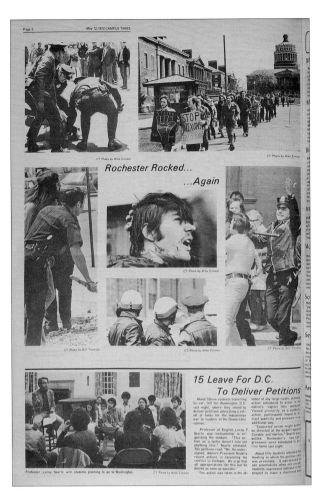

in the city in 1964—sought an employment agreement for hundreds of African Americans. "It would be no easy task to count the number of times the word 'protest' appeared in the *Campus-Times* during that period," Waxman wrote. "As Ronnee Press Lipman '70 was to recall later: 'Everyone in our crowd would go to Todd for the mail, then play bridge, then go protest.'"

Among the largest of the protests unfolded in the fall of 1967 over student and faculty opposition to a campus visit from recruiters of Dow Chemical. Wallis tried to head off a planned sit-in, telling a gathering of 700 for a student government meeting that such an act would represent coercion and that disciplinary charges would be placed. A standing ovation went to history professor Arthur Mitzman when he declared that a student wishing to interview with a recruiter for a firm producing napalm must "be prepared to walk over my body and render bodily harm to secure his job." More than 100 students and faculty members sat in corridors of the third floor of the dining center, forcing

In November 1967, students and faculty protested a recruiting visit by Dow Chemical by staging a sit-in and strike.

the Dow interview to move to Taylor Hall. Provost McCrea Hazlett subsequently suspended 23 graduate students—91 undergraduates had been placed on probation—despite a faculty committee's recommendation against punishing the upper-level students.

Faculty also were disturbed deeply when they believed Wallis blocked the appointment of Professor Eugene Genovese. Genovese had drawn attention at Rutgers University, where he publicly supported Marxism and socialism. Wallis blamed the Rochester controversy on inappropriate handling of private negotiations by members of the history department and, ultimately, hired Genovese as its new chair.

Dissension grew further over the administration's decision to continue to manage the Center for Naval Analyses, a research organization designated to perform unbiased studies on military problems. Faculty and students objected to the University's involvement in a military-related operation that performed classified work at its Washington, D.C.,–area location.

Wilson, increasingly involved in causes outside the University after the end of his term as Board chair in 1967, nonetheless continued in a significant support role and by all accounts still was perceived as a Board leader. Faculty members would appeal to Wilson—a less rigid figure than Wallis. He stood by the president, urging all parties to regain confidence in each other, in a significant meeting in the fall of 1969.

In that meeting, Wallis said changes in governance to give more power to students and faculty would be wasted energy. "After all, the structure and governance of the university—including the presidency and even the faculty senate—are merely instruments to advance the goals of the university," the president said. "What is of overriding importance in a university, what makes all of us cherish ours, is the fascination of learning what others have known and thought and felt, the excitement of discovering something for the first time, the joy of introducing the young to the life of the mind, the satisfaction of seeing others grow from our teaching or build on our discoveries, and the sharing of the intellectual adventure with students, with colleagues, with men long since dead, and with unknown men yet to be born."

Eugene Genovese

Demonstration during a student strike, May 1970

THE RATTLE OF

XOXOX

RECOGNITION
ISSUE

*To my brothers
of Theta Chi -
with all good wishes!
Ed Gibson*

Clockwise from top left, Edward Gibson with homecoming queen Ruth Van Lare '57, '65N (MS); receiving honorary degree at convocation, where he also received the keys to the City of Rochester; and with Don Lyon on the set of "University Open House" in 1974

University Convocation

Eastman Theatre
University of Rochester
April 3, 1974

Edward G. Gibson

ASTRONAUT MATERIAL

Engineering graduate Edward G. Gibson '59 was among the first chosen by the National Aeronautics and Space Administration to train as a scientist-astronaut in 1965, as the Apollo space program accelerated. At the time, he was a research scientist with Philco. Gibson's fellow recruits were Owen Garriott, an electrical engineering professor at Stanford University; Duane Graveline, a physician specializing in aerospace medicine; Joseph Kerwin, a naval flight surgeon; Curt Michel, a space sciences professor at Rice University; and Harrison Schmitt, a geologist and the 12th and last man to walk on the moon as of 2013.

Gibson, who had been active in University football, swimming, wrestling, and track teams—as well as engineering clubs—earned a master's degree in engineering from the California Institute of Technology and then a PhD there as well, after graduating from the University of Rochester.

With NASA from 1965 to 1974, Gibson marked many achievements. He served as a member of the astronaut support crew and as a communicator with astronauts from Mission Control for the Apollo 12 lunar landing. Gibson was the scientist-pilot aboard Skylab 4, the third and final manned visit to the Skylab space station, according

to his NASA biography. Gibson was the crew member primarily responsible for Apollo telescope operations, which made extensive observations of solar processes. He was credited with capturing images for the first time of the birth of a solar flare.

Gibson left NASA to perform research on Skylab solar physics data for the Aerospace Corp. of Los Angeles. He later served in a variety of consulting roles. Gibson wrote an introductory guide on solar astrophysics, *The Quiet Sun*, as well as a novel. Gibson also edited *The Greatest Adventure*, a compilation of stories on space missions from astronauts.

The Eastman Wind Ensemble rehearsing while on a West Coast tour in 1968

Wallis, in a private interview with Meckling in 1982, sketched out recollections of the turmoil. He described sending a letter every summer to students at home so it would be received in the presence of adults "and not just on campus where they would immediately be swamped with propaganda."

"For the most part, I personally stayed out of any kind of confrontational situation," Wallis recalled. "If anybody said or 'demanded'—you know, these students were always saying, 'we demand this, or that'—if they demanded that I see them, or do something, I just absolutely never did it or even answered them if they talked that way. I had somebody tell them, 'Well, the president just doesn't respond to demands.'"

The president was sometimes accompanied by security guards; extra locks were placed on doors, and the entrance to his office was reconfigured so that a small waiting room could cause a "bottleneck" for intruders. "For a long time, I made a point of using a different route every day going to and from the campus," the president said. "None of that, I think, was ever really necessary here, but it certainly was at some places, and you never knew for sure here.

"Really the worst thing about it, I'd say from the point of view of its effect on me, was the faculty reaction. A lot of the faculty . . . tried to find out which way the mob was going and run around and get in front of them . . . some of them were among our most eminent people. . . . I guess I'd say that after that I never had my heart in the university to anything like the extent I did before."

Provost Robert Sproull, a physicist and administrator at Cornell University before joining Rochester, worked closely with Wallis to manage campus unrest. In 1970, Sproull was named president, and Wallis became chancellor—the second and only other individual to hold that title in Rochester's history. The title change had little effect on function, Sproull said; he continued managing day-to-day operations while Wallis remained the University's top executive.

Wallis and Wilson would lead a significant financial change at the University in 1970. Rochester was among several universities to adopt new methods for defining appropriate spending from endowment income. The University based its change on analysis by Meckling and Jensen of stock market results since 1926, which showed that total return on common stocks historically had been 9 percent, leaving 5 percent available for use after inflation of about 4 percent. The Board approved a policy that would let the University use 5 percent of the previous five-year moving average of endowment income, insulating the institution from annual dips in earnings.

Wallis handed over the chief-executive role in 1975 but stayed with the University for several years, focusing on long-range planning, including studying the feasibility of a law school. He served in the Nixon and Ford administrations as a member of the National Council on Educational Research and the National Commission on Productivity, and as chair of the President's Commission on Federal Statistics and of the Advisory Council on Social Security. In addition, Wallis served on the Nixon presidential commission that recommended ending the military draft. In 1976, he published *An Overgoverned Society,* a critically acclaimed collection of essays and speeches describing how bureaucratic rules were shackling both the economy and individual freedoms.

On a late fall day in 1971, Wilson died of a heart attack in Gov. Nelson Rockefeller's apartment, where he was having lunch following Xerox meetings in New York City. Wilson, 61, recently had been named chair of President Nixon's Committee on Health Education and also led Rockefeller's Steering Committee on Social Problems. A lengthy piece in the *New York Times* detailed his business success and social leadership, including his efforts at the University. "Mr. Wilson saw to it that the company's success enriched causes he believed in," the *Times* said. "Before the Xerox stock captured the public imagination, the University of Rochester invested $196,000 in it; only a few years later the stock was valued at close to $100 million."

Mary Anne Krupsak '53 was New York State assemblywoman from 1968 to 1972 and state senator from 1972 to 1974. She became the first woman to serve as lieutenant governor of New York State in 1974.

Both Wallis and former President de Kiewiet, however, said Wilson's involvement had outweighed any financial contributions. "He had extraordinarily broad cultural, intellectual, and social interests," Wallis said. "He had great personal warmth, wit, sensitivity, generosity, and modesty . . . more important than his gifts, it was his character, counsel, guidance, and spirit that made the University worthy of the support that he and many others have given it."

Wilson's wife, Marie—known as Peggy—carried on his philanthropy, donating her home, art collection, and other support through the Marie C. and Joseph C. Wilson Foundation.

After Wallis retired from the University in 1982, he served as Under Secretary of State for Economic Affairs in the Reagan administration. He coordinated U.S. economic programs and policies abroad and served as President Reagan's advance man and advisor for several international economic summits.

President Wallis with his wife, Anne, and their Welsh terrier, Penthy

Peggy Wilson formally broke ground for Wilson Commons on February 19, 1973, using the same spade used by Rush Rhees at the groundbreaking for the River Campus in 1927.

In recognition of Wallis's dedication to the combined study of economics and politics, the W. Allen Wallis Institute of Political Economy at the University of Rochester was named in his honor. The institute, which opened in December 1992, would support study on how market forces are influenced by political institutions.

Wallis died in 1998 in Rochester after falling ill during a visit from his home in Washington, D.C., to attend a memorial service for Meckling. Wallis had continued to visit Rochester for events involving the College and the business school, which in 1986 was named in honor of leading benefactor William E. Simon. The University administration building was named in honor of Wallis during memorial events.

Sproull credited Wallis as the principal architect of the University. "He had the greatest respect for universities as institutions and the highest principles in defending them," Sproull said.

Thomas H. Jackson, University president when Wallis died, said Wallis's legacy was "permanent and extraordinarily positive. He was a man of absolute integrity and perseverance, who had a clear academic vision and an insistence on the highest academic standards. Not only was he instrumental in the transformation of the University to a national institution of the first rank, but his continuing mark on this institution is clear today, as many of our strongest schools and programs can be directly traced back to leadership that Allen was instrumental in bringing to Rochester."

Dandelion Day poster, mid-1970s

The Carillon

At times, the melodies from the top of the Rush Rhees Library tower can be heard on the other side of the Genesee River. They're produced by 50 bells that make up one of the few carillons in New York State.

The Hopeman Memorial Carillon, dedicated in 1973, replaced the 17-bell Hopeman Memorial Chime, which was installed in the tower when the River Campus was opening in 1930. The original chime was donated in memory of Arendt W. Hopeman by his daughter and two sons. Arendt Hopeman founded A. W. Hopeman Builder in 1869; the company served as the general contractor to the River Campus from 1927 to 1930 and also built the Eastman Theatre, Eastman School of Music, Eastman Kodak headquarters, and other Rochester landmarks. The Hopeman Engineering Building is also named

for him. Arendt Hopeman's daughter, Margaret, graduated from the University in 1903 and earned her master's degree at Rochester in 1906. His sons, Albert and Bertram, held leadership positions with the construction company.

The carillon is much bigger than the chime but is much lighter; the new bronze bells from the Netherlands weigh 6,668 pounds. The chime, cast at Meneely Foundry in Watervliet, N.Y., weighed 34,000 pounds, with its largest single bell weighing 7,800 pounds.

A carillon is an instrument consisting of at least 23 bells that are tuned so that bells can be sounded together harmoniously. The bells are stationary; only their clappers move. They are operated by a keyboard of a double row of rounded wooden levers. A carilloneur plays the instrument by hitting

the keys with loosely clenched fists.

Rochester's first bellman was John R. Slater, chairman of the English department. Alumnus and honorary trustee Robert Metzdorf—who earned his undergraduate, master's, and PhD degrees at Rochester—operated the instrument for a time. Dozens of students have operated the bells over the years, including for major University events, weddings, and memorial services.

The wall in the bell tower carries an inscription by Slater:

Hear them at the evening chime
Bells of the future, bells of the past,
Bells of beautiful things that last
Eternity, telling time.

Donald Slocum '56 and Hinda Manson '56 examining one of the bells up close in Rush Rhees Library, 1956

Joseph T. Alling

This bell summoned students to class at the United States Hotel and at the Prince Street Campus until 1876. The bell ringer, typically the janitor, would take it out of a locked cupboard and ring on the hour. "At that time Anderson Hall was the only University structure, and this bell was loud-voiced enough to be heard throughout the building," Board chairman Joseph T. Alling, Class of 1876, remembered. With the addition of Sibley Hall, the handbell was replaced by one that was rung using a rope and could be heard in both buildings. Some University relics turn up in unexpected places: the handbell spent about 30 years in a workshop in the Eastman Building at the Prince Street Campus after physics technician Fred Baumgartner recovered it from debris in the basement of Anderson Hall.

The original bells of the Hopeman Memorial Chime before installation in 1930

The C. E. K. Mees Observatory in New York's Bristol Hills

THE LONGEST VIEW OF TIME

ROBERT L. SPROULL, 1970–1984

FRESH IN HIS ROLE AS PROVOST ON A JULY MORNING IN 1968, ROBERT LAMB SPROULL HEARD sirens screaming through campus. He rushed out from Bausch & Lomb Hall to see fire trucks next door at Rush Rhees Library. Sproull, who had just come from Cornell University to become Rochester's provost, stepped inside the iconic library building and instantly recognized an odor from his early lab work as a physicist. A plastic known as Bakelite was burning, Sproull knew, and this material, used in electrical insulation, had to be in the elevator. He told the fire officials, who narrowed their search and extinguished the fire before much was damaged.

If there were metaphors for Sproull's tenure at Rochester, this would be one. Sproull, in effect the chief operating officer of the University through the tumultuous late 1960s, president from 1970 to 1975, and president and chief executive until 1984, played a critical role managing urgent problems among students and faculty. By all accounts a high-energy, hands-on leader, he navigated the University of Rochester through a distressed economy marked by an energy crisis, double-digit inflation, and escalating unemployment—as government mandates multiplied. Simultaneously, he supported the University's newfound strength in its young graduate programs and, thanks to his shrewdness about scientific matters, was able to promote development of one of the world's most powerful lasers.

Sproull accepted the role of provost at a high point in campus unrest. As was the case at universities across the country, the United States' involvement in the conflict in Vietnam affected much of campus life and administrative decision making. The previous fall at Rochester, more than 100 students had protested a recruiting visit by Dow Chemical, and the administration's harsh penalties for graduate students had embittered faculty. By mid-1968, students and faculty were raising questions over the University's contract to

Robert L. Sproull

manage the Center for Naval Analyses, an independent research group for the U.S. Navy. Civil rights strife peaked; Sproull would negotiate a peaceful end to a weeklong takeover of the University Faculty Club by the Black Students' Union, which pressed for better support of African-American students and faculty. Sproull would recall in interviews much later that for a time, administrators seemed able to focus only on limiting disturbances rather than on advancing the institution.

An exceptional era of growth was coming to a close. By the late 1960s, Rochester's enrollment had reached roughly 8,000. Faculty had swelled to 700—many recruited under President W. Allen Wallis as federal research funding and tuition revenue grew. Rochester held national stature in several programs, including its new efforts in economics and political science. But financial adversity would hobble development in the new decade. Enrollment growth tapered off nationally for the first time since World War II, especially in the Northeast. Competition grew: numerous high-quality colleges, including Amherst and Dartmouth, moved toward coeducation, eliminating one edge Rochester had held. Annual inflation bumped to nearly 6 percent in 1970 and 11 percent in 1974. Fuel prices quadrupled in a span of three years after the OPEC oil embargo. The University, famously wealthy since George Eastman's munificence, retrenched in stock market declines, including one year when its endowment lost 40 percent in absolute value. By 1974, as Sproull transitioned to full leadership, an ambitious, 10-year growth plan was essentially scrapped, and his administration would focus largely on trying to maintain Wallis's gains.

The spring of 1968, when Sproull considered President Wallis's invitation to become provost at Rochester, had been a particularly wrenching period for the nation. Martin Luther King Jr. was assassinated that April. Columbia University shut down when students took over administration buildings in protest of the war and perceived discriminatory decisions by university leadership. As Sproull visited the Rochester campus in early June, Robert F. Kennedy was mortally shot in Los Angeles.

Sproull evaluated the University. Most of his education and career had been at Cornell University, at the pastoral southern end of New York's Cayuga Lake. His responsibilities had grown since joining Cornell's faculty after World War II. A native of rural Illinois, Sproull had transferred to Cornell after two years at Deep Springs College, a work-study junior college on an isolated California cattle ranch, where he enrolled after his parents lost their savings in the stock market crash of the Great Depression. Deep Springs offered no physics instruction, but Sproull became intrigued through his own reading. He graduated from Cornell with a bachelor's in English—precision in writing would be a Sproull hallmark at Rochester—and then earned a doctorate in physics at Cornell at the height of the war in 1943, studying under Nobel-winning theoretical physicist Hans Bethe.

Countless academic scientists were drawn into the war effort, and Sproull, with a classified experimental thesis relevant to microwave

Walter Cooper

Walter Cooper earned his PhD in physical chemistry at the University in 1957 and worked at Kodak as a research scientist until retiring in 1986 with three patents and many research publications to his credit. Simultaneous with his contributions and honors in the world of science, Cooper worked on behalf of civil rights and his commitment to the power of education as the primary means to improve the opportunities and circumstances of young people. He served as a founding member of the Rochester Urban League and of Action for a Better Community and in leadership roles in the National Association for the Advancement of Colored People (NAACP). Cooper was awarded the University's Hutchison Award in 1994 and its Frederick Douglass Award in 2008.

The *Campus-Times* of April 9, 1968, reported that Bernard Gifford '68M (Mas), '72M PhD (left) addressed a memorial gathering in downtown Rochester. Jackson Collins '71 is pictured at right. Gifford, at the time part of the Rochester FIGHT organization, would later become deputy chancellor of New York City's public school system and then vice president for student affairs at the University of Rochester. The Black Students' Union was established in the wake of Martin Luther King Jr.'s death.

Charles Strouse '47E

Entering the Eastman School of Music at 15, Charles Strouse felt intimidated by a sense of seriousness at the school. A talent who had skipped two grades in his native New York City, the eventual Tony, Grammy, and Emmy award winner immersed himself in classical composition despite a knack for the lighthearted. He would recall an Eastman teacher slamming the keyboard lid down as he made fun of an assignment to mimic 18th-century style.

Strouse continued to see himself as a classical composer beyond his Eastman years and until the 1960 success of *Bye Bye Birdie*. But even as *Birdie* drew acclaim, he didn't mention his Broadway work to then private instructor Aaron Copland, who saw a poster for the show and wondered whether the Strouse on the poster was his student. Strouse would credit renowned Parisian composition teacher Nadia Boulanger with opening his mind to playful work when she praised his talent for "light music," according to a 1985 feature in *Rochester Review*.

Strouse's *Annie*, which debuted in 1977, would run for more than 2,000 performances and generate countless productions, including movies, worldwide. Many of Strouse's compositions became American popular classics, from "Those Were the Days," the theme song of television's *All in the Family*, to *Birdie*'s "Put on a Happy Face."

magnetrons, went to work in the Princeton, N.J., laboratory of RCA, focused on U.S. Navy radar. After the war, he returned to Cornell for an assistant professorship.

Rising through administrative roles in the growing physics programs at Cornell, Sproull also became known at Rochester. His path would cross with University scientists in regional consortiums, and he became acquainted with Joseph C. Wilson through advisory work for Xerox. Sproull, leading much of the recruiting and funding, became Cornell's first director of the Laboratory of Atomic and Solid State Physics. After the creation of the U.S. Defense Advanced Research Projects Agency (DARPA) in response to the Soviet launch of Sputnik, Sproull earned one of the first—and the largest—of its contracts for interdisciplinary materials science and became director of Cornell's efforts in that burgeoning field. He left Cornell for two years to serve as director of DARPA, reporting to the secretary of defense, before being named Cornell vice president in 1965. His Defense experience would bring him to lead a national committee evaluating the search for a missing U.S. hydrogen bomb, ultimately found, after a B-52 and an Air Force tanker collided off the coast of Spain in 1966.

The prospect of the University of Rochester and its diverse, robust city—10 times the population of Cornell's Ithaca—held appeal. With top-ranked graduate schools in music and medicine, the University had within the past 15 years merged its colleges for men and women and formed new schools in business, education, and engineering. Growth at industries with fresh technologies had prompted the metropolitan area population to swell to close to one million. Xerox was building a 30-story tower downtown. Kodak, its Instamatic a household word, had expanded camera-making operations at a sprawling suburban plant. Bausch & Lomb, which had created the lenses used in the cameras that first took satellite images of the moon, was fine-tuning the world's first soft contact lenses. Sproull recalled that his only hesitation came from Wallis's reputed far-right political interests, but his concern was assuaged by descriptions from former Wallis colleagues at Chicago: "strictly honest and principled."

"He knew what was necessary to make a major university and he was determined to get the resources to do it," Sproull recalled.

A partnership developed. Wallis would gravitate toward long-range goals and cultivating external relationships. Sproull, characterized as a direct, plainspoken executive who moved fast and worked long hours, managed most routine executive decisions and budget planning. Some saw him as practical. He would on occasion ground Wallis's soaring vision, which included a distinct, economics-based law

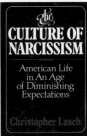

THE CULTURE OF NARCISSISM

Christopher Lasch surprised even himself with *The Culture of Narcissism*. His 1979 analysis of American culture brought history to a broad audience, becoming a national bestseller and earning Lasch a consulting invitation from President Jimmy Carter.

Lasch, the Don Alonzo Watson Professor of History and Political Science, who joined the University of Rochester in 1970, achieved lasting distinction for his observations of social trends through the lens of times past. His generally progressive, wide-ranging books and essays critiqued industrial capitalism and its effects on American politics, social arrangements, modes of thought, and personal psychology.

In *The Culture of Narcissism,* Lasch described postwar America as a society of dangerously self-absorbed individuals, fixated on personal goals, fearful of their impulses, and easily

controlled by power elites. President Carter consulted with Lasch on his July 1979 "national malaise" speech. Lasch later told an interviewer he was surprised by the popularity of the book, which he considered "difficult, even somewhat forbidding."

As recently as 2010, in the wake of scandals with Sen. John Edwards and golfer Tiger Woods, reviewer Lee Siegel revisited the book: "Just over 30 years ago, in *The Culture of Narcissism,* Lasch, a historian at the University of Rochester, took what was still mainly a narrowly clinical term and used it to diagnose a pathology that seemed to have spread to all corners of American life."

Lasch, a native of Omaha, graduated summa cum laude from Harvard University with a bachelor's in history in 1954. After earning a master's from Columbia University in 1955 and a doctorate there in 1961, he became an

associate professor at the University of Iowa in 1964 and a full professor the next year. He was a professor at Northwestern University from 1966 to 1970.

Lasch became chair of the Rochester history department in 1985 and was credited with much of its national prominence. He was a frequent contributor to publications such as *Time* and the *New York Times.* When he died of cancer at 61 in 1994, a University statement noted that his work earned him a much wider audience than typical of academic historians. "His focus always was to show how the individual is alienated in a consumer culture," the statement said. "Difficult to label politically, Lasch hit plenty of hot buttons alternately espoused and condemned by both neoconservatives and liberals."

Ronald Thomas '71, president of the Black Students' Union, spoke at a press conference at the close of a student occupation of the Frederick Douglass Building.

In 1977, Thomas, then a sports writer, would be featured in the *Rochester Review*. His book, *They Cleared the Lane: The NBA's Black Pioneers*, was published in 2002 by the University of Nebraska Press.

school. He would temper Wallis's tensions with faculty, forming advisory groups for research and academic affairs that helped give professors a greater sense of participation in management decisions.

Their early collaboration centered on keeping peace. Sproull at times was the lone, but successful, opponent to a law-enforcement presence on campus, mindful of the escalation of turmoil when police intervened at other schools. "I really can't convey adequately the poison that the Vietnam War inserted into anything we did, or anything anyone else did, for that matter," Sproull said in an interview. He shared recollections in extended interviews—in 1992, with presidential assistant Kenneth Wood, and nearly 20 years later, in 2011, as part of more recent University history research.

"You couldn't argue with the students because there was nothing to argue about," Sproull said. "They didn't like the draft—they didn't like the Vietnam War, we didn't like the draft, the administration and faculty—but we couldn't turn it off. And it boiled down to two things—one is making some kind of statement that the University is opposed to the war, which I refused to do because I didn't believe the University should be in the business of hamstringing faculty and other participants by saying what side they're on no matter what the side was. So that went round and round, with no intellectual content at all. The other was a very local kind of wart on the academic body, which was CNA, the Center for Naval Analyses. It really was just a tiny bump on the road, but nevertheless it was a bump that you had to get over because it took up everybody's time."

The Kent State University shooting deaths of four students by National Guardsmen in May 1970 triggered a climactic episode in Rochester unrest. While aggressive disturbances at other campuses followed the tragedy, Rochester students embarked on a peaceful petition drive calling on Congress to pull troops out of Vietnam. The *New York Times* noted the Rochester drive had reached 41 states.

Tensions eased each year, Sproull recalled. The United States gradually reduced its involvement in the increasingly unpopular war. The U.S. voting age dropped from 21 to 18, giving college-age citizens a greater voice in government decisions. The military draft ended in 1973, influenced in part by research of Wallis, Meckling, and University economist Walter Oi advocating an all-volunteer military. *Campus Times* articles revealed less about fierce objections of students to government actions and more about signature 1970s escapades: A streaker T-shirt went into the time capsule of the Class of 1974; a tow-truck operator's contract was cancelled after he threatened the students who threw eggs at his loathed vehicle.

Still, the Reverend Hays Rockwell's words in a *Rochester Review* essay would characterize lasting changes in student behavior. Interests and concerns had become more diverse, less "monolithic" than in the Protestant chaplain's 1950s college days, when undergraduates rallied around Homecoming and worried most about how to come up with cash to cover a bar tab. "It is precisely because this university offers the chance to be free," Rockwell wrote, "that it is an ambiguous and complex place."

As tensions settled, Sproull turned more attention to academic advancement. A leading endeavor centered on laser experiments led by Moshe Lubin, a vigorous engineering professor who became convinced Rochester could be a leader in the quest for laser fusion—a potential source of inexhaustible energy.

Lubin, a plasma physicist, had realized Rochester held the elements necessary to create conditions in which thermonuclear reactions might be made, recalled James M. Forsyth, a graduate student involved in Lubin's early experiments. Forsyth wrote in *A Jewel in the Crown,* a history of the Institute of Optics, "He needed expertise in pulsed laser technology . . . ready access to state-of-the-art optical fabrication facilities . . . advanced optical design . . . and a pool of talented graduate students. It was all here!"

"Moshe Lubin and Engineering were attracting the ablest young people on campus," Sproull recalled. "When you see the best students going into an area, you pay attention to it." He remembered aiming funding at Lubin's lab under the same theory as Stanford University's longstanding practice of concentrating resources to grow distinct programs of excellence.

Sproull supported early University funding and lobbied for the project with government funders. The Laboratory for Laser Energet-

Walter Oi with his guide dog Karl. At his final commencement as president, Robert Sproull asked Oi to walk in the procession. Oi agreed but—as a joke—only if appropriate regalia were provided for Karl. Several weeks later, a trustee's hood tailored to fit Karl arrived in the mail. It was worn by each of Oi's successive dogs for all commencement ceremonies.

Moshe J. Lubin, founding director of the Laboratory for Laser Energetics, with a prototype liquid-cooled neodymium-glass slab amplifier

ics, established in 1970 as a center for investigations of the interaction of intense radiation with matter, grew from 13 faculty members and an annual budget of $250,000 to 40 faculty members and a $1 million budget by 1972. In 1983 Robert L. McCrory, former senior scientist and director of the lab's theoretical division, was named director of the LLE. McCrory's research and leadership were recognized in a number of honors, including the 1995 Edward Teller Medal for work in the use of lasers for controlled thermonuclear fusion.

Lab officials reflecting on the its 40-year history in 2010 said 191 scientists had received doctoral degrees based on research carried out there. The University's early investment, $30 million, generated nearly $1.4 billion for the University and the regional economy by 2010, with Rochester consistently on the forefront of expertise in high-power lasers and laser fusion. Also in 2010, the laser lab was one of four institutional partners in the U.S. Department of Energy's $3.5 billion National Ignition Facility at Lawrence Livermore National Laboratory, which aimed at achieving the beginning of a self-sustaining fusion reaction.

On Wallis's recommendation, the Board of Trustees named Sproull president in 1970, designating Wallis as chancellor. Records show the new title was intended to give Sproull more influence with-

Rosemary Leary and Bob Hutchison in front of the Omega 24-beam laser after it was fully converted to ultraviolet operation in 1985

out changing duties of the two executives. Transition took a more significant step in 1973, when Wallis urged the Board of Trustees to take the unusual measure of designating his successor five years before his planned retirement. The Board concurred with Wallis's recommendation for an orderly change as the institution prepared to carry on its brisk advancement.

That November, Wallis and leaders from every division of the University outlined aspirations for the coming decade. There were economic warning signs, but assumptions apparently were optimistic; the U.S. economy had not sustained a prolonged downturn since the Great Depression. Stock prices had slid; the Rochester endowment lost nearly 9 percent in absolute value the year ending June 30, 1973. Inflation, despite wage-price controls by the Nixon administration, climbed bewilderingly through the year to reach 8 percent when trustees gathered to hear the new 10-year plan. The Organization of the Petroleum Exporting Countries, or OPEC, had declared its embargo just a few weeks earlier.

Each division conveyed confidence. The libraries were exploring new information technologies. The College would fine-tune its faculty and programs, with a special focus on quickly responding to student ap-

Nursing Innovator

Loretta Ford transformed the nursing profession and changed the delivery of health care by cofounding the nurse practitioner model at the University of Colorado in 1965 with Henry Silver, MD.

In 1972, she became the founding dean of the University of Rochester School of Nursing, where she implemented the unification model of nursing education, practice, and research. Also during her tenure, the educational mission of the School of Nursing expanded beyond the bachelor's and master's degree programs to provide both doctoral and postdoctoral training, placing the School of Nursing in a position of academic leadership nationally and internationally. She retired in 1985.

Among many honors and awards, Ford was inducted into the National Women's Hall of Fame in Seneca Falls, N.Y., and was named one of only a few dozen Living Legends by the American Academy of Nursing.

praisals: "We would like our freshmen to feel . . . that this is a hotshot institution that does everything right," Dean Kenneth Clark commented. The College of Engineering and Applied Science planned to double its undergraduate enrollment. Seventeen new faculty members from prestigious universities throughout the country were putting programs in place at the School of Nursing, reported Dean Loretta Ford. She said the school, a pioneer in its unification of patient care, teaching, and research, already was recognized as a national resource since its designation as a college a year earlier. The Medical Center, considered among the top 10 nationally, would seek to refine strength, especially in graduate and post-doctoral subspecialty education and neuroscience. The Eastman School of Music, exploring curricular changes—to incorporate non-Western music, computers, and other themes—would step up enrollment by 12 percent and upgrade facilities significantly, perhaps even by building a new school at the River Campus, said Director Robert Freeman.

Economic conditions continued to deteriorate, however. The United States would mark its longest recession since 1929 between that November and March 1975, with national unemployment peaking at 9 percent. The stock crash of 1973–74 sank Rochester's endowment by 40 percent in absolute terms, to $240 million, its lowest total since 1964. Budget reports showed annual endowment spending exceeding limits by as much as $660,000.

Wallis remarked that he felt he was "passing the buck instead of the torch" to Sproull, named as his successor as the 1974–75 academic year kicked off. In a simple inaugural in the Eastman Theatre in February 1975, Sproull outlined the challenges facing the University but underscored the hope inherent in a commitment to its progress: "Of all man-made institutions, the university takes the longest view of time. The primary missions of universities are to help succeeding generations prepare themselves for lives of service and to create new knowledge that will enrich the lives and enlarge the opportunities of succeeding generations. One does not give his life to a university unless he is optimistic about the twenty-first century."

The 10-year vision abruptly faced severe revisions: $73 million, rather than $41 million, of a planned $100 million capital campaign would have to go to the endowment. In perhaps the starkest example of thwarted plans, the Eastman School tabled notions of significant upgrades or a possible move when executives determined they could invest only $5 million in improvements to the 50-year-old school rather than $40 million.

Board of Trustees' financial reports lamented the University's heavily invested position through the crisis. New strategy in 1971 had

shifted funds away from conservative bonds toward potentially higher yielding growth companies as officials sought returns to counter inflation. Even the University's customarily successful investments plummeted: its roughly 700,000 shares apiece in Kodak and Xerox dropped 45 percent and 68 percent in market value, respectively, in 1974. "The major mistake we made last year was to remain fully invested through the worst market selloff in the postwar period," the Trustees' Investment Committee wrote in a report to the full Board in May 1975.

Many higher education institutions shared the grief, having been influenced by the prominent Ford Foundation, whose president, McGeorge Bundy, urged more aggressive investments in the late 1960s. Previously, most schools had been using post-Depression strategies of cautious balance between stocks and bonds, reported *Fortune* magazine in a 1987 analysis. "[Bundy's] recommendations—that endowments take on a heavier equity weighting, emphasize growth stocks

Robert Witmer, left, and his father, G. Robert Sr., pictured at the inauguration of President Joel Seligman, 2005

G. Robert Witmer Jr. '59

G. Robert Witmer Jr. '59 embarked on a more than 35-year role in University leadership in 1977, when he was elected chair of the Trustees' Council, the University's top alumni advisory group at that time. Witmer joined the Trustees' Council in 1972 and served as president of the University Alumni Council in 1974 and as president of the River Campus Alumni Board of Directors from 1966 to 1970.

A prominent lawyer with Nixon, Hargrave, Devans & Doyle—later Nixon Peabody—Witmer joined the University Board of Trustees in 1979

and was elected chair in 2003. He led the search that culminated in the selection of Rochester's 10th president, Joel Seligman, who would remark in 2008 that Witmer, a gentleman of uncommon wisdom, sensitivity, and quiet strength, seemed to know—and be respected and liked by—everyone in Rochester. "He puts people at ease with an infectious smile and chuckle," Seligman said.

After earning a bachelor's degree with honors from Rochester and being elected to Phi Beta Kappa, Witmer earned his law degree from Harvard

Law School in 1962. He joined Nixon in 1963, serving as chair of the management committee there from 1984 to 1987 and in 1991. Witmer led the firm's environmental law department from 1976 to 1983.

Cocaptain of the varsity basketball team during his undergraduate years, Witmer was named a charter member of the University's Sports Hall of Fame. His father, the Hon. G. Robert Witmer Sr., was a 1926 graduate of the University; since 1922, more than a dozen Witmers have attended the University.

over blue chips, and spend principal, if necessary—proved ill-timed," *Fortune* said. "No sooner had colleges loaded up on stocks than the Dow Jones Industrial average crashed from 985 in 1968 to 631 in 1970. Endowment administrators would prefer to forget some other trying times: 1973 and 1974, when stocks dropped again, and the late 1970s and early 1980s, when few endowments kept pace with double-digit inflation and many had to dip deep into principal." It would be the early 1980s before Rochester's endowment again reached pre-1973 levels.

Sproull set out to raise $102 million for the campaign. Early overtures to Rochester's largest employers, which contributed a third of Wallis's $38 million campaign a decade earlier, would fall short of expectations. Industries were facing stronger international and technological competition. Kodak responded to the University's request for $10 million—and upping its annual giving by 50 percent, to $300,000—with a pledge of

Robert Freeman

A well-known music educator, musicologist, and pianist, Robert Freeman was director of the Eastman School of Music from 1972 to 1996. He also has been on the faculty of or in leadership positions with other renowned music schools in the United States. Freeman, a Steinway Artist since 1973, has performed throughout North America and Europe and has made several recordings, some with Eastman colleagues. He publishes works on 18th-century music and on the history and future of music education. He has served on various boards and advisory councils for music and the arts throughout New England; New York; and Texas, where he was dean of the College of Fine Arts at the University of Texas at Austin and where he was in 2006 named the Susan Menefee Ragan Regents Professor of Fine Arts. Rochester, Freeman's hometown, in 1983 awarded him its Civic Medal in connection with his work on downtown revitalization.

Freeman, at right, and renowned cellist Yo-Yo Ma both were guest artists on the program with then quartet-in-residence, the Cleveland Quartet, for a September 1983 recital in Kilbourn Hall at the Eastman School.

Library Friends

A group of University library supporters decided in 1972 to formalize a system for helping the libraries in a variety of ways. "As this University's search for excellence in learning and research becomes more diverse and ambitious, its need to add to and enrich library collections with materials of scholarly importance and research value becomes greater," a 1972 pamphlet introducing the Friends explained.

The next year, the Friends organized its first antiquarian book fair, featuring 25 dealers, including one offering a 1779 copy of *The Book of Common Prayer*. At least 200 people attended the fair, which raised $4,200. The 1976 fair raised $35,000, with attendance of 1,300.

Rowland Collins, chair of the English department, wrote to Ben Bowman, director of University Libraries, in 1974: "What a difference the Friends organization has made in our sense of ourselves."

Activities of the group have expanded to include annual awards for library staff and to student book collectors and a graduate dissertation fund. The annual sale became a general book sale. Members of the group received invitations to lectures, book sales, readings, dinners, and borrowing privileges at River Campus libraries.

$6 million and continuation of its $200,000 yearly commitment. "It's in effect less than the 1960s campaign . . . spread over a longer period as well," Sproull observed confidentially to Wallis. A pitch to Xerox, which included tallying the number of copiers on campus (91), also fell short, with a pledge of $2 million rather than $6 million.

The University could highlight many points of pride as the campaign proceeded. The American Council on Education's most recent review of graduate education had rated 12 University departments as "distinguished and strong," a mark achieved by only three Rochester departments in 1964. A new, $70-million Strong Memorial Hospital offered one of the nation's most modern health care facilities. Six faculty members were in the National Academy of Sciences, 19 faculty and staff were fellows of the American Academy of Arts and Sciences, and three alumni had been awarded the National Medal of Science in the previous five years.

Ultimately the campaign would close at $104 million, $2 million above its goal. The University tallied 26,637 donors, with 12 gifts of $1 million or more. Thirty percent of alumni contributed. Separate from the campaign, officials celebrated a $2.8 million award from the National Cancer Institute toward a $5.7 million cancer research center to consolidate research, treatment, and support services. The University also inherited more than $25 million from the estate of Charles F. Hutchison, Class of 1898 and longtime trustee and Kodak executive. The 1974 bequest was believed to be the largest to any college or university in five years.

Government pressures cascaded through the era. A previous federal emphasis on competitive research shifted toward greater undergraduate, need-based financial aid, with funding aimed directly at students rather than institutions through instruments such as Pell Grants, said historian John R. Thelin.

New administrative efforts at Rochester would include strategy in admissions. Projections showed a 40 percent drop in high school graduates in New York State from 1977 to 1987. Staff were recruited to intensify marketing and outreach—in 1977, Rochester representatives would visit 1,000 high schools versus 300 a year earlier, and alumni were asked to use their influence to bolster the University's image. "It was clear that we could not continue to think of the Admissions Office as simply an organization which selected a few people out of a vast array of applicants and offered admissions to them," Sproull said. "We had to start recruiting the way every other institution was doing, and considering our clientele and considering what we had to offer and how to offer it."

A press for recruiting and fostering a more welcome environment for African-American students and faculty coincided with admissions

Charles F. Hutchison

Charles F. Hutchison, Class of 1898, was active in University affairs as a trustee and advisor for roughly 40 years. When he died in 1974 at age 98 his bequest of $25 million made him one of the institution's largest benefactors.

Hutchison, who studied chemistry, joined Kodak in 1902 and eventually became controller of film and plate emulsion for the United States and Canada. A close associate of George Eastman, Hutchison is recognized as the primary developer of the Kodak Park facilities for emulsion making.

He retired from Kodak in 1952. Hutchison volunteered in a variety of roles in the community but devoted much of his time to his alma mater. He was named to the Board of Trustees in 1932 and served in leadership roles on the Board until 1961 and served on the Board of Managers of the Eastman School of Music. Named an honorary University trustee in 1959, Hutchison continued to attend meetings well into the 1970s.

Hutchison Hall, which houses the departments of chemistry, biology, and earth and environmental sciences, was dedicated in his honor in October 1971. The Charles Force Hutchison and Marjorie Smith Hutchison medal is awarded each year to an alumnus or alumna for outstanding achievement and notable service to the community, state, or nation. From 1951 to 1976, the University owned Hutchison's home on East Avenue, which was used by the Eastman School first as a student union and recital hall and later as the residence of the school director.

Russell Peck

A student taking a class with Russell Peck would be unlikely to forget him. Peck, by 2012 the longest-serving active faculty member of the University, would draw in students with his teaching style, which at times included playing on a tuning harp.

An authority on Middle English literature, Peck joined the University in 1961. A Wyoming native, Peck earned a doctorate from Indiana University in 1963 and a bachelor's from Princeton in 1956. Engaging students in countless ways, from an annual theater course in England to trips to Rochester's Seneca Park Zoo, Peck became known as a force of nature in Rochester's English department.

Peck served as faculty director for the Medieval Society and the Drama House and led the acquisition in 1987 of the collection of medieval texts that became the Rossell Hope Robbins Library. Since the late 1980s he created and was the chief editor for the Middle English Text Series to retain authoritative texts that can be read easily in the original Middle English.

In 2012 trustee Janice Willett '78 and her husband Joseph Willett '75 pledged $3.5 million to the University's capital campaign, designating a significant part of the gift to honor Peck and his wife with the Russell and Ruth Peck Professorship.

enterprises. Provost Richard D. O'Brien wrote in a March 1983 *Campus Times* article the University had, among several initiatives, tailored financial aid packages to offer superior packages to minority students, created new graduate fellowships for minorities in three departments, and was working with the Urban League of Rochester to develop undergraduate scholarships. The previous year, nine African-American full-time faculty members had been hired, O'Brien said. "This list of activities is not presented with any complacency," he concluded. "There is still only a small number of black graduate and undergraduate students and black faculty and administrators at the UR. The whole climate of the UR for minorities should be a continuing matter of study and possible improvement."

Admissions publications of the era highlighted names of renowned professors, including Eugene Genovese in history; Pulitzer-winning poet Anthony Hecht; Paul R. Gross, a national authority on developmental and molecular biology; pathbreaking child psychologist David Elkind; and Russell Peck in English, the Mercer Brugler Distinguished Teaching Professor, the John Hall Deane Professor of Rhetoric and Poetry, and winner of the Danforth Foundation award in gifted teaching.

Faculty work of the period would have lasting impact. T. Franklin Williams, MD, the J. Lowell Orbison Distinguished Service Alumni Professor at the Medical Center and director of Monroe Community Hospital, helped redefine care and perception of the aged. He would later serve as director of the National Institute on Aging of the National Institutes of Health. Meckling and Jensen published their pathbreaking paper on agency theory. The work of professors Ross L. Watts and Jerold L. Zimmerman, the Ronald L. Bittner Professor of Business Administration, in positive accounting helped established that academic discipline with research first published in 1978.

The University also would celebrate its ranking in 1977 among the top 15 universities in the nation in the number of faculty members awarded research fellowships from the Guggenheim Foundation. *Rochester Review* noted the remaining 14 institutions had faculties twice the size of Rochester's. In 2011, more than 90 academic leaders at foremost research institutions across the country had earned doctoral degrees from Rochester between 1975 and 1984.

Sproull received national attention in 1983 for resisting an attempt at patronage in administration of the Center for Naval Analyses, which the University had managed since 1967. The CNA provided independent research for the Navy. The University received pressure from Secretary of the Navy John Lehman to replace the CNA president with an individual of his choice. Sproull refused. The University lost the contract that summer to the Hudson Institute, a conservative-leaning research center.

"We had to hold firm to the principle, mostly for the University but also for the whole structure of quasi-independent studies and analyses groups," Sproull said later.

Sproull recalled in interviews that he was intent on completing Rochester's transition from a liberal arts college to a university. He paid particular attention to the appointment and support of department chairs and deans. More specific procedures were put in place to guide decisions on promotions and tenure. "It involved making the selection of faculty and particularly the selection of tenured faculty more according to established procedures and safeguards, and it meant making the selection of deans and the care and feeding of deans a major project in the president's office," Sproull said.

Sproull also would look for ways to give greater clout to graduate programs—appointing the prominent political science chair William Riker dean of graduate studies and steering fellowship money to Riker's control rather than to individual departments. "This gave him a chance to invade the little fiefdoms in the individual colleges, because when the colleges had all the money for the graduate fellowships, a college which was very weak could still give fellowships to very weak candidates, whereas if the fellowships were in University hands, they would have to face the University competition and that would cause them to shape up."

On Sproull's retirement in 1984, trustees honored him by naming the graduate fellowships in honor of him and his wife, Mary. Sproull remained an active member of the Board of Trustees committee over-

William Riker

Construction under way at the Memorial Art Gallery, 1966. The 30,000-square-foot addition, finished in 1968, doubled the size of the gallery and moved the entrance to the north side of the building. The gallery was closed during construction, with works on long-term loan to other museums and to traveling exhibits for schools and community organizations.

Cleveland Quartet

The Cleveland Quartet found a home at the Eastman School of Music in 1976, where it was based for most of its world-renowned career.

Eastman School director Robert Freeman worked with President Sproull to craft an unusual tenure agreement for members of the group in which their teaching—and their performance as a quartet—were evaluated. The group, founded at the Cleveland Institute of Music and based for five years at the State University of New York at Buffalo, originally included Paul Katz, cello; his wife, Martha Strongin Katz, viola; Peter Salaff '63E, violin; and Don Weilerstein, violin. Salaff and Paul Katz remained with the quartet through its 26-year run; Atar Arad and James Dunham joined at different points on viola; and William Preucil replaced Weilerstein on violin in 1989.

The group counted more than 2,500 concert performances between its inception in 1969 and retirement in 1995 and created award-winning recordings, including a 1996 Grammy for best chamber music performance.

seeing the laser lab. He and Mary in 1999 donated $2 million toward faculty research and study in the arts, sciences, and engineering. In recognition of that gift, the title of dean of the faculty of the College also includes their names.

Reflecting on his legacy, Sproull cited Wallis's major increment of quality in faculty and programs. "I'm proud of the fact we [continued] that in impossible conditions," he said. "We kept an administration. We did this and at the same time made the institution a more human institution. We have the advantage of an institution with a solid core and a solid approach to its future."

Robert Sproull sailing, 1969

WILSON COMMONS

Three years under construction, the I. M. Pei–designed Wilson Commons hosted 4,500 visitors on its opening day in 1976. Chancellor Allen Wallis recollected a student telling him he had never seen anything so beautiful.

The steel-framed brick-and-glass student center featured an 18,000-square-foot glass area 84 feet high.

Wallis, who commissioned Pei, said it took at least six months to convince the architect, then in great demand, to take the project. "I think you feel that the thing is built for the people and the activity that goes on in the Commons," Wallis told an interviewer. The $9.5 million building includes dining areas, meeting rooms, club headquarters, and an art gallery. While students and faculty were critical of the project as it unfolded—faculty called it "the world's largest cloud chamber"—critics quieted when they entered.

The diagonal axis of the six-level building was intended to put the Rush Rhees Library tower, the center of the University's identity, in focus, Pei said at the time. "The glass links the academic world symbolized by the tower to the residences." The Commons features entrances from every direction—bridges above and tunnels below.

An evening prank by Rick Levine '74 became a symbol for the project. For opening day, Commons decorations included reproductions of his graffiti on boards that had walled off construction: "THE SHORTEST DISTANCE BETWEEN TWO POINTS IS WHERE WILSON COMMONS IS."

"I felt like doing something," Levine explained to Rochester Review, "and I remembered that there was all that nice blank space on the boards overlooking this muddy pit that had evolved from the nice piece of land where we used to play football and soccer. . . . it occurred to me, mathematician that I am, that the site really was in the middle of everything—that if you drew a line between any of the dorms and the Eastman Quad, it was in the way. Anyway, it just kind of dawned on me and I wrote it. If I'd known you were going to make a poster out of it, I'd have tried to make the printing a little neater."

Hugh Smith

ROCHESTER REVIEW

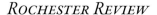

Since 1921, a magazine has helped keep graduates connected with activities of the University and with each other.

The *Rochester Alumni News* debuted with other efforts by part-time alumni secretary Raymond Ball '14 to more systematically forge ties. Hugh A. Smith '07, took over as full-time alumni secretary in 1922 and managed the publication until his death in 1936. Charles R. Dalton '20 and then Harm S. Potter '38 each held substantial tenures as alumni secretaries.

The magazine name changed with the institution, for a time called the *Alumni-Alumnae Review* and then *Rochester Review*. Its cover design also reflected changes.

Margaret Bond '47 edited the *Review* for 22 years, retiring in 2001. Public relations vice president Robert Kraus summed up Bond's service: "She has shown the institution truthfully but in its very best light."

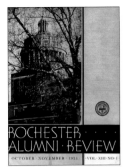
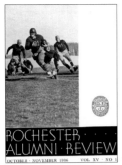

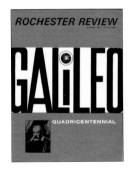

Margaret Bond

Students protested the idea of a University name change in 1986.

Passion for the Place

G. Dennis O'Brien, 1984–1994

A DROP IN UNDERGRADUATE APPLICATIONS AND A POPULATION FORECAST OF FEWER teens in the decade ahead drew concern as President Sproull readied for retirement. Provost Richard O'Brien attributed a 13 percent decline in applicants for fall 1983 to a demographic shift—"as a selective institution the University is more affected by this trend than the average college or university"—intensified by growing appeal of state universities. Rochester also was analyzing a decline in applicants to doctoral programs, reliant on University revenue such as undergraduate tuition for graduate stipends. As in previous administrative transitions, the Board of Trustees and faculty set fresh priorities in the search for a president. Enhancing the appeal of the College of Arts and Science and promoting the University's image would assume high importance.

Higher education institutions generally looked forward with trepidation. The number of 18-year-olds nationally peaked in 1979, and the age group declined by 26 percent in the next 12 years, according to historian Roger L. Geiger. Economic returns of an undergraduate degree reached a plateau in the 1970s while the cost of going to college escalated. Students drifted from universities' traditional core humanities subjects toward professional studies.

The University's home city began to experience signal economic change. Kodak, the dominant employer—and leading force in the city's identity—cut jobs by the thousands through the 1980s as it faced sharper global competition and changing technology. *Time* called 1983 "the year the company's glossy image lost much of its luster. . . . Profits of the world's leading maker of photographic equipment plunged nearly 50 percent in the first nine months . . . as key products faltered both at home and abroad." By 1997 Kodak's local workforce would drop by nearly half to 35,000.

February 2, 1984, special edition of
the *Campus Times* announcing the
selection of the University's eighth
president.

G. Dennis O'Brien

Other leading employers strongly identified with Rochester—
Xerox and Bausch & Lomb also would begin cutbacks. At the same
time, downtown suffered as retailers and offices shifted to the suburbs.
Main Street's Sibley, Lindsay & Curr, the city's oldest and largest department store, closed in 1990. New business names, however, would
enter local consciousness, such as Paychex, whose CEO B. Thomas
"Tom" Golisano eventually would run for governor and become a
prominent philanthropist. The Golisano Children's Hospital was
named in honor of his multimillion-dollar gifts to the Medical Center.

Rochester's continued economic and political clout warranted a 1984 re-election speech by President Ronald Reagan, who called it "a town . . . synonymous with America's industrial might and our scientific and technological leadership in the world."[1]

Faculty members consulting with the trustee search committee identified qualities most wanted in the new president. Chief were outstanding academic credentials and an ability to articulate and lead the faculty in goals of excellence. But circumstances also dictated a leader gifted in public relations. "The time has passed when a university can sit back and expect the students to come to it," the faculty advisory committee wrote to the trustees in April 1983. "Advertising and name recognition are essential. We need to mount a sophisticated campaign designed to make the public better acquainted with our name and what we stand for." The committee floated the idea of changing the University's name to differentiate it from public universities—a concept that resurfaced to become a heated test for the next president.

An internal study on doctoral education also informed the search. Applications to Rochester's science programs were down 28 percent from 1970 to 1980 while they had risen 2 percent on average among schools in the Consortium on Financing Higher Education (COFHE), a group of roughly 30 selective private institutions. A 1982 assessment of graduate education by the Conference Board of Associated Research Councils ranked five Rochester departments—chemistry, physics, economics, history, and political science—among the top fifth in quality, but placed eight departments at or below 60th percentile. Rankings had dropped since 1969 in several departments. Provost Richard O'Brien raised questions about appropriate funding. Some universities reliant on graduate students as teaching assistants were making "very attractive offers" to candidates, he said.

The provost underscored in the report the importance of drawing both graduate and undergraduate students to maintain Rochester's appeal: "Gifted graduate students are an essential part of this community. A faculty able to work at the frontiers of disciplines enjoys and, in the sciences, depends upon top-notch graduate students; undergraduates are attracted to an institution offering the intellectual excitement and richness of a university without losing the warmth of a college. Substantially altering the composition of the graduate constituency could upset the other constituencies and damage the University's distinctiveness. As the college-age population shrinks, we do not want to

Flyer posted on campus announcing the November 1, 1984, appearance by President Ronald Reagan at the War Memorial downtown

---

1 Ronald Reagan, "Remarks at a Reagan-Bush Rally in Rochester, New York, November 1, 1984," The Public Papers of President Ronald W. Reagan, Ronald Reagan Presidential Library, www.reagan.utexas.edu/archives/speeches/1984/110184e.htm.

WITMER HOUSE

A Mt. Hope Avenue estate that had been with Rochester's Barry family since its nursery heyday became the University president's home in 1984. The house had most recently been the residence of former mayor Peter Barry, great-grandson to Ellwanger & Barry Nursery cofounder Patrick Barry.

The house was designed by J. Foster Warner—who also was the architect of George Eastman's home—and built in 1906 for William C. Barry Jr., grandson of Patrick Barry. William C. Barry became a full partner in the nursery business. His son, William C. Barry Jr., headed the Ellwanger & Barry Realty Co., which evolved as

the nursery business faded. The realty company developed neighborhoods in the Mt. Hope area. His son, Peter Barry, who occupied the house until his death in 1973, served as mayor of Rochester from 1955 to 1961 and encouraged the development of downtown's Midtown Plaza.

On Peter Barry's death, the University bought the property for $105,000. The building's first significant use was as the residence of the O'Brien family. The Georgian Revival home featured a gambrel roof with pediment dormers, massive end chimneys, and fine detailing and craftsmanship throughout, including marble fireplaces, a ceiling

medallion, and key-stoned, archway doors.

In 2006, the house was dedicated as Witmer House in honor of G. Robert Witmer Sr. '26 and his wife, Marian Witmer, and in recognition of his family's nearly 80-year role in helping guide the University. Trustee G. Robert Witmer Jr. '59 and his wife, Nancy, were the chief benefactors in a drive to expand and renovate the historic property.

risk losing our appeal to prospective undergraduates. Recruiting and maintaining a corps of top graduate students will help us keep our best faculty, attract colleagues for them, and, in turn, remain attractive to our traditional undergraduate audience."

A trustee search committee reviewed 261 names, and University representatives visited 19 candidates across the country. A few warranted a trip to Rochester via private jet with David Kearns, chief executive of Xerox and chair of the University Board of Trustees. Among them was George Dennis O'Brien, the charismatic president of Bucknell University, who had quickly raised $40 million in a record campaign. O'Brien—no relation to Rochester's provost—earlier was dean of the faculty at Middlebury College. A philosopher and authority on Hegel, he also was admired for his warmth and wit. His experience lay decidedly in undergraduate education. Bucknell, which offered master's degrees but no PhD, had been ranked "first in the East" by college presidents among comprehensive universities in *U.S. News & World Report*'s inaugural rankings—a review that overlooked Rochester.

Students supported O'Brien. "The University of Rochester needs someone who can represent well on the outside and inspire people," education professor Walter Garms reported on his work with a student committee advising on the search. Administrators with a focus on graduate education, however, expressed confidential concerns. "None of the candidates stand out . . . as having potential for leadership the way Sproull or Wallis had when starting out," remarked one. Another questioned whether O'Brien could manage the complexities of a research university and whether faculty and deans in research would respect him. It was noted that the institutions in O'Brien's administrative background did not include any with a medical school—a demanding enterprise in higher education management. Others saw in O'Brien exciting potential for better public relations and internal morale that balanced lack of experience in a research setting. Some believed external relationships, including those in the Rochester community and with alumni, had been inadequately cultivated during the University's previous two decades of focus on graduate programs and campus infrastructure. "He would be able to build spirit and morale," said George Angle, vice president for public affairs.

O'Brien liked the prospect of taking his liberal-arts perspective to a high-quality university. After seven years at Bucknell, he was open to considering a different experience when search committee chair Walter Fallon, CEO of Kodak, reached out. O'Brien saw wonderful possibilities in refining undergraduate education at Rochester, more than twice as large as Bucknell, while advancing recognition for the institution

William E. Simon

The University's growing business school was named in honor of lead benefactor and former U.S. Treasury secretary William E. Simon in 1986. Simon contributed not only financially but also as an advisor on the school's executive advisory committee from 1986 until his death in 2000.

Simon served as U.S. Treasury secretary from 1974 to 1977 under presidents Richard Nixon and Gerald Ford. He previously served as deputy Treasury secretary, launching the Federal Energy Administration, or FEA, during the 1973 oil embargo. FEA was the first federal agency primarily focused on energy—collecting and analyzing data. It became part of the U.S. Department of Energy formed in 1977.

Simon, a financial entrepreneur involved in the creation or growth of a number of businesses, founded William E. Simon & Sons, a firm focused on venture capital, with his sons, William E. Simon Jr. and J. Peter Simon, in 1988. Simon served on the boards of more than 30 companies and was a member of the U.S. Olympic Committee.

We are the Champions!

Basketball Championship

With two seconds left on the clock, guard Adam Petrosky '92 slapped the ball from a DePauw University player to score and seal the Yellowjackets as the NCAA Division III titleholder for 1990. The 43-42 game was recorded as one of the lowest scoring championships in DIII history.

Center Chris Fite '93, voted the tournament's most outstanding player, was featured as *Sports Illustrated*'s small-college Player of the Week following the game.

Rochester Review celebrated the victory and highlighted the efforts of basketball players. Team captain Erik Rausch '90 had juggled demanding coursework with games every other day and practices on days between. Coach Mike Neer worked with players before the season began to set a practice regimen to accommodate academic schedules.

Neer had a noteworthy, 34-year run as Rochester's basketball coach, starting in 1976. When he stepped down in 2010, Rochester had not only earned the 1990 title but also reached the Final Four three other times. His record was 563-326 (.633), making him one of the most successful coaches in NCAA Division III history.

overall. Long after accepting the presidency in spring 1984, O'Brien would recite a colleague's observation: "Congratulations, Dennis. You're going from a reputation better than reality to a reality better than reputation." O'Brien shared his recollections in interviews in 2011 and in a manuscript soon after leaving Rochester in 1994.

Education ran deep in the O'Brien family. A grandmother had been among the first graduating class of the University of Wisconsin, and a grandfather had been a professor of sociology at Ripon College in Wisconsin. O'Brien's father, a leading cardiologist in Chicago, had chaired the department of medicine at what became Stritch School of Medicine at Loyola University in Chicago and treated high-profile patients, including Mayor Richard J. Daley.

O'Brien grew up in what he called the "Catholic ghetto" of south Chicago. His Catholic faith would thread through O'Brien's research career and into administrative decision making. Moralistic interference could make him uneasy. Such discomfort caused some reluctance to appease protestors when Rochester shifted investments to companies including those doing business in South Africa during the anti-apartheid movement of the mid-1980s. He never forgot his father's caution early in his academic career that, as a Catholic, he would not be selected as a university president at a secular institution. "I understand that quite well, having lived with Catholicism and the kind of intellectual interference that they like to get involved in," O'Brien observed.

O'Brien, a Phi Beta Kappa graduate of Yale University, earned his doctorate in philosophy from the University of Chicago, where he held a Carnegie fellowship in university teaching. Accepting his first teaching position at Princeton University, O'Brien heeded the advice of a Chicago mentor, philosopher Warner Wick: "Be useful." O'Brien volunteered for administrative tasks such as helping students with registration in the philosophy department. He was asked to become assistant dean of the college, a role that gave him an early window into the intricacies of undergraduate achievement. "These young people were people who on paper should have done very well, but something was going on in their lives that made them unable to function," O'Brien said. "Education is more than putting bright faculty in front of bright students."

O'Brien moved to Middlebury College in Vermont as dean of men with an appointment on the teaching faculty in philosophy. He followed a similar route into administration, successively becoming dean of the college and dean of faculty. He formed a lasting rapport with President James Armstrong. Among their undertakings was recruitment of African-American students after the assassination of Martin

Luther King Jr. The night King was shot, O'Brien saw an interview with civil rights activist Roy Wilkins. "Somebody asked, 'Who's going to be the new leader of the black community if King dies?' And Roy Wilkins said, 'That's the wrong question. Because the question is what will the white community do in this case. So don't look around and say, well, why don't we find a good black leader to do something for us? What is the white community going to do about this?' And I said to Jim, 'That's the question. What are we going to do about this situation?'"

Arriving in Rochester in the summer of 1984, O'Brien set out quickly to establish stronger connections with Rochester's African-American community, first lifting the suspension of a graduate student accused of striking an editor who had rejected his story at the student newspaper. The penalty had been viewed by some as harsher than the treatment a Caucasian student would have received. He met with and maintained relationships with a dozen pastors of local African-American churches. The University would play host to special events, such as a Martin Luther King Jr. School Day, when 500 students from city schools attended an Afro-Brazilian dance show, conflict resolution workshops, and a slideshow about Africa.

Before long, plans were in place for the University's Frederick Douglass Institute for African and African-American Studies. In 1985, the University bestowed an honorary doctorate on Bishop Desmond Tutu, South African Nobel laureate. O'Brien formed close ties with Urban League of Rochester president William A. Johnson Jr., later mayor of Rochester, and James McCuller, president of Action for a Better Community, an agency focused on helping low-income individuals and families.

International Fiesta, 1988

Diversity remained a high priority. O'Brien appointed Frederick C. Jefferson a presidential assistant on matters of race, and a presidential commission including top administrators, faculty, staff, and students examined and recommended actions on recruiting and campus life. "No response to these issues can be regarded as wholly definitive," O'Brien wrote in an introduction to the recommendations, shared widely in the Rochester community in early 1985. "Some of the problems that face us—both the university and the minority community— are so deep, so long standing, and so difficult that solutions have evaded men and women of good will on all sides.

"Nevertheless, progress can be made and must be attempted. The only final commitment must be the elimination of racism as a divisive factor in our common life. We must all remain sensitive to modes and methods of accomplishing that goal which may not even be imagined in this memorandum."

O'Brien similarly supported a center dedicated to women's issues in the Susan B. Anthony Institute for Gender and Women's Studies. "Professional academics basically look at people in terms of their brains," O'Brien explained in 2011. "Whether they're men or women or black or white, it doesn't make any difference. But in an undergraduate situation that's a different story. Now you're dealing with people in terms of levels of socialization, how they perceive themselves, how they perceive the institute, 'Do I belong here?' I remember feeling, when I was at Yale, a little odd. Talk about being a Catholic. I suddenly discover that all of my roommates are Catholics. And I'm convinced that that was deliberately done . . . to segregate us so we would be protected or segregate everybody else so that they would be protected from us."

He laughed, but continued, "And so, that becomes part of your whole perception: 'Is this a place I really belong? Am I really welcome here?'"

With initial priorities defined in undergraduate education, O'Brien did not expect to face a raft of appointments to replace departing executives or to head new initiatives. O'Brien later would thank his own ignorance for his successes; it led to placement of effective people leading critical functions around him. He sought professionals from within and outside: "I knew what I didn't know and I had to find people who did know about those things." The president made his first key selection in Brian Thompson as provost to succeed Richard O'Brien, who became executive vice chancellor and provost of the University of Massachusetts at Amherst. Thompson, a respected engineer who joined the University as director of the Institute of Optics in 1968, had become dean of engineering in 1975 and maintained a pathbreaking research career in coherent optics and holography.

O'Brien next recruited James Scannell, admissions dean at Cornell with earlier recruiting success at Boston College, to oversee a revamped admissions operation. The president envisioned a "cradle to grave" service for applicants, students, and alumni. Scannell developed outreach efforts including scholarships sponsored by local corporations and a community grant program. By 1994, the undergraduate college admitted as many students as it had applicants 10 years earlier.

Other administrative changes cascaded. Twenty-five year veteran treasurer LaRoy B. Thompson retired, and business manager Robert France suffered serious illnesses. Frank Young, leading the Medical Center, left to become chief of the U.S. Food and Drug Administration. College of Arts and Science dean Paul Hunter returned to teaching. Influential individuals brought into the central office—some still

James Scannell oversaw enrollment, placement, and alumni relations in a new strategy to integrate the three areas.

Desmond Tutu, the first black archbishop of Cape Town and 1984 Nobel Peace Prize laureate for his role in the effort to eliminate apartheid in South Africa, received an honorary doctor of divinity degree at the 1985 commencement ceremony.

dynamic in University leadership more than 30 years later—included treasurer Richard Greene, budget director Ronald Paprocki, development vice president Richard Miller, and vice president and University dean of students Paul Burgett. Prominent neurologist Robert Joynt, MD, assumed leadership of health affairs.

O'Brien named a committee on University goals with administrative, student, and faculty representatives across the institution to recommend programs geared toward improving student life and distinguishing Rochester. "I felt that the graduate education really worked well," O'Brien said later. "It tends to be . . . dominated appropriately by faculty professional disciplines. You're looking for the best chemists, the best physicists, philosophers, whatever it may be. In a way, it should run pretty much on its own. Undergraduate education is rather a different dish of tea because it's not just discipline-oriented. At least

Judith Pipher

Judith Pipher's work in infrared technology was an important influence on the study of our astronomical origins. In 1983 Pipher, a professor of astronomy, was among the first in the United States to turn an infrared array toward space. She and colleagues mounted a prototype infrared detector on a telescope in a small campus observatory, taking the first infrared telescopic pictures of the moon.

Pipher's work in near-infrared detector arrays helped move her field from single-pixel devices to virtually flawless multimegapixel arrays. In 2003, NASA launched the Spitzer Space Telescope, which is equipped with infrared detectors Pipher helped design. With the telescope in orbit, Pipher investigated, among other things, clusters of forming stars and brown dwarfs—planet-like objects too small, cool, and dark to be seen by ground-based telescopes.

Pipher joined the University as an instructor in 1971 after earning her PhD from Cornell University. She has served as scientific editor of the *Astrophysical Journal* and on the board of trustees of the Universities Space Research Association. Pipher was inducted into the National Women's Hall of Fame in 2007 for her work in infrared detector array development.

From left, Nobel laureate Arthur Kornberg '41, Medical Center vice president Robert Joynt, and provost Brian Thompson during the 1987 Rochester Conference on Creation

that's the way I've always looked at it. Eventually people will major in a discipline, but in the meantime you've got to get them involved in the whole idea of university study, a greater level of sophistication. I felt what we needed to do was to somehow find a way of making a University of Rochester education intriguing."

One initiative became publicly known before any announcement—and fell apart. The committee had looked at a possible name change, perhaps along the lines of Rochester University or Eastman University, a notion that had been raised previously within the school and by mentors of O'Brien in higher education. An independent consultant's analysis supported a change. The local *City* newspaper, one of many critics, wrote: "The University of Rochester, apparently worried about its image, is considering changing its name. Is somebody pulling our leg? Apparently not. University officials are considering the name change, because, consultants have suggested, the name may not send the right signals. Schools named after cities don't have enough prestige, say the consultants. And the word 'Rochester' creates images of a 'cold and distant outpost.'" Students protested.

Alumni letters poured into O'Brien's office. "I must object to any attempt to change the University's name," wrote a medical school alumnus. "My degree, my relatives' degrees, my Steiff teddy bear's sweater, and my baseball cap all bear U of R logos . . . all in all quite an investment. Once again I've been asked to work the telethon in Seattle to ask for nickels and dimes for the University. At the same time I'm paying full freight for two students at 'back East' schools. I find it hard to understand or forgive the spending of $50,000 for a name change study." A graduate from the 1940s vented in the *Roch-*

ester Review: "I think the president has more important things to do than build images."

In a spring 1986 announcement of a five-year plan coming out of the committee on University goals, O'Brien put the issue to rest: "Lots of people wrote and called and a few yelled to make sure that I understood how much they loved and supported 'the University of Rochester.' What we need now is passion for the place, not just the name. This University by any name could have great days ahead. The University of Rochester can draw on its heritage, it can believe in its strengths, it can venture ahead."

Other plans drew mixed results. An annual weeklong Rochester Conference—named to capitalize on the famed physics consortium—with renowned speakers on philosophical topics was dropped in budget cuts. University Day, a midweek pause in classes to free students for seminars or other enriching events, was abandoned because of weak attendance by students. "Turns out most people did their laundry," O'Brien quipped.

But one invention turned, almost overnight, into a Rochester signature. Electrical engineering chair Sidney Shapiro, seeing his students with few opportunities for electives during their standard four years of study, suggested an additional, tuition-free year for especially bright students to pursue studies of their choice. O'Brien had doubts at first, imagining students marveling at how they could bear even four years. Testimonials soon spoke to Take Five's effectiveness, and it became a model for programs at other schools. Optics major Jeff Bugenhagen

Beautiful Way

Composer, recording artist, and Rochester native Chuck Mangione '63E received an honorary degree and a dandelion-yellow and blue fedora during commencement exercises in 1985. Mangione conducted the Eastman Wind Ensemble in a performance of "Bellavia," his 1977 Grammy Award–winning composition.

"Bellavia"—meaning "beautiful way" in Italian—honors his mother, second from left in this photograph.

Barbara Duncan,
first Sibley librarian, 1922–47

Manuscript of Debussy's *La Mer*

SIBLEY MUSIC LIBRARY

The Eastman School of Music's Sibley Music Library, said to hold the largest music collection in an academic setting in the United States, received a spectacular upgrade in 1989. The library had been housed in an increasingly crowded Swan Street building since 1937 and earned three floors in the new, $18 million Eastman Place—later named Miller Center in honor of the family of Mitch Miller '32E.

The library predates the Eastman School by nearly two decades. Hiram W. Sibley, son of Western Union lead founder Hiram Sibley, donated a collection to the University in 1904, calling it "the Sibley Musical Library for the music lovers of Rochester." The collection, open to the community,

featured musical scores, journals, and books on music in a reading room of Sibley Hall, home of the University library on the Prince Street Campus and named for its benefactor, the senior Sibley.

When Hiram W. Sibley died in 1932, the University assumed responsibility for its care. Barbara Duncan, recruited in 1922 from the Boston Public Library, designated the library's rare book collection and helped found the Music Library Association. In 1947, Ruth Watanabe succeeded Duncan and led the library for nearly 40 years. Watanabe, who earned her doctorate in musicology at Rochester in 1952, recalled Eastman director Howard Hanson telling her, "You will buy every-

thing, I mean everything." By the 1990s Sibley Music Library ranked among the three largest in the country, behind the Library of Congress and the New York Public Library.

"There aren't many places in the world where you can look at Brahms' penmanship, or survey the first American edition of what may be the first violin sonata ever published in this country," *Democrat and Chronicle* music critic Robert Palmer said in a *Rochester Review* report.

In 2012, the collection included 334,000 books and scores, a listening room with 50 stations, and an in-house conservation lab.

Ruth Watanabe '52E (PhD), librarian of the Sibley Music Library for nearly four decades. "Her training as a scholar, her thorough approach to building research library collections, and her love of music resulted in collections of international importance, which continue to support and sustain music performance and research, study, and teaching at the Eastman School," said librarian Dan Zager when Watanabe died in 2005.

'87 was quoted in Waxman's *Beside the Genesee:* "It gave me a way to find out what else there was."

Less conspicuous were modifications in night class schedules, improved academic advisement for students, and more busing to the Eastman School of Music.

The president's vision also would place the University in a leading role forming the University Athletic Association. O'Brien worked with chancellor William Danforth of Washington University in St. Louis to create an enduring conference of nine research universities, including Brandeis, Carnegie-Mellon, and the University of Chicago. "I remember talking to a member of the tennis team, who'd gone down to Emory for the tennis tournament," O'Brien said. "I said 'Well, What was it like?' 'Oh,' she said, 'it was wonderful, it was the first time when nobody asked me why I was reading a book between the sets.'" The University would create its Athletic Hall of Fame in 1992, honoring key players in shaping its intercollegiate sports history.

The national mood toward higher education improved. By 1983, government appropriations for higher education picked up, and gubernatorial candidates campaigned as "higher-education governors," wrote historian John R. Thelin. The notion of universities as economic incubators took hold: the University of Rochester would be a founding partner, with the Chamber of Commerce and Rochester Institute of Technology, in the business incubator High Tech Rochester in 1987.

O'Brien took a leading role in a number of community endeavors. He was a major participant in meetings of a committee of political, business, and public school leaders focused on a youth, family, and community plan to strengthen health and human services to support student learning in city schools. He supported a city and county plan to improve the Genesee River area in Rochester's 19th Ward and at the University, which included building a pedestrian bridge across the river to connect the two. Bausch & Lomb gave the University $2 million toward park-like, riverside improvements on its property. The bridge was a controversial topic among many at the University who feared it would provide greater access for criminal activity, but the administration viewed the connection as providing access to students living off campus and to a neighborhood where it hoped a college-town atmosphere could develop.

Serious complications in some efforts would occupy much of O'Brien's attention. Intense controversy unfolded in 1987, when under perceived pressure from Kodak, action was taken to withdraw the admission of a Simon Graduate School of Business student who was an employee of Fuji. O'Brien and Provost Thompson had understood that Kodak, convinced of industrial espionage, would withdraw up to

Peter Lyman

A premier tennis and squash player in his prime, Peter R. Lyman '47 coached Rochester's programs into national prominence. The River Campus's outdoor tennis and indoor squash complexes both are named in his honor.

He coached squash and men's tennis for 44 and 42 years, respectively. Lyman was inducted into the University's Athletics Hall of Fame and the Frontier Field Walk of Fame in 2000.

His men's tennis team was represented at the national championships for 22 consecutive years. His players earned a total of 20 All-America honors. Lyman's tennis teams were ranked in Division III's Top 30 every year from 1983 to 1997; five were ranked in the Top 10. He was honored as the Intercollegiate Tennis Association's Division III National Coach of the Year in 1990.

Lyman coached the squash team to a consistent Top 20 ranking. Five squash athletes earned a total of nine All-America awards. He received a Lifetime Achievement Award from the National Intercollegiate Squash Racquets Association in 2000.

Lyman, center, congratulates his 1982 national doubles champions, Bob Swartout '83, left, and Alex Gaeta '83.

The first pedestrian bridge connecting the campus with Rochester's 19th Ward opened in 1991.

200 employees, financially crippling Simon. The student was admitted to Massachusetts Institute of Technology's Sloan School of Management. The story seeped to the *New York Times*—and raced around the globe. "It was an unusual show of corporate influence even in the long, close relationship between American business and the nation's business schools," the *Times* said. "And it was even more striking because the University of Rochester's William E. Simon School of Business is known for its free-market principles, which advocate minimum of regulatory constraint."

"Abhorrent," said $30-million benefactor William Simon in a United Press International Report. O'Brien said he expected Kodak to validate claims of espionage when the issue became public, but executives denied intending any threat and offered no specifics. The University reversed its decision and invited the student to enroll, but he opted to stay at Sloan. Students and faculty were outraged. Writers pegged it "Kodak-scam" in the *Campus Times,* and alumni wrote to O'Brien declaring they would not donate. "You may contact me again next year, if the University has not done something else to humiliate itself and its alumni," wrote one. After months of review by Rochester faculty and trustees, a Board of Trustees ad hoc committee recommended clear procedures for consultations with deans, faculty, trustees, and representatives from any school involved in comparable situations in the future.

Before the Fuji storm subsided, a second tempest hit. The endowment portfolio underwent significant diversification credited with improving its performance. The changes included purchases in large corporations. Those companies, however, included a handful doing business in South Africa while many institutions were disinvesting in dissent with apartheid. A University committee had examined the ethics of such investments and recommended following the Sullivan principles, a set of guidelines for corporate social responsibility by the Rev. Leon Sullivan, a member of General Motors' board and a prominent African-American minister. Most universities followed the same guidelines without much reaction. At Rochester, criticism mounted. "UR president Dennis O'Brien's skin ought to be as thick as a hippopotamus hide by the time the latest round of boos and hisses subsides," Rochester's *Times-Union* editorialized. The *Democrat and Chronicle* said groups tracking involvement in South Africa believed the University's revised investment scheme marked the first time a major institutional investor had taken on South African–related holdings where none previously existed. "As part of his mission . . . O'Brien pledged to give the school the national visibility he thought it deserved," the *Democrat and Chronicle* said. "The events of the past month, however, are not what he had in mind." Faculty and students worried that the Kodak and South Africa incidents would undermine University efforts to recruit top faculty. Three hundred faculty members petitioned for an end to South African investments. Within weeks, the administration's committee on investing and ethical considerations recommended divestiture, saying the policy was damaging the University in the eyes of its own faculty and students as well as in the eyes of the larger community. O'Brien and the Board agreed. O'Brien would confide by letter to a former colleague: "I am greatly gun-shy of having universities adopt general moral stances on anything which is not directly related to their own immediate educational interest. I haven't yet been convinced that divesting in South African related stocks is in the immediate vital interests of universities as such. It is in the immediate vital interests of universities if it means that we can no longer serve minority students and faculty. That is a consideration and I think will be the basis on which we will divest."

The endowment restructuring nonetheless was believed to well serve the University's long-term interests. Analysts had observed that in the portfolio before restructuring, heavily weighted toward venture capital and idiosyncratic, small-cap stocks from 1970 forward, Roch-

The *Campus Times,* October 5, 1987

Duncan Moore

When the $1.5 billion Hubble Space Telescope dispatched blurry images worthy of a home camera, the director of Rochester's Institute of Optics became a natural choice for leading the effort to solve the problem.

Duncan Moore had established a reputation as a lens and mirror expert. He was appointed in 1992 by the National Aeronautics and Space Administration to lead a panel that would pinpoint the error in the 8-foot primary mirror aboard Hubble, which was launched in 1990. As it turned out,

the spacing of a test lens was incorrect in the telescope.

Moore joined the Institute of Optics faculty in 1974 after earning a PhD there. He later served as director for optics, then as dean of engineering and applied sciences. In 1997, Moore was appointed associate director of technology in the White House Office of Science and Technology Policy, where he served until 2000. In that role, reporting to President Clinton's science advisor, Moore would influence policies concerning clean cars,

the Internet, nanotechnology, and technology to help individuals who are aging.

Moore, the Rudolf and Hilda Kingslake Professor in Optical Engineering and professor of biomedical engineering, as well as professor of business administration in the Simon School, served on several high-profile science panels and developed a significant role in University entrepreneurship programs. He was named vice provost for entrepreneurship in 2007.

ester missed out on a significant surge in value, especially among large corporations. By one estimate, the 1987 endowment of $564 million could have been twice that. Coupled with spending that often exceeded the annual 5 percent limit, Rochester's relative wealth dropped substantially. The eighth-richest university in 1984, it was 15th in 1986. O'Brien recruited investment banker Edmund Hajim '58 to the Board. Hajim took the lead of the Board's investment committee and in contracting with professional investment managers to significantly diversify holdings.

Financial pressure would cause some upheaval in the College of Arts and Science. O'Brien and Provost Thompson urged deans, including Jack Kampmeier of the College of Arts and Science, to find ways to cut spending at least 5 percent. The administration also would propose consolidation of the liberal arts college with the College of Engineer-

Art, Identity, and Politics

Douglas Crimp, the Fanny Knapp Allen Professor of Art History and professor of visual and cultural studies (VCS), is the author of *Melancholia and Moralism—Essays on AIDS and Queer Politics*. His work on AIDS has been seen as an important contribution to the development of queer theory in the United States. In 1992, Crimp was a featured speaker at the University's Craig Owens Memorial Lecture, presented in memory of his friend and colleague who died at the age of 39 from an AIDS-related illness. Owens was one of the founders of VCS, the first graduate program of its kind that provides students with an opportunity to study critically and analyze visual culture from a social-historical perspective. Crimp helped establish the lecture as an annual series in 1996. Owens speakers are chosen for their interest in gender, feminism, sexuality, and identity.

Crimp has been an important critic in the development of postmodern art theory. His most important work on postmodernist art and institutional critique was published in the 1993 book *On the Museum's Ruins*.

Margaret Warner Scandling

In 1993, the University's education school was named the Margaret Warner Graduate School of Education and Human Development in honor of its chief benefactor's late wife.

Margaret Warner Scandling, who died in 1990, was described as bright, determined, and humorous. She had attended the University as part of the Class of 1944. She and her husband, William F. Scandling, a founder of Saga Corporation, became especially interested in the well-being of the education school and made several significant donations.

"One of Margaret's concerns," said William Scandling at the school's dedication, "was that this school, being smaller, less well funded—and having an alumni group who, by their own choice, were not in high-paying professions—did not have a long list of people to tap for major support."

This portrait of Margaret Warner Scandling by Sascha Lautman, in oil on canvas, was donated by William Scandling and is on display in Raymond F. LeChase Hall, which opened in 2013 to house the Warner School.

ing and Applied Science. Correspondence among the three showed Kampmeier expressing the impossibility of such cuts when certain programs needed substantially more funding, and he pressed for revenue sharing to the College of Arts and Science from other University divisions. Ultimately, in 1991, Kampmeier was removed as dean and returned fully to his professorship in chemistry. Recipient of numerous teaching awards, he was nationally known for development of the Peer-led Team Learning Workshop model for teaching chemistry and left a powerful legacy in his department. The Colleges of Arts and Science and Engineering merger were implemented by O'Brien's successor.

There were significant highlights. The Memorial Art Gallery underwent a renovation that expanded its exhibition area by nearly 60 percent, making the museum bigger than New York City's Guggenheim or Whitney. New features included a main entrance facing University Avenue, as it had originally; a glass-roofed sculpture garden; and children's discovery room. Roughly 28,000 visitors attended opening week festivities.

The education school was named the Margaret Warner Graduate School of Education and Human Development in 1993 in honor of the late wife of William F. Scandling, whose endowment and operating gifts over the years exceeded $14 million. Schlegel Hall, named for the parents of lead benefactor Helen Schlegel Moretz '37, opened in 1991. The University of Rochester Press, founded in 1989 in collaboration with British academic publisher Boydell & Brewer, established a reputation for contributions to scholarly dialogue in a range of disciplines, including music, gender and race, and medical history. Eastman director Robert Freeman, appointed in 1972 to succeed Walter Hendl, expanded the school through construction of the Student Living Center and Eastman Place. One of Eastman's best-known alumni, soprano Renée Fleming, graduated in 1983.

Medical Center researchers David H. Smith and Porter Anderson developed the Hib vaccine, first licensed in 1985. The vaccine, refined in 1999, effectively eradicated the major cause of childhood bacterial meningitis. Nursing professor Jean Johnson's self-regulation theory, based partly on analysis of stress and illness with cancer patients in the 1980s, gave doctors and nurses tools to help patients cope with their illnesses and treatment. Leonard Mandel of optics broke new ground in a 1991 quantum experiment demonstrating that it was not necessary to directly observe a photon's motion to change its behavior from wave-like to particle-like.

Rochester ranked 25th among *U.S. News and World Report's* top national universities in 1991. It ranked ninth that year in faculty re-

sources, a category that examined the ratio of students to faculty; the percentage of full-time faculty with doctorates; and the average salary and benefits for tenured professors.

O'Brien timed his retirement in the spring of 1994 with that of two of his most trusted colleagues, provost Thompson and health affairs vice president Joynt. A tribute to the president in *Rochester Review* included accounts of his influence in ways large and small. Student Kim Babat '94 remembered bringing up with him in a meeting her challenges in using a desk for right-handers. "Everybody else laughed, but he didn't. And sure enough in the spring I had a left-handed desk to take my exams in." Board of Trustees chair Robert Goergen '60 credited O'Brien with enabling the University to change its endowment management, improving admissions processes, and launching a $375 million capital campaign. The campaign finished in 1996 at $421 million under O'Brien's successor.

Much later, reflecting on his legacy, O'Brien said he believed his appointments moved the administration in a more diverse, professional direction. "I suppose the other thing that I'd like to be remembered for is just raising the question of undergraduate education."

A Working Desk

President O'Brien participated in many events geared toward improving undergraduate morale. Dressed as Santa Claus, O'Brien is shown in 1985 at the desk of first president Martin B. Anderson. The desk mysteriously disappeared from Anderson Hall on the Prince Street Campus and was discovered under unexplained circumstances at Cornell University some 30 years later. It was identified by a brass plate inscribed, "Working desk of Martin B. Anderson, LL.D., First President of the University of Rochester." When Cornelis de Kiewiet, then acting president of Cornell, accepted the presidency at Rochester, some of his colleagues at Cornell had the desk restored to its original condition and sent to his Rochester home with a note expressing their "warmest best wishes" and pointing out that it was a "working desk."

THE UNIVERSITY HAS CELEBRATED ITS MILESTONES

At 50 years, Prince Street buildings were decorated with American flags and dandelion yellow streamers. Events included dedication of the Alumni Gymnasium and speeches, including a sermon by Baptist clergyman Thomas E. Brown, who spoke of "the permanent influence of sacrifice."

The University in 1925 celebrated not only the University's 75th anniversary but also President Rhees's 25th year as president and a successful 1924 capital campaign. Alumni competed in balloon games at Oak Hill—soon to become the River Campus—and wore blue and yellow "diamond jubilee caps." A record 600 graduates attended festivities.

For the centennial in 1950, events took place throughout the year. A student convocation highlighted the fall of 1949, when professor John R. Slater sketched the institution's history. "The University closes no door to ambition, sets no age when minds cease to grow," Slater said. Visiting speakers through the year included Eleanor Roosevelt, Nobel laureate Ralph J. Bunche, and diplomat Gen. Walter Bedell Smith.

Sesquicentennial commemorations in 2000 included the first Meliora Weekend, 22 smaller celebrations throughout the country, and publication of the pictorial history book *Beside the Genesee*. Two years of planning created a large pool of volunteers who remained involved in future events and created new fundraising offices targeting different groups.

A model cake of Rush Rhees Library tower was commissioned for the sesquicentennial celebration. The 21-inch model appeared on many of the publications promoting the event.

MELIORA
ONE HUNDRED FIFTY YEARS

University of Rochester

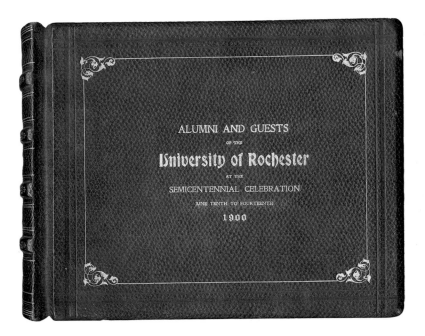

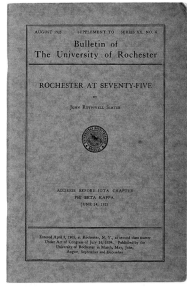

Rush Rhees Library tower lighted for the "freedom" theme of Meliora Weekend 2001

Renaissance

Thomas H. Jackson, 1994–2005

THE PRESIDENTIAL SEARCH FINALISTS OF 1993 LEARNED OF AN INSTITUTION FACING FI-
nancial challenges. Enrollment was robust but so was the tuition discount rate to attract students, leaving revenues weak and endowment spending high. Departments across the University had endured recent wage and hiring freezes. Thomas Humphrey Jackson, then a young
provost and vice president at the University of Virginia, had a sense that the Board of Trustees expected
Rochester's next leader to enact difficult job cuts. But Jackson, a leading bankruptcy scholar who had risen
fast in administration, thrived on complex intellectual challenges, and he began to see one at Rochester.

Few, if any, other institutions had followed such a trajectory, Jackson recalled in a 2012 interview.
George Eastman's largesse thrust Rochester, previously a small liberal arts college, to a place among the
country's wealthiest universities—where it stayed for nearly 50 years. Its first systematic growth outside
the world-class schools of music and medicine—and focused areas such as optics and physics—came in
the 1960s, when the Wallis administration, backed by Xerox executive and then Board chair Joseph C.
Wilson, built elite graduate programs in the College of Arts and Science, the College of Engineering and
Applied Science, and the business school. Rochester, still small and young as a research institution, was
drawing high-quality students comparable with the Ivies by the late 1960s, Jackson observed. Then, poor
investment performance, coupled with higher endowment spending, pushed the University not only out
of the richest five but also out of the best-endowed 25. The University also slipped from the top 25 of *U.S.
News and World Report*'s annual ranking of the best universities—a metric that within a decade of its 1983
debut had cemented itself in the consciousness of higher education decision makers. "It was sort of like
you built your dream house," Jackson said. "There you are living in your dream house, but the money you

Thomas H. Jackson

were going to pay for the house is in your mattress and the mattress burns up, and so here you are living in this house and trying to figure out, 'How do I pay for it?'"

"You don't find institutions that have that kind of rollercoaster ride," Jackson said. "Higher education institutions tend to be much more subtle and gradual in their rise and fall. So I was just fascinated by how an institution did that and what you do about it."

Jackson saw strong faculty and programs—"good bones," he called it. He also was impressed with an extraordinary level of teamwork on the presidential search committee among faculty and trustees, two constituencies vital to any presidential initiative. Early in the process Jackson asked about the faculty's potential receptiveness to a legal academic as president in an institution without a law school. Faculty search committee leader Charles Phelps, a professor of economics and political science and chair of the Medical Center's Department of Community and Preventive Medicine, and others had studied Jackson's work and could assure him of scholarly respect where diverse disciplines benefited from working together. "Here's a place without a law school that actually knew how to handle the question," Jackson said.

Jackson was an academic superstar. A 1972 summa cum laude graduate of Williams College, he had earned his law degree at Yale University in 1975 and clerked for U.S. Supreme Court Justice William H. Rehnquist. Jackson then held professorships at Stanford and Harvard law schools, and at age 36, while at Harvard, published one of the more significant bankruptcy law books of the era, *The Logic and Limits of Bankruptcy Law.* Two years later he became dean of the University of Virginia School of Law.

Justice Rehnquist remarked in a UVA law magazine article collected during the search that Jackson had arrived at work at 6:30 a.m. daily and carved out his own research time on top of demands for the court. "He's just an awfully nice fellow," Rehnquist stated. "He has none of the arrogance that you find in some bright people." Richard Aslin, College of Arts and Science dean, attended a dinner with Jackson and Board member Robert Witmer in late August where, according to Aslin, Jackson seemed "very mature, poised, articulate, and knowledgeable about public and private higher education. He immediately understood Rochester's 'market' in the undergraduate sphere." Jackson, Aslin added, embraced an open management style and recognized that change would need to come with faculty contribution. Rochester Board chair Robert Goergen '60, the governing body's most forceful leader since Wilson, supported the choice of Jackson heartily.

The Jackson inauguration in October 1994 would foreshadow refined and swift change. New academic robes in blue were ordered to replace bright yellow gowns worn since the 1960s, when then president Wallis had wanted Rochester representatives to be noticed during events elsewhere. Jackson's address touched on the visions of prior presidents stretching to Martin B. Anderson, who had advocated education available to students based on "talent and industry" versus social standing. Jackson announced a $5,000 tuition grant for undergraduate students from New York State. Larger strategies would unfold to draw top-quality students.

He outlined criticisms facing research universities as the 21st century approached: that they ignored undergraduate education in pur-

Invitation to President Jackson's inaugural festivities

suit of research; they were controlled by fanatics of political correctness; that they were focused too much on theory rather than practical problems; and that they were expensive. Jackson observed that this was a sort of reversal from a hundred years earlier, when the role and future of liberal arts colleges were questioned as research universities rose. He had studied the successful response of colleges then in an undergraduate honors thesis. His advisor was Frederick Rudolph, higher education historian at Williams, who received an honorary degree during Jackson's inaugural.

"Today symbolically marks the beginning of my time as president," Jackson said, "but it also provides a time to reflect on the underlying continuity and change of the University of Rochester. When we reflect as well at the enormity of the changes in higher education since 1850, when this University was founded, we can take great comfort in the ability of an institution of higher education, committed to the right values, to survive and flourish through periods of change more dramatic than the present. The challenges the critics see provide opportunities for us."

The decade ahead brought a concerted refocus in undergraduate and graduate education at Rochester. Across Elmwood Avenue, a dynamic new chief executive, Jay H. Stein, MD, selected by Jackson in

Imaging the Eye

The groundbreaking contributions to vision science by David Williams, director of the Center for Visual Science since 1991, were recognized in 2012 when he received the prestigious Antonio Champalimaud Vision Award in Lisbon, Portugal. Williams's team applied adaptive optics techniques developed by astronomers to the human eye, so that it is possible to image individual retinal cells—even individual cone photoreceptors in the living human retina. The methods Williams's group developed in the 1990s are used in many of the LASIK procedures conducted worldwide today.

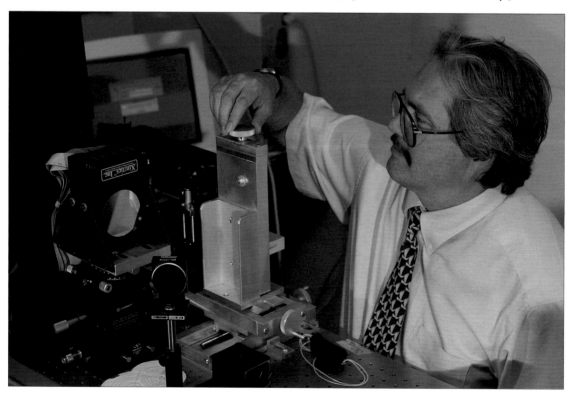

Robert B. Goergen

Robert B. Goergen '60 began a long history of support for the University soon after graduation, when he was asked to join alumni groups interacting with the administration. Goergen, who earned an MBA from the Wharton School of the University of Pennsylvania and followed a successful entrepreneurial career, was elected to Rochester's Board of Trustees in 1982.

Goergen founded Blyth, a designer and marketer of home products with more than $1 billion in sales in 2012. He also founded the Ropart Group, a private-equity investment firm. He began his career at Procter & Gamble, moving on to McCann-Erickson, where he became a senior account executive.

He also worked with consultants McKinsey & Co. and as managing general partner of the venture capital group at Donaldson, Lufkin & Jenerette.

Goergen chaired the University of Rochester Board of Trustees from 1991 to 2003. He led the search that resulted in the selection of Thomas Jackson and was a strong and decisive supporter throughout Jackson's 11-year tenure. They worked closely on plans around limiting enrollment, decentralizing the University, and revitalizing the Medical Center.

In an interview, Goergen said the principles of business apply in University decision making as well, although an institution of higher education has

a plurality of objectives versus a business's focus on growing profitability. "At a university everyone thinks they're in charge," he joked.

He and his wife, Pamela, have committed more than $20 million to the University, and both the biomedical engineering-optics building and the athletic center bear his name. One of their gifts established in 1997 the Goergen Awards for Excellence in Undergraduate Teaching.

"I'm proud to be a graduate of the University and proud to be on the Board of Trustees," Goergen said, "and I'm happy I've been able to pull on the oar a little bit. It takes a whole team."

Esther Conwell

Esther Conwell, research professor of chemistry and physics, won the Edison Medal of the Institute of Electrical and Electronics Engineers in 1997. Conwell's research focuses on how electric fields affect the movement of electrons in semiconductors. She has earned uncommon triple membership in the National Academy of Sciences, the American Academy of Arts and Sciences, and the National Academy of Engineering. In 2002 she was named one of *Discover* magazine's Most Important Women of Science. Conwell earned her master's in physics from Rochester in 1945 and a doctorate in atomic physics from the University of Chicago in 1948.

1995, led the Medical Center on a $500 million strategic plan to enhance its national standing. The University and its home city weathered a chaotic national economy marked by the burst of the dot-com bubble and the horrific terrorist attacks of September 11, 2001. Technology profoundly sped the exchange of information: in 1994, a special section of the *Campus Times* offered a tutorial on navigating the Internet; a decade later near-instant communication was the norm.

The University began to embrace its role as a local leader, both as an employer and as a hope for a new economic foundation, as manufacturers continued to struggle. Research universities generally assumed greater visibility nationally, wrote Wilson Smith and Thomas Bender in *Higher Education Transformed, 1940–2005:* "Knowledge became the engine of economic development, and in that process universities . . . assumed an unprecedented role."

By the time Jackson was inaugurated, consequential appointments and organizational changes had begun. Charles Phelps became provost. Phelps, who joined the University in 1984 as a professor of political science and economics, had earned an MBA in hospital administration and a doctorate in business economics from the University of Chicago. He was elected in 1991 to the Institute of Medicine of the National Academy of Science. Phelps was considered a leader with cross-disciplinary experience who thought broadly about University-wide issues.

He and Jackson forged a strong relationship that underpinned substantial changes for the institution. After a year as provost, Phelps wrote to the president: "It's hard, as you know, for either you or me, let alone outside observers, to figure out what happens that is 'you' and what is 'me,' so let's begin by recognizing that there is an enormous amount of 'co-authorship' involved in all of this. We have established a very productive working relationship with each other. . . . This, it turns out, was quite easy (and very fun), but from stories we hear, it often differs with other president/provost pairs. . . . I expect this to continue and grow."

Under Jackson, the College of Arts and Science and the College of Engineering and Applied Science were merged to become "The College" following the recommendation of a faculty committee. Each entity now had its own dean, who reported to Richard Aslin, former dean of the College of Arts and Science, in the new role of dean of the faculty. The essential drivers for the new structure, Jackson explained, were the links between the two colleges' revenues from tuition and endowment draw, combined activities such as admissions and student services, and the need for a single leader for the entities. "I am very sensitive to the notion that academic decision making needs to be the focus, to which support units respond," Jackson assured a faculty member who complained of the change. Soon undergraduate admissions services moved from the central administration to the College, one step in a broad process of decentralization in moving many responsibilities to individual schools or departments.

In the spring of 1995, the administration told the faculty the University would take a longer view addressing what had then become annual budget problems, especially in the College. Preparation for the roughly $150 million, 1995–96 College budget showed a potential $6 million shortfall. The previous year's tuition discount had surpassed 50 percent.

Carl Bonner '96 (PhD) is shown in Professor R. J. Dwayne Miller's research lab with an ultra-high vacuum instrument used for surface science spectroscopy studies.

Steven Chu at Commencement in 2013

Steven Chu

In 1997, Steven Chu '70 became the fourth University alumnus to receive the Nobel Prize.

Chu, who shared the prize in physics for developing a way to cool and trap atoms using lasers, was appointed U.S. energy secretary in 2009, marking the first time a Nobel laureate was named to lead the energy department. Before his federal appointment, Chu directed the Lawrence Berkeley National Laboratory, where he helped guide research into carbon-neutral energy sources.

Chu, the son of Chinese immigrants who moved to the United States during the World War II period to pursue advanced education, enrolled at Rochester after being rejected by Ivy League schools. He earned degrees in both math and physics, finishing third out of a class of 733. "The pull towards mathematics was partly social: as a lowly undergraduate student, several math professors adopted me and I was invited to several faculty parties," Chu recalled in an autobiography for the Nobel Foundation.

As a senior at Rochester, Chu won the Stoddard Prize for the most outstanding term paper. A *Rochester Review* account of Chu's undergraduate experience noted he played trombone in the concert band, took music lessons at the Eastman School, and played intramural sports.

After graduating, he entered the graduate physics program at Berkeley, where he earned his PhD. Chu then worked for AT&T's Bell Labs, where he and his team carried out the work for which he shared the Nobel with Claude Cohen-Tannoudji and William Daniel Phillips. He then joined the Stanford University faculty. Chu was named a University of Rochester trustee in 1999 and served until his cabinet appointment.

Other Rochester graduates to win the Nobel Prize are Vincent du Vigneaud '27 (PhD), the 1955 prize in chemistry; Arthur Kornberg, MD, '41M (MD), '62 (HNR), the 1959 prize in physiology or medicine; Daniel Carleton Gajdusek '43, the 1976 prize in physiology or medicine; and Masatoshi Koshiba '55 (PhD), the 2002 prize in physics.

Charles Phelps

Memos from Jackson, Phelps, and Aslin together to the faculty underlined basic assumptions. Continued development of graduate programs and research was an important focus, and Rochester's reputation depended on having several peaks of excellence. The University was one of the nation's preeminent research universities, whether measured by its inclusion in the Association of American Universities, its Category I ranking in Carnegie Foundation groupings, or its program quality as measured by peers in the field.

Also, the University had an intrinsic interest in undergraduate education and a desire for the "best and brightest" students, ensuring highest-quality interactions in and out of the classroom, the admin-

William Scott Green, 1983

istrators said. "Not only is a flourishing undergraduate educational experience important to alumni perceptions of the College, to the development of future alumni leaders for the University, and to future development efforts for the College, but it is also critical to our ability, immediate and long range, to sustain and increase the core tuition revenues that are derived from undergraduate students and that lie at the core of the financial health of the college. Without vibrant undergraduate education, we cannot sustain many nationally prominent graduate and or research programs."

Rochester's traditionally small enrollment actually had climbed to the extent that its undergraduate population in 1995 was larger than that at Princeton, Chicago, or Columbia Universities, the administrators wrote. Enrollment growth in the previous 20 years—from 3,703 to 4,433 undergraduates and from 772 to 1,126 graduate students—had come as a reaction to pressing fiscal needs and to departmental decisions rather than conscious institutional policy, the administrators said.

Jackson, Phelps, and Aslin concluded that the student body size needed to be addressed in a systematic way. The College also would have to examine the number of programs it offered and associated faculty size, with an eye toward investing in programs that would provide the greatest benefit in the future. They called for improving the undergraduate experience to become more residential—with enrollment growth, a fourth of undergraduates were then living off campus—and cultivating a more intellectual and cohesive environment. Faculty opinion would help shape the planning. "Rochester," the administrators said, "in common with most universities at this time, generally added without subtracting, with the result that the University carries too many programs and specialties in the sense of being able to nurture and sustain them successfully into and through the 21st century. . . . Once conceived of as virtually an Ivy League institution, Rochester now does not seem entirely sure with whom it competes or why, an issue of critical importance both when examining what our image is among prospective undergraduates and in looking at who comes here."

Faculty members throughout the College began pulling together data to determine each department's priorities, and the president began a review of costs in administrative functions. While the Board of Trustees had seemed to anticipate across-the-board spending cuts, Jackson articulated to the governing body an important difference he saw between corporate operations and higher education management.

"The only currency of academic institutions is quality, and if you did this, you degraded quality and so you didn't get the equilibrium," Jackson recalled in 2012. "[If] you cut faculty, you'd hurt student-

faculty ratios, good faculty would leave, and you'd look and say, 'OK, this year I got the budget in balance but the quality has declined.' The next year is going to put you right back into it. So I became real worried that you weren't going to cut your way into anything that was particularly sustainable. And I said, 'You know, you guys in business, you can sometimes innovate your way out of this stuff. You can come up and invent a radically different car or a radically different product and gain market share because you're different. But my experience in higher education is: being different doesn't work. There's a uni-dimensional model of what it is to be a successful university, and that's all based on quality.'"

There were cuts, but a larger foundation of the plan grew from a theory that if the University admitted fewer undergraduate students, a policy of greater selectivity would result in not only stronger students but also higher net tuition.

Jackson, Phelps, and Aslin consulted weekly for more than a year, looking closely at potential savings through reduction of doctoral programs while preserving or enhancing undergraduate education. They talked with 75 faculty members individually and reviewed information across three broad spectrums in every discipline: faculty and graduate-

Joanna Scott

The MacArthur Foundation wrote about Joanna Scott: "In highly textured and analytical prose, Scott's insights touch on the origins of modern sensibility."

Scott, the Roswell Smith Burrows Professor of English, is a MacArthur Fellow and a Guggenheim Fellow. She received the Lannan Literary Award in 1999. Scott joined the University faculty full time in 1988 teaching courses in creative writing, contemporary literature, and the works of Charles Dickens. Her novel *The Manikin* was a finalist for the Pulitzer Prize in 1997. A member of the American Academy of Arts and Sciences and PEN, Scott's honors also have included the Ambassador Book Award from the English-Speaking Union of the United States, the Rosenthal Award, and an honorary doctorate from Trinity College.

NEW YORK STATE

Rochester University Plans More Spending Per Student

By WILLIAM H. HONAN

At a time when shrinking budgets are forcing most colleges and universities to cut their costs per student, the University of Rochester announced yesterday a plan to raise its spending on each undergraduate.

It is the second time in little more than a year that the small research university has taken a bold step to compete better with lower-cost public institutions for the best students. Last year, the university introduced a $5,000 tuition discount for in-state students. This time, it is seeking to create a more intimate environment by increasing the professor-to-student ratio. The plan is similar to — but more far-reaching than — one undertaken three years ago by Tulane University in New Orleans.

At Rochester, the sweeping changes are expected to reduce the size of the undergraduate student body over the next four years by 20 percent, from 4,500 to 3,600, and the number of graduate students in the liberal arts college and the engineering program by 25 percent, from 1,100, to 850.

To partially offset the loss of income from 900 fewer undergraduates, the university plans to reduce its faculty from 343, to about 306, and four doctoral programs — comparative literature, linguistics, mathematics and chemical engineering — are to be discontinued. Four other doctoral programs are to be refocused and reduced.

The faculty reductions will be achieved, university officials said, through attrition and early retirement programs.

"We are unambiguously going to spend more per undergraduate," said Thomas H. Jackson, president of the university. "The trustees have authorized us to take $10 million to $15 million more from endowment earnings over the five-year period for the program than we normally would have." The university's endowment is now $707 million.

In addition to offering smaller classes, the university plans to renovate classrooms, improve the campus computer center and require faculty members to work more closely with undergraduates.

Richard N. Aslin, dean of the university's college, said the revamping would ultimately improve the student-to-faculty ratio to about 11 students to each faculty member — on a par with Ivy League institutions.

Founded in 1850 as a Baptist-sponsored institution, the University of Rochester, now nondenominational, is one of the smaller research universities in the country — comparable in size and reputation to Rice University in Houston and Tulane.

The restructuring will coincide with the long-planned introduction of a new curriculum intended to give undergraduates a deeper exposure to the liberal arts, and the opportunity to pursue their interests in much the same way as the research professors on the faculty.

"It's an important development," said Ernest L. Boyer, a former chancellor of the State University of New York and now president of the Carnegie Foundation for the Advancement of Teaching.

"Since the end of World War II, we have built many great research universities as well as colleges with an exceptional climate for undergraduate study, but there are also those in a gray, middle ground that have not achieved world-class research status nor a reputation for the best teaching," Dr. Boyer said. "For this latter group to make themselves distinctive, it calls for this sort of boldness."

One college president who spoke on condition of anonymity said the plan appeared to be aimed at raising the caliber of the student body and simultaneously weeding deadwood from the faculty.

Sanford Segal, a professor of mathematics and chairman of the faculty senate, said that while he supported a number of the initiatives, he thought the discontinuation of the doctorate program in math was "ill considered."

"As a result, we will attract fewer science-oriented students," he said.

University officials insisted that the plan was not undertaken in an atmosphere of financial crisis but was the result of a yearlong study. And that the discount offer had been a good start.

"With undergraduate applications up 18 percent, we're now in a position of strength," Mr. Jackson, referring to the university increased ability to be more selective.

It now costs a Rochester student $25,460 a year for tuition, fees, room and board. At the best New York State universities, the comparable cost for in-state students is approximately $9,000.

In 1995 the *New York Times* highlighted the announcement of Rochester's Renaissance Plan.

student quality; the importance of a subject to undergraduate education; and a discipline's potential for distinctiveness to Rochester. They looked at faculty honors, grant funding, publications, placement of students, external rankings, and the role of graduate students in undergraduate instruction and faculty research.

In the meantime, William Scott Green, dean of the College and the Bernstein Professor in Judaic Studies, led a faculty redesign of the undergraduate curriculum, giving students greater freedom in course selection and the ability to choose focused clusters in the humanities, social sciences, and life sciences—a design still distinctive more than 20 years later. Three central features of learning were at the core of the Rochester Curriculum: curiosity, competence, and community. Sets of intellectually connected courses outside of a student's major, rather than a standard curriculum in which students were required to take various courses, were offered to provide an opportunity to attain depth and breadth geared toward nurturing a lifetime habit of learning.

The Renaissance Plan, announced in November 1995, emerged as the most significant strategy in Rochester's core programs in arts and sciences and engineering in 30 years. The plan, subjected to some revision after a passionate campaign by one department, suspended four doctoral programs, added some funding to others, and, most dramatically, lowered undergraduate admissions to 900 a year. The plan would reduce College undergraduate enrollment by 25 percent in the next five years.

"We are refocusing the University from a position of strength and will make our excellent undergraduate and graduate programs significantly stronger by carefully redirecting our resources and energy," Jackson said as the plan was made public in November 1995.

Four doctoral programs were targeted for suspension in the fall of 1996: chemical engineering, comparative literature, linguistics, and mathematics. Graduate stipend spending was reduced in the history department. No tenured or tenure-track faculty members were let go, and all commitments to current graduate students were honored. A memo to the faculty by Aslin shed light on decision making. Chemistry, for instance, earned continued support because grant income for the department was high and it served a large number of undergraduate nonmajors. Further, the National Research Council ranked it among the best 20 percent in the country. In *U.S. News,* only 16 of the 28 higher-ranked universities had chemistry departments with higher stature. "Despite the relatively high cost of a chemistry department," Aslin said, "this is an investment that is worth maintaining, particularly given the strong market for PhDs in chemistry."

Reaction varied. National publications noted Rochester was among a number of colleges and universities restructuring, others with more drastic measures. "Among institutions with the highest national prominence, Rochester has probably put the most pieces on the table with its re-engineering," said David L. Warren, president of the National Association of Independent Colleges and Universities, in the *Chronicle of Higher Education*. A *New York Times* piece highlighted that Rochester's plan raised spending per undergraduate "at a time when shrinking budgets are forcing most colleges and universities to cut their costs per student."

Students expressed some misgivings. "Some think that the campus, located on the fringe of the city—between the Genesee River and a large cemetery—will feel too small," the *Chronicle* reported. "Some are worried that the pursuit of well-heeled students will hurt some groups of applicants." The *Campus Times* poked fun in its April Fool's edition, calling it the "Rochester Late-Leap Forward Reformation Plan."

The *New York Times*, February 4, 1996

CAMPUS TIMES

Serving the University of Rochester community since 1873

Vol. 45, No. 6   ©1999 CAMPUS TIMES   —Rochester, NY—   Thursday, February 25, 1999

Inside:
- Kurt Vonnegut, Page 11

ROCHESTERTODAY.COM weather: *Today:* Gray skies with light snow expected. High 33, low 20. *Friday:* Cloudy in the morning. High 37, low 20. *Saturday:* Clouds in the afternoon. High 43, low 26.

MSAB protest ends in compromise

KELLY EGAN/*SENIOR STAFF PHOTOGRAPHER*
Freshman Ricalder Valentine joins 200 other students lining hallways of Wallis Hall protesting over several minority issues. The students remained in the building for over four hours, until MSAB leaders and the administration reached a compromise.

BY MICHAEL S. MILLER
SENIOR STAFF WRITER

On Monday, approximately 200 UR students staged a sit-in on the second floor of the Wallis Hall administration building to protest the treatment of minority issues at UR. The protest, organized by the Minority Student Advisory Board, lasted over five hours and ended in UR President Thomas H. Jackson agreeing to most of MSAB's demands.

MSAB members and supporters organized in the Interfaith Chapel and, after a short prayer, processed single file into Wallis Hall promptly at 11 a.m. They proceeded up the stairs to the second floor where they sat down, lining the hallways between the Office of the President and the Office of the Provost.

Some protesters carried signs. "Put it in writing," one said. "Don't give us the runaround we want answers now," another read.

The students presented the administration with a four-page document, called the "MSAB Agreement," and refused to leave until administrators signed the document.

Although officers from UR Security and the Rochester Police Department met the protesters at the entrance to Wallis Hall, they did nothing to stop the procession. RPD left shortly after the protesters arrived. Security, however, did confine the protestors to the second floor and outside of the building.

Security contacted MSAB negotiator and Speaker of the Students' Association Senate Sean Vereen, a senior, early that morning. "We had a sense for what they were about," Security Director Walter Mauldin said. "That was reassuring to us."

"The rule of protest is not to disrupt or interfere with the business of the university," Vice President and University Dean of Students Paul Burgett said. "I don't think we should hide these things. I don't think we should be afraid of them. It's the students saying 'Let's do better.' It's the university's motto at work. That's a good thing."

At one point, protesters who were sitting in the Admissions Office were asked to leave.

"Security told us that not only were we distract-

SEE PROTEST, PAGE 3

Sports complex changes begin

BY BREE BROWN-ROSA
STAFF WRITER

On March 5, the Friday before Spring Break, the Alumni Gym Field House will lock its doors at 7 p.m. The gym will not fully reopen until March 2000. This is the first phase of the River Campus Sports Complex renovation schedule.

The renovation will begin on Monday, March 1, with the closing of the Alumni Gym locker rooms. On March 5, several parts of the complex will be moving. The Fitness Center, varsity weight

ment, said. "While the work is being done we don't want to disturb the students," he added.

"It looks like a party is happening on Court C, everything is moving there. It will be an inconvenience for the students who will be here over break but I'm sure it will be worth the long-term benefits," junior Meredith Pelton said.

'It looks like a party is happening on Court

SIT-IN

Roughly 200 students concerned about diversity issues on campus staged a peaceful sit-in outside President Jackson's office in Wallis Hall in February 1999. The demonstration ended when students and administrators agreed to efforts on several issues, including recruitment of minority students and faculty and enhancement of academic and cultural life for minorities.

An incident that spring contributed further to tension. Four African-American students were arrested outside Rush Rhees Library after University security guards approached the students, who were socializing in the bus stop lobby of the library, and requested University identification. The episode escalated to the point that city police were summoned.

That August the administration announced renewed efforts to understand the perspectives of diverse cultures and backgrounds. Administrators including Paul Burgett, vice president and University dean of students, and Richard Miller Jr., senior vice president and operating officer, would examine ways to encourage a more inclusive community. A committee of students, faculty, and staff also would work on recommendations.

In November, Jackson and Provost Phelps announced a number of initiatives. The efforts included a mission statement focused on diversity; developing a diversity website; a review of diversity programming in residence life; formation of a College Diversity Roundtable Committee; having each

dean in the University develop school and department-specific plans for recruiting faculty members from under-represented groups, expanding minority staffing, and expanding minority graduate student presence.

"We intend these responses . . . to signal the beginning, rather than the end of our ongoing efforts to increase diversity and inclusiveness at the University of Rochester," Jackson and Phelps said. "We pledge our energy, attention, and leadership to bring these goals to fulfillment, not ending with our responses to these specific recommendations, but rather with the hope and promise that our actions in this regard will indeed help to fulfill the University's promise—*Meliora!*"

Photographs of children who were treated at the Children's Hospital at Strong, renamed the Golisano Children's Hospital in 2002

Intense debate developed on one piece of the plan and closed with reinstatement of a PhD for mathematics—a reversal that Jackson described as a very good surprise. Rochester professors and associations of that discipline across the country raised grave concerns about elimination of advanced studies in a subject central to science. "If Rochester could take such a step in tough financial times, they say, so could other leading universities," reported the *New York Times* in February 1996. "They are also concerned that it is a recipe for disaster at Rochester, a university respected for its strength in science and technology."

The math department had been considered heavily theoretical, Jackson remembered. Aslin's 1995 memo showed admissions to its advanced programs had declined, and it ranked 58th among 139 departments with the National Research Council. Among 28 universities ranked higher by *U.S. News,* almost all had higher-rated math graduate programs. "They had a reputation as being sort of uncaring on the teaching front," Jackson recalled. "They had a couple of really top-notch people but it wasn't a department that was rich in reputation."

Jay H. Stein, MD

Douglas Ravenel, a young theorist in algebraic topology and the Daniel Burton Fayerweather Professor of Mathematics, had encouraged a national letter-writing campaign and pursued alternatives with Jackson, Phelps, and Aslin. Physics chair Paul Slattery offered one of his department's graduate slots to math—a gesture administrators saw as significant. With math department leadership a factor in its troubles, Jackson remembered telling Ravenel: "If you want to save this department, you're going to have to become the department chair. And if you become department chair, and if you commit to revitalizing the undergraduate education component, we'll consider, with Paul Slattery's help, reinstating a small PhD program for you.

"Well, that was kind of a breakthrough," Jackson said. "And Doug went into that position, was a brilliant chair, delivered everything he said he was going to deliver. We got a much better math department capably led by the best person in the department. I never would have

Meliora Weekend

The tradition that became Meliora Weekend began in 2000 with the commemoration of the University's 150th anniversary. The Sesquicentennial celebration included events throughout the year, culminating in four days of festivities in October that combined reunions, homecoming, panel discussions, entertainment, and fireworks.

The University also released its pictorial history, *Beside the Genesee,* that year. Sesquicentennial chair Joseph P. Mack '55 noted in its foreword that the anniversary offered an opportunity to celebrate "a record of extraordinary accomplishments, including . . . one

hundred years of coeducation and 75 years of distinguished teaching, research, and health care at the Medical Center. In great variety, programs throughout the institution serve to reinforce our reputation as one of the nation's leading research universities."

An estimated 8,000 alumni, students, faculty, and staff participated in events that October weekend. Prominent speakers included political satirist Mark Russell, actor Robert Duvall, NASA chief Dan Goldin, and Pulitzer Prize–winning historian Doris Kearns Goodwin.

Meliora Weekend, modeled after the successful 150th party, kicked off

in 2001. Only weeks after the September 11 terrorist attacks, the event, coincidentally themed "Freedom," included speakers Norman Mineta, U.S. secretary of transportation, and Jeane Kirkpatrick, former U.S. ambassador to the United Nations.

Keynote speakers later included former President Bill Clinton and former U.S. secretaries of state Hillary Rodham Clinton and retired Gen. Colin Powell. During Meliora Weekend 2011, the University kicked off its largest comprehensive campaign to date, the $1.2 billion *The Meliora Challenge: The Campaign for the University of Rochester.*

imagined that two or three years later I would view the math department as one of the great successes of the Renaissance Plan. It provoked them into changing, or it provoked the really good people in the department to step up."

As the Renaissance Plan took shape, a second important area of challenge was at the Medical Center. Jackson held off appointing a vice president for health affairs to replace Robert Joynt, MD, whose retirement coincided with the end of President O'Brien's tenure. Jackson wanted to understand more about the health care enterprise, including dynamics between leadership of Strong Memorial Hospital and the medical school. "I didn't quite have a finger on it," he recalled, "but there was something . . . the Medical Center didn't seem to me to be performing particularly well, seemed to me a little complacent, and led to, I think, one of [Provost Phelps] and my first significant decisions: that we needed a change agent over there; we needed somebody who was going to come in and shake things up a little bit."

Jackson hired Jay Stein, MD, in the summer of 1995 from the University of Oklahoma Health Sciences Center, where Stein reportedly was credited with "more changes in two years than many others in 30."[1] His successor at Rochester, McCollister Evarts, MD, described Stein's leadership more colorfully in a Q&A with the *Rochester Business Journal:* "He took my university, my medical school, and shook it by the hair of its head and really brought it, with some kicking and screaming, into the 21st century." Stein, a respected nephrologist, previously served 15 years as chair of the Department of Medicine at the Univer-

1   Carlos Zapata, "Presidential Candidate Jay Stein Visits Campus," Newspeak of Worcester Polytechnic Institute, March 29, 1995, http://www.wpi.edu/News/TechNews/950404/STEIN.html.

Finishing touches were put on the James S. Gleason Hall in September 2001. This addition to Schlegel Hall increased the Simon Business School's usable space by nearly 64 percent.

CHAPTER 8

sity of Texas Health Science Center in San Antonio. The Chicago native had earned his bachelor's and medical degrees from the University of Tennessee.

A month before Stein's August arrival as vice president and vice provost for health affairs, Stein told Medical Center executives he wanted a strategic plan in place by year-end. The incoming executive identified key issues, including information systems, interdisciplinary programs, areas of focus for research, the economic relationship between academic and clinical disciplines, Medical Center governance, and both undergraduate and graduate medical education.

This was a period of upheaval in the nation's health care system. Stein distributed to dozens of Medical Center representatives for a fall 1995 strategic planning conference articles from *Academic Medicine* magazine and the *Journal of the American Medical Association* sketching concerns. National reforms could include universal access to health care, federal mandates in benefit packages, a stronger orientation toward health promotion and disease prevention. "Physician groups, hospitals, and insurance companies are in a buying and selling frenzy

The Arthur Kornberg Medical Research Building opened in June 1999. When Medical Center CEO Jay Stein, MD, and other executives visited Nobel laureate Arthur Kornberg '41M to tell him they would like to name the 240,000-square-foot facility for him, Kornberg gave them his 1959 Nobel medal, which is displayed in the foyer.

Students gathered in Wilson Commons to watch as events in New York City unfolded live on television.

Candlelight vigil on Eastman Quad, September 15, 2001

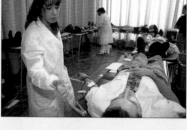

Members of the University community gave blood in support of the relief efforts.

Jeremy Glick

Jean Hoadley Peterson

Jeffrey Smith

Zhe "Zack" Zeng

Brendan Dolan

Aram Iskendariam

September 11

The terrorist attacks on the World Trade Center and Pentagon stunned the nation, and the University of Rochester mourned six alumni who died in the attacks and in the downed plane headed for Washington, D.C., on September 11, 2001.

Jeremy Glick '93 was believed to have been one of the passengers on United Flight 93 who fought to prevent terrorists from turning the flight toward Washington. Glick, a sales executive for an e-commerce consulting company who had been a national collegiate judo champion when he was a student at Rochester, spoke with his wife, Lyzbeth, for several minutes during the ordeal. "We both decided that this is what he

had to do," Lyzbeth said. "He said 'I love you, stay on the phone. I'll be right back.'" Moments later, the plane crashed, killing all 45 on board, including Rochester alumna Jean Hoadley Peterson '69N and her husband, Donald Peterson.

President Jackson wrote to survivors. He told Lyzbeth Glick, "the University is honored and proud to count Jeremy as one of its own. His memory is alive here and, because of this tragedy, is certain to be permanently fixed in the pantheon of Rochester heroes who have graced our history over the past 150 years." Alpha Delta Phi Fraternity at Rochester created a memorial scholarship to honor Glick, who had served as the chapter's president.

Four alumni died in the attack on the World Trade Center. Jeffrey Smith '87, '88S (MBA) worked on the 104th floor of the South Tower for Sandler O'Neill and Partners. Zhe "Zack" Zeng '95, '98S (MBA), trained as an emergency medical technician, went there to help victims. Brendon Dolan '86 was vice president in charge of the energy group at Carr Futures, and Aram Iskendarian '82 was vice president of global risk management at Cantor Fitzgerald.

A group of benches at Meliora Hall, a gift of the Class of 2002, commemorates the six students, and the fourth-floor patio at Gleason Hall is dedicated to the memory of Smith and Zeng.

to develop integrated service delivery networks at the local level," *Academic Medicine* reported. *JAMA* noted that a system previously based on solo practitioners and hospitals was now being led by health maintenance organizations, managed care, group practices, and integrated health networks.

Stein soon focused on a precipitous slide in Rochester's research funding from the National Institutes of Health, the leading measure of prestige in academic medical centers. From 1988 to 1996, URMC had fallen from the 15th-highest-funded institution to 27th, and it fell further. Stein also saw a need for improvement in the University hospital's competition for regional health care dollars. He clarified administrative roles to ensure a united enterprise of clinical, research, and educational divisions. He became a very visible spokesman for the University's potential as a new leader of the region's economy; phrases like "technology transfer" became part of the local economic lexicon. In 2000, a *Rochester Business Journal* survey identified Stein as the second most influential local businessperson of the previous 15 years, behind Paychex founder Tom Golisano and tied with Wegmans grocery superstore leaders Robert and Danny Wegman. "Stein's prominence reflects the area's growing hope that biotechnology in this century will become

Students staging a protest against the war in Iraq, 2003

With President Jackson (third from left, standing), provost Charles Phelps (second from right), and dean of graduate studies Bruce Jacobs (far right) are the 2003 recipients of the Edward Peck Curtis Award for Excellence in Teaching by a Graduate Student: (from left) Jeremy Grimshaw '02E (MA), '05E (PhD); Dana Symons '00 (MA), '04 (PhD); Pamela Bedore '02 (MA), '05 (PhD); Betsy Huang '99 (MA), '04 (PhD); and Kelly Dyer '05 (PhD).

what manufacturing was for the local economy through much of the last century," the newspaper noted.

By early 1997, URMC had the first phase of a $500 million strategic plan in place to recruit 50 top scientists, build new scientific facilities, and solidify its position as the region's most recognizable medical care provider. The centerpiece of the plan was the Aab Institute of Biomedical Sciences, housed in a new, $73 million research building named for Nobel Prize winner Arthur Kornberg, a 1941 graduate of the medical school. An additional $40 million was planned for renovating existing space and reallocating resources to focus on three broad areas: aging and development, vaccine biology and immunology, and cancer. Oral hygiene and cardiovascular research later became additional areas of focus. The medical school introduced its "Double Helix" curriculum, weaving basic science and clinical education throughout the four-year program. Organizational changes resulted in a new board of trustees for the Medical Center and formation of Strong Health, a sort of parent company for all clinical components of the enterprise.

Key recruits included Tim R. Mosmann, credited with crucial discoveries in immune system response; Hartmut K. Land, among the most cited investigators in molecular biology and genetics; and cardiologist Bradford C. Berk, who later became chief executive of the Medical Center. Investigators brought staff members with them; in total nearly 100 were hired in research.

The Medical Center also acquired Highland Hospital as an affiliate, started a new health maintenance organization, integrated the Eastman Dental Center—formerly a standalone entity though on the Medical Center campus—began construction on a second new research building, and embarked on a $10 million expansion of the pediatric intensive care unit of the children's hospital that was renamed in honor of benefactor Golisano. Stein in 2002 chose David Guzick, the Dr. Henry A. Thiede Chair in Obstetrics and Gynecology, as dean of the medical school. Guzick would be the leader in 2006 in Rochester winning its largest-ever National Institutes of Health award, $40 million toward clinical and translational science endeavors. Rochester was among the first 12 institutions selected in the new NIH program.

University-commissioned studies by the Center for Governmental Research underlined potential for economic growth with a particular focus on medical discoveries. "No longer are manufacturers like Kodak or Xerox the economy's 'center of gravity,'" said a 2002 CGR report. "For their contributions both to economic growth and quality of life,

AIDS Research

Michael C. Keefer, professor of medicine, has worked for more than 20 years to identify one of the most sought-after weapons in the fight against AIDS—an HIV vaccine. He has directed the University's HIV Vaccine Trials Unit since 1991 and is codirector of the Center for AIDS Research, part of a National Institutes of Health program. "To have a Center for AIDS Research here is quite exceptional and confirms the University's place in the big leagues of AIDS research," said Keefer. "This gives us the opportunity to reach out more broadly across the institution than ever before in search of new ideas, talent, and inspiration."

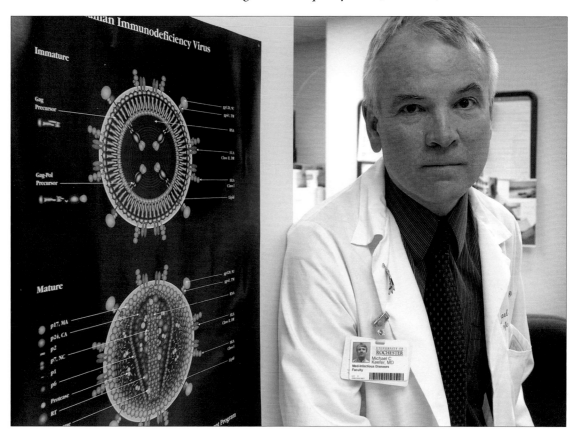

Tom Golisano

Tom Golisano, the founder of one of Rochester's most successful businesses of the latter 20th century, became one of the Medical Center's leading benefactors. His philanthropy at the University, throughout western New York, and in Florida would prompt comparisons with George Eastman.

Golisano founded Paychex in 1971. The company specializes in payroll and human resources services to small and midsized companies and by 2010 had grown to serve more than 500,000 businesses across the country. Golisano also founded the B. Thomas Golisano Foundation, among the country's largest private foundations focused on supporting programs for people with disabilities.

In 2002, Strong Memorial Hospital's children's hospital was named for Golisano in honor of his $14 million gift at that time. The gift helped the Medical Center recruit faculty and expand programs in cardiac care, general surgery, and neuromedicine.

In 2011, Golisano committed $20 million toward a new, $134 million Golisano Children's Hospital. Plans included a 245,000 square-foot hospital with a 60-bed neonatal intensive care unit, pediatric imaging, private pediatric rooms, and a family-oriented lobby.

Golisano's foundation had given $2 million to the Medical Center by 2013.

At the time of the 2011 gift, University President Joel Seligman called Golisano, who had donated roughly $145 million to Rochester-area institutions and charities, as "this generation's George Eastman."

Rochester's colleges and universities are replacing manufacturing at the center of the regional economy."

Stein also dealt with repercussions of the Manhattan Project of World War II. Shortly before his arrival, news reports detailed secret injections of plutonium in patients at Strong Memorial Hospital and at hospitals in Chicago; San Francisco; and Oak Ridge, Tenn., where scientists were evaluating the health effects of atomic-bomb-making materials. Stein explained to reporters that the experiments were done in a different era, when the nation was rapidly trying to understand the effects of radiation and that no one now could condone the work or even consider it.

The University pursued a high-profile and costly effort to gain royalties based on Medical Center researchers' patented discovery of the ability to suppress an enzyme that enabled pain relief medicine that did not cause stomach problems associated with many pain relievers. When the pharmaceutical company G. D. Searle (now Pfizer) produced the immensely popular Celebrex, which inhibited the single Cox-1 enzyme, the University sued for patent infringement, envisioning potentially billions in royalties. Stein was quoted in the *New York Times:* "It could obviously make it easier to do what we're planning and help us compete better with the Harvards, Stanfords, and so-ons." Jackson, University lawyers, and outside counsel worked on the case for four years, and the University spent millions on the case. The U.S. Court of Appeals for the Federal Circuit in Washington, however, in an opinion that sharply split the court, ruled the patent invalid in that while it identified the mechanism for suppressing the enzyme, it did not identify a compound for doing so.

Jackson recalled a productive relationship with Stein. The administration had explored a new organizational structure that would have created a parent company of the University, effectively separating other divisions from the Medical Center and potential liability associated with hospital finances. The change would have given the Medical Center substantial autonomy. After considerable examination of the idea, Jackson concluded, however, that the process needed to be slowed significantly. Stein was disappointed deeply.

The president accepted Stein's resignation May 16, 2003, and released a statement praising Stein's leadership and contributions while alluding to concerns about coordination between the Medical Center and University. Jackson wrote to a troubled alumnus that rather than focus on the circumstances of Stein's resignation he wanted to point to Stein's enormous contributions to the Medical Center, the University, and the community: "Those are the events that he justly should be remembered for." Stein soon became senior vice president and dean of clinical affairs at the Baylor College of Medicine in Houston.

Phelps stepped in briefly as an interim CEO; then McCollister Evarts, MD, assumed the role of senior vice president for health affairs. Evarts, a Rochester graduate and orthopedic surgeon, recently had retired as chief executive for health affairs at Pennsylvania State University at Hershey and returned to Rochester. Phelps had tapped Evarts to help him as interim CEO and quickly realized Evarts should assume the position. Evarts was credited with reinforcing a vision of the Medical Center as part of a cohesive University.

Approaching his 11th year at Rochester, Jackson announced in March 2004 that he would leave the presidency at the end of the next academic year. "Leadership change and evolution is good for an institution, and . . . a successful tenure as an academic leader is likely to be measured in an eight- to twelve-year period," Jackson said. "As measured by projects, or accomplishments, I believe that I have completed virtually all of the major goals that I set for myself, and for the institution, upon my arrival."

He could report to the Board that SAT scores of enrolled students averaged 1300, up from 1125 in 1994; that the freshman discount rate had declined from 55 percent to 45 percent; and that net tuition per student had risen from $10,000 to $16,000. Medical Center funding from the National Institutes of Health had reached $140 million annually, and Strong Memorial's market share had risen by 10 percentage points, to 50 percent.

After a yearlong sabbatical, Jackson returned to become the Trustees' Distinguished University Professor with courses in the Simon

Mary Kay Perillo, pediatrics nurse, circa late 1980s

Cathy Troisi Stoll and her daughter Jessica Troisi Stoll '06 on Freshman Move-in Day in 2002. The College returned to a weeklong orientation program for all first-year students (a tradition dating back to 1918) in 2000 after experimenting with other formats. The longer program helps freshmen to establish a community, take care of academic business, and have some fun before classes begin.

President Jackson donned a tie-dye shirt and helped volunteers during the annual Wilson Day activities in 1999.

WILSON DAY

A day designated in 1972 in memory of Joseph C. Wilson '31, founder of Xerox and chairman of the University Board of Trustees from 1959 to 1967, has evolved into a significant annual day of service.

A year after Wilson died suddenly, president and chancellor Allen Wallis announced an annual event to honor Wilson's involvement in the University. "Wilson Day will not be a day of mourning his death," Wallis said, "but a day of celebrating his life, a day full of the kinds of things that Mr. Wilson prized about the University: music, art, poetry, science, scholarship, education, research."

Until 1987, Wilson Day celebrated intellectual engagement by featuring talks, concerts, or symposia by No-bel- and Pulitzer-winning scientists, musicians, and writers. Everyone at the University and from the Rochester community was welcome.

Prompted by a student, Theresa Guenther '90, the format evolved to focus on Wilson's generosity, kindness, and service to the community. Since 1989, more than 21,000 students, faculty, and staff have contributed more than 90,000 hours to help social agencies, hospitals, schools, and parks.

School of Business and in the College's political science department. "Higher education institutions, I think, are America's great resource," Jackson reflected in 2012. "I'm a passionate believer in higher educational institutions and just making small differences. Presidents often get credit for things that they didn't do or get blamed for things that they couldn't have avoided, but at the margin it's, 'Do you think you made a difference? Is it a better place than when you came?' And, my sense now that I'm teaching on the faculty side and watching the wonderful students we get here . . . I think we have made a difference, and that's what really gives me great satisfaction."

Board Chairs

John Nicholas Wilder, 1850–1858
William Kelly, 1860–1872
John Bond Trevor, 1872–1885
Edward Bright, 1886–1893
Edward Mott Moore, 1893–1902
Rufus Adams Sibley, 1902–1903
Lewis Pratt Ross, 1903–1915
John Pixley Munn, 1916–1931
Joseph T. Alling, 1931–1937
Edward G. Miner, 1937–1945
M. Herbert Eisenhart, 1945–1952
Raymond Nathaniel Ball, 1952–1959
Joseph Chamberlain Wilson, 1959–1967
Mercer Brugler, 1967–1970
Donald A. Gaudion, 1970–1978
David T. Kearns, 1978–1985
Edwin I. Colodny, 1985–1988
Virginia A. Dwyer, 1988–1991
Robert B. Goergen, 1991–2003
G. Robert Witmer Jr., 2003–2008

Through many years and myriad changes on the River Campus, the Eastman Quadrangle, anchored by the iconic Rush Rhees Library, remains—as Rhees said—at the heart of the development in which George Eastman took delight.

Paul Burgett '68E, '72E (Mas), '76E (PhD), right,
with John Braund '53, '61W (Mas), September 1967

Afterword

By Paul Burgett

O N MY ARRIVAL AT THE OLD PRINCE STREET CAMPUS AS AN EASTMAN SCHOOL OF MU-
sic freshman in the mid-sixties, I remember asking, "What's this University of Rochester I
see lurking in the form of the University seal that appeared in Eastman's printed literature,
in the ornamentation on Eastman edifices such as the dorms, the Eastman Theatre, the main
building of the school, and Cutler Union?" I didn't know Eastman was part of the University . . . or, for
that matter, particularly care; in fact, I daresay that most Eastman students back then didn't. I had some
vague awareness of an association, but we students referred to the River Campus as *The University* and to
our domain as *The Eastman School*—two distinct and separate institutions that may as well have been on
different planets. Of course, I now know differently thanks to a half-century's association with the University . . . as an undergraduate and graduate student at Eastman, as that school's dean of students, as vice
president and University dean of students, University general secretary to the Board of Trustees, senior
advisor to the president, as a faculty member in the music department in the School of Arts & Sciences,
and, of course, as a loyal alumnus.

Now, in the twilight of my professional career, I've become fascinated by the story of the University
that educated and trained me; sent me out into the world as a well-prepared and confident high school and
college music teacher, performer, and music administrator; and then welcomed me back 34 years ago and
turned me loose on its campuses and in its halls and classrooms to join with faculty, students, and staff in
the work of its auspicious and noble mission. I have become a serious and passionate student of our history
and believe that all of us who claim an association with the University, in any form or manner, will want to
learn more about the institution that affected our lives deeply.

Thus, the reader will understand my enthusiasm for Janice Bullard Pieterse's marvelously detailed narrative that advances our knowledge of the University's history and builds on the earlier efforts of her predecessors, including Professor Arthur May's 1977 seminal *History of the University of Rochester: 1850–1962,* Jan Waxman's 2000 pictorial history *Beside the Genesee,* and several other historical documents. I believe Janice's monograph will stand the test of time, and generations of faculty, alumni, students, staff, trustees, and the many other friends of the University will enjoy and be edified by its contents.

It was a pleasure to exchange insights and opinions with Janice during the book's preparation. She welcomed my comments, and it was fun to engage with her about many details, including University myths and legends. For instance, where are Thomas Swinburne's remains buried? Swinburne, Class of 1892, composed the lyrics to the University's alma mater, *The Genesee.* Legend had it that his ashes were buried in a bronze box under the Swinburne rock located on the banks of the Genesee River. When the rock was moved in 1968 to make way for construction of the Interfaith Chapel, no remains were found. It's a mystery.

Tradition dictates that only verses one and three of *The Genesee* are ever sung. Why? Well, only those two verses are inscribed on the bronze plaque of the Swinburne rock. A 1950s alumnus related another legend that involved famous Eastman Wind Ensemble founder and conductor Frederick Fennell. After football games in Fauver Stadium, Fennell also led the marching band in playing *The Genesee.* One bitterly cold November Saturday, so the story went, as the band prepared to play, Fennell directed that only verses one and three should be sung because it was just too cold. Take your pick of the story you prefer . . . or better yet, perhaps you know another.

On the origin of the University motto, *Meliora:* It has long been thought that the word, chosen by Professor Asahel Kendrick in 1850 and approved by the first faculty as our motto in 1851, is taken from the phrase *video meliora proboque . . .* in Book VII of the Roman poet Ovid's *Metamorphoses . . .* and so it might have been. However, an undergraduate student, Laura Zimmerman '10, who studied Latin at the University, pointed out to me that the phrase that translates, *I see and approve of the better,* while correct, fails to include the second half of Ovid's phrase *deteriora sequor,* which translates, *but I follow the worse.* Hardly inspiring, thought Laura. But inspiration aside, she and I agreed that Ovid's complete phrase probably reflects the human situation more accurately . . . and I proudly add that it was a bright Rochester student who was curious and industrious enough to consult the primary source, translate it, and bring it to my attention.

On the statue of Martin Brewer Anderson on the Wilson Quadrangle (which many older alumni will remember by its original name, the Residential Quad): The myth persists that it is positioned so that President Anderson can always see the Rush Rhees tower. A variation on that myth continues to circulate that concerns were raised when Wilson Commons was planned that the building would block President Anderson's view of the tower and should he not be able to see it, the tower would collapse and fall. This worry was remedied by creating walls of glass on either side of the Commons so as not to obscure our first president's view. Though the story is apocryphal, President Anderson likely would appreciate the sentiment.

Improvised washtub light fixtures in Kodak Hall at Eastman Theatre

Campus myths abound and persist. Despite what some say, I could find no evidence that George Eastman's will declared that no houses of worship be located on the River Campus. Then there's the persistent tale that the River Campus is rife with tunnel systems to which the University refuses to allow students access against winter's bitter bite. Again, only partially true . . . some tunnels are impassable to pedestrians, and others, for safety and security reasons, are off limits.

The reader of this book will be fascinated to learn that although women were officially admitted to the University in 1900 thanks to the dogged efforts of Susan B. Anthony and others, attempts to provide higher education for women were initiated much earlier. In 1852, University of Rochester leadership including trustees John Wilder and Azariah Boody, faculty members John Raymond and Chester Dewey, and a leading Rochester citizen and scholar, Lewis Henry Morgan, organized Barleywood Female University. The effort failed for lack of funds, but, as Janice reports, the initiative by University of Rochester leaders to arrange collegiate education for women has existed almost as long as the University itself.

Let's not leave out a couple of memorable legends involving the Eastman School of Music. The ceiling light fixtures on either side of the upper balcony of Eastman Theatre (now Kodak Hall) are original though were not part of the initial lighting plans. The intention was to install small crystal chandeliers, miniature versions of the grand central chandelier suspended in the center of the ceiling. The smaller ones didn't arrive in time, so an enterprising construction worker acquired two washtubs, painted them gold, decorated and wired them, affixed light bulbs, and hung them from the ceiling. Those original washtubs remain in place today. Should you be in the theater, have a look at the base of these fixtures, and you'll recognize the familiar concentric washtub circles.

And of course, there's the 1951 Valentine's Day legend in which mischievous Eastman students positioned themselves in the catwalk above the ceiling in the Eastman Theatre. During a Rochester Philharmonic Orchestra performance of Tchaikovsky's "1812 Overture," at the climactic moment of the piece, as the cannon fusillade exploded with its intended din, the miscreant students dumped a "snow storm" of pillow feathers through the spotlight openings that drifted slowly onto the audience below. As if to reprise this "heroic" exploit and perhaps create a tradition, 30 years later, during my years as Eastman's dean of students, University Security and I discovered an electric bubble machine abandoned on the stairs leading to the catwalk, presumably by students whose actions, almost certainly, were interrupted by the threat of detection. A concert was scheduled that evening in the theater. I could only imagine the chaos that bubble machine might have wrought. Just as Eastman's Dean Flora Burton never discovered the culprits in 1951, neither did I in 1981.

The University's proliferation of traditions, myths, legends, and lore, some true . . . others fanciful . . . and all persistent, could fill a book. But the fundamental facts of the University's birth, adolescence, and maturity and the individuals who were responsible for shaping its history remain the substantive story, and Janice Pieterse's book adds facts and updates the history that enhances the reader's understanding of that history.

We are a scrappy University. Imagine the *chutzpah* (couched in Baptist fervor to be sure) of our early pioneers, described in Janice's book: Wilder, Kendrick, Raymond, and Richardson throwing off what they saw as a limited future in Hamilton, N.Y., and emigrating to Rochester where they enlisted in their efforts Dewey, Quinby, Mixer, Lattimore, Morey, Gilmore, and Robinson and Martin Brewer Anderson, our first president, on whose shoulders bore the heavy challenges of leadership.

In contemplating the University's history, two defining principles seem to prevail; and while not unique to Rochester, these evolve in distinctive ways. The first is the vigorous pursuit and commitment to quality of the highest order, and the second is the identification and cultivation of inspired, effective, and generous leadership. These principles constitute the existential nucleus, the foundational values that lie at the heart of every substantive development over the past 164 years.

Pieterse reports on the administration of David Jayne Hill, our second president, whose relatively brief six-year tenure was the fulcrum between the astonishing 35-year tenures each of Presidents Anderson and Rush Rhees. The curriculum was expanded, competitive sports were welcomed (including football, though our first game, against Cornell, resulted in a humiliating 106-0 defeat; but redemption followed that season with the defeat of Syracuse 36-0); and, importantly, the movement to admit women gained serious momentum. After his wife gave birth to twins, a boy and a girl, Hill was alleged to observe, "If the Creator could risk placing sexes in such near relations [the womb] they might safely walk on the same campus and pursue the same curriculum together."

The 20th century issued in the era of Rush Rhees, our third president, whose tenure was a masterpiece of leadership, imagination, and accomplishment that resulted from inspired, effective, and generous leaders. The 1920s was a watershed decade that yielded astonishing growth and expansion of the University from a regional college of quality during its first half-century to a modern university that would take its place in the pantheon of America's great research universities.

George Eastman and President Rhees forged a productive relationship that cannot be overstated. In the course of slightly more than a decade, together they established the Eastman School of Music and recruited composer Howard Hanson, Prix de Rome and Pulitzer Prize winner, who during his 40-year tenure, built an American school of music that combined musical performance, scholarship, and education into an internationally renowned school of music with a coherent and comprehensive program and brilliant faculty that was connected to the University.

They established the School of Medicine and Dentistry and Strong Memorial Hospital and recruited the Nobel Prize winner and founding dean George Whipple, who during his 34-year decanal tenure, implemented the Flexner model of medical education that established Rochester in the forefront of 20th-century clinical, research, and educational health care and service.

They coordinated, together with George Todd, the extraordinarily complex acquisition of Oak Hill Country Club, now known as the River Campus, and in five years or so oversaw the master planning of the campus's buildings and grounds and the construction of the facilities and relocated the College for Men to the completed site in 1930.

In the midst of this decade of transformative activity of historic proportions, the University awarded its first PhD degrees; and one of the recipients, biochemist Vincent du Vigneaud, went on to win the Nobel Prize in Chemistry in 1955. The University's Institute of Optics was established in 1929. By the end of the 1920s, the University of Rochester was firmly established in the galaxy of American research universities as a fully enfranchised participant of the highest quality . . . a university of world-class intellectual, scientific, artistic, and cultural might.

Janice Pieterse's book has all this and more. With assistance and collaboration of the University archivist Melissa Mead, we had great fun sleuthing and sharing information. Pieterse brings her readers up to date, detailing the stewardships of the successors to the leadership of the University's first 85 years . . . including Presidents Valentine, de Kiewiet, Wallis, Sproull, O'Brien, and Jackson . . . and she augments their stories with sidebars about important events and people that help fill in the interstices of this epic saga.

As the University moves through the second half of its second century, important familiar and new challenges remain. The University's commitment to a more diverse community of faculty, students, and staff is stronger than ever, but much more work remains to be done. The shrinking globe is creating collaborative opportunities and competitive challenges that our forebears couldn't have imagined. The explosion in the creation of information and the fast-paced developments in technology have sped up production and dissemination of knowledge, acquisition of new intellectual and technical skills, and development of entrepreneurial activity that were unimaginable even a generation ago.

I sometimes muse about the conversations that Presidents Anderson, Hill, and Rhees; Director Hanson and Dean Whipple; George Eastman and Joseph C. Wilson; Susan B. Anthony and Annette Gardner Munro; Professors Kendrick, Dewey, and Lattimore; Perkins and Slater, Schilling and Marshak might now be having in the great beyond. I believe they would be pleased and satisfied that subsequent generations in the University have been faithful and effective stewards of the legacies they established, gratified that their successors have steered the University to greater heights of quality and accomplishments and confident of the University's ability to navigate future challenges and opportunities. The prospects are promising, I think; and Janice Pieterse's book provides persuasive evidence.

Kilbourn Hall, Eastman School of Music

Frederick Douglass's friends in Rochester commissioned a marble bust when Douglass moved to Washington, D.C., in 1872. Sculptor Johnson Mundy visited Douglass to mold his features. The bust, now in the Frederick Douglass Building, was first placed in Sibley Hall on the Prince Street Campus. When the bust was unveiled, the *Democrat and Chronicle* reported, "Rochester could do nothing more graceful than to perpetuate in marble the features of this citizen in her hall of learning."

Acknowledgments

IT HAS BEEN AN HONOR TO WORK ON THIS NARRATIVE. I THANK PRESIDENT JOEL SELIGMAN for the opportunity.

The project came to fruition with the extraordinary help, counsel, patience, and inspiration of Melissa Mead, Bill Murphy, Nancy Martin, Paul Burgett, and President Seligman. The staff of the University of Rochester Department of Rare Books, Special Collections and Preservation provided wonderful assistance.

Many others made important contributions by offering recommendations on manuscripts, performing research, copy editing, typing transcripts, or handling administrative matters, including Maureen Baisch, Michelene DeFranco, Stephen Dow, Joyce Farrell, Eileen Fay, Elizabeth Goodfellow, Frank Interlichia, Karl Kabelac, Sonia Kane, Robert Kraus, Jack Kreckel, Melissa Lang, Phyllis Mangefrida, Erin Moyer, Lamar Murphy, Jonathan Schwartz, Sue Smith, and Kristine Thompson. Michael Osadciw's design work was remarkable.

I am grateful also to presidents emeritus Robert L. Sproull, G. Dennis O'Brien, and Thomas H. Jackson and to Board of Trustees chairs Ed Hajim and Bob Goergen for their participation and candor.

I appreciate deeply the friendship and support during this work from several of the above as well as Alice Bower, Katharine Becker, Patsy McBride, JoAnne Pedro-Carroll, Lee Ann Daigle, David R. Fries, Svetlana Blitshteyn, Frank Bilovsky, Marcia Greenwood, and Kathryn George. Finally, a heartfelt thank you to Todd H. and Ella Bullard for everything they were, and to William and Ella Pieterse for everything they are.

Janice Bullard Pieterse
June 2014

In 1998, the Periodical Reading Room in Rush Rhees Library was restored
to its original splendor through a gift from Martin E. Messinger '49
and named in his honor.

Sources

I HAVE RELIED PRIMARILY ON MINUTES FROM UNIVERSITY BOARD OF TRUSTEES MEETINGS; AR-chival papers of the University's presidents; and interviews with former presidents, trustees, and executives.

I consulted and quoted other University resources, most notably the indexed, unabridged typescript of historian Arthur J. May's *A History of the University of Rochester: 1850–1962* (www.lib.rochester.edu/index.cfm?PAGE=2347). May was a professor of history at Rochester from 1925 to 1964 and University historian from 1964 to 1968. Other helpful books published by the University or by the University of Rochester Press were Jesse Leonard Rosenberger's *Rochester: The Making of a University* (1927); Jan LaMartina Waxman's *Beside the Genesee* (2000); Robert Kraus and Charles E. Phelps's *Transforming Ideas* (2000); Carlos Stroud's *A Jewel in the Crown* (2004); Vincent Lenti's two volumes on the history of the Eastman School of Music, *For the Enrichment of Community Life* (2004) and *Serving a Great and Noble Art* (2009); and the Medical Center histories *To Each His Farthest Star: University of Rochester Medical Center 1925–1975* (1975), edited by John Romano; *The University of Rochester Medical Center: Teaching, Discovering, Caring,* edited by Jules Cohen and Robert J. Joynt (2000); and *The Quarter Century: A Review of the First Twenty-Five Years, 1925–1950,* edited by George H. Whipple, Basil C. MacLean, Karl M. Wilson, John A. Benjamin Jr., Jacob D. Goldstein, Hilda DeBrine, Dorothy O. Widner, and Wallace O. Fenn (1950).

Student newspapers, yearbooks, and the alumni magazine, as well as the University's recording of Winston Churchill's address during 1941 commencement exercises, helped illuminate the story.

The following sources, several quoted, were indispensable in understanding developments at Rochester and the progress of American higher education.

Areen, Judith. *Higher Education and the Law: Cases and Materials.* New York: Thompson/Reuters Foundation Press, 2009.

Blake, Casey, and Christopher Phelps. "History as Social Criticism: Conversations with Christopher Lasch." *Journal of American History* 80, no. 4 (1994): 1310–1332.

Bonner, Thomas Neville. *Iconoclast: Abraham Flexner and a Life in Learning.* Baltimore, MD: Johns Hopkins University Press, 2002.

Brayer, Elizabeth. *George Eastman: A Biography.* Rochester, NY: University of Rochester Press, 2002.

Brubacher, John S., and Willis Rudy. *Higher Education in Transition.* New Brunswick, NJ: Transaction Publishers, 2008.

Cole, Jonathan R. *The Great American University: Its Rise to Preeminence, Its Indispensable National Role, Why It Must Be Protected.* New York: Public Affairs, 2009.

Corner, George W. *George Hoyt Whipple and His Friends: The Life-Story of a Nobel Prize Pathologist.* Philadelphia: J. B. Lippincott, 1963.

Ellis, Charles D. *Joe Wilson and the Creation of Xerox.* Hoboken, NJ: John Wiley & Sons, 2006.

Geiger, Roger L. *Research and Relevant Knowledge: American Research Universities since World War II.* New Brunswick, NJ: Transaction Publishers, 2009.

The George Eastman House. Frequently Asked Questions, George Eastman. Accessed January 13, 2014. http://www.eastmanhouse.org/museum/faq/eastman.php.

Glotzer, Richard. "C. W. de Kiewiet, Area Studies, and the American Post-war Research University." *American Educational History Journal* 32, no. 1 (2005): 34.

Goodstein, Judith R. "Lee A. DuBridge (Part II)." Oral History Project, California Institute of Technology Archives, Pasadena, CA, 2003.

Hanson, Howard. "Music Was a Spiritual Necessity." *University of Rochester Library Bulletin* 26 (1971).

Hayes, Catherine. "The History of the University of Rochester Libraries—120 Years." *University of Rochester Library Bulletin* 25, No. 3 (1970).

Holzer, Harold, ed. *Lincoln's White House Secretary: The Adventurous Life of William O. Stoddard.* Carbondale: Southern Illinois University Press, 2007.

Kean, Kristen Elizabeth. "First Flute: The Pioneering Career of Doriot Anthony Dwyer." PhD diss., Louisiana State University, 2007.

Kendrick, Asahel Clark, and Florence Kendrick Cooper. *Martin B. Anderson, LL.D.: A Biography.* Philadelphia: American Baptist Society, 1895.

Kerr, Clark. *The Uses of the University.* 5th ed. Cambridge, MA: Harvard University Press, 2001.

Lazerson, Marvin. "The Disappointments of Success: Higher Education after World War II." *Annals of the American Academy of Political and Social Science* 559 (September 1998): 64–76.

McKelvey, Blake. *Business as a Profession: The Career of Joseph C. Wilson, Founder of Xerox.* Rochester, NY: Office of the City Historian, 2003.

———. "A History of Social Welfare in Rochester." *Rochester History* 20, no.4 (1958).

———. *Rochester on the Genesee.* Syracuse, NY: Syracuse University Press, 1973.

———. "Rochester's Hesitant Promotion of the Image of Quality." *Rochester History* 34, no. 4 (1972): 1-24.

Memorial Art Gallery. "The Permanent Collection of the Memorial Art Gallery—a Community Treasure." Accessed March 10, 2014. http://mag.rochester.edu/collections/.

National Aeronautics and Space Administration. "Edward G. Gibson (Ph.D.): NASA Astronaut (Former)." Accessed January 14, 2014. http://www.jsc.nasa.gov/Bios/htmlbios/gibson-eg.html.http://www.jsc.nasa.gov/Bios/htmlbios/gibson-eg.html. Accessed January 14

Noyes, W. Albert. *A Victorian in the Twentieth Century.* Austin: University of Texas, 1976.

Parkman, Aubrey. *David Jayne Hill and the Problem of World Peace.* Lewisburg, PA: Bucknell University Press, 1975.

Raymond, John Howard, and Harriet Raymond Lloyd. *Life and Letters of John Howard Raymond.* New York: Fords, Howard & Hulbert, 1881.

Reagan, Ronald. "Remarks at a Reagan-Bush Rally in Rochester, New York, November 1, 1984." The Public Papers of President Ronald W. Reagan. Ronald Reagan Presidential Library. http://www.reagan.utexas.edu/archives/speeches/1984/110184e.htm.

Ricker, Joseph. *Personal Recollections: A Contribution to Baptist History and Biography.* Augusta, ME: Burleigh & Flynt, 1894.

Rosenberg-Naperstek, Ruth. "Frankfort: Birthplace of Rochester's Industry." *Rochester History* 50, no. 3 (1988): 14.

———. "Rochester's Pioneer Builders: Relinquishing the Reins of Power." *Rochester History* 47, nos. 3 and 4 (1985): 3-4.

Rosenberger, Jesse Leonard. *Rochester and Colgate: Historical Backgrounds of the Two Universities.* Chicago: University of Chicago Press, 1925.

Rudolph, Frederick. *The American College and University: A History.* Athens: University of Georgia Press, 1990.

Samet, Jonathan M. "A Conversation with D. A. Henderon." *Epidemiology* 16, no. 2 (2005).

Slater, John Rothwell. *Rhees of Rochester.* New York: Harper & Brothers, 1946.

Smith, Wilson, and Thomas Bender. *American Higher Education Transformed: 1940–2005.* Baltimore, MD: Johns Hopkins University Press, 2008.

Thelin, John R. *A History of American Higher Education.* Baltimore, MD: Johns Hopkins University Press, 2004.

Valentine, Alan. *Trial Balance.* New York: Pantheon Books, 1956.

Zapata, Carlos. "Presidential Candidate Jay Stein Visits Campus," *Newspeak of Worcester Polytechnic Institute,* March 29, 1995, http://www.wpi.edu/News/TechNews/950404/STEIN.html.

Dutch elm disease took its toll on the Eastman Quadrangle's original American elms, which were gradually replaced by oaks in the 1970s. The ivy, seen here at one of its high points, is cut back annually to protect the buildings and to allow the details on their façades to be seen.

Some of the earliest photographs of the University's buildings and grounds
were taken by Herman LeRoy Fairchild, who joined the faculty as professor
of geology in 1888 and retired in 1920. One of Fairchild's first projects was to
reorganize the University's collection of more than 40,000 scientific specimens
purchased from Henry Augustus Ward. The museum was located on an upper
floor in Sibley Hall on the Prince Street Campus.

Image Credits

UNLESS OTHERWISE NOTED, ALL OF THE MATERIALS SHOWN IN THIS BOOK ARE DRAWN FROM THE photographic and historical collections held in the University Archives (UA-RBSCP) of the Department of Rare Books, Special Collections, and Preservation, River Campus Libraries. Credit for photographic reproductions of objects, along with the names of photographers whose pictorial work appears, is listed below.

The following staff photographers have contributed to the University's photographic archive during its recent history: Richard Baker, Linn Duncan, Don Eddy, J. Adam Fenster, Joe Gawlowicz, Jeff Goldberg, Sandy Hill, Elizabeth Lamark, James Montanus, Chris Quillen, Shannon Taggart, and Brandon Vick.

Many photographs in the collections have no indication of the source or photographer. The following list attempts to record those who are known to have contributed to the preservation of the University's history on film and who were not already credited with images; in some cases, a full name is unknown: Lee Alderman, George Baker, Greg Becker, Talis Bergmanis, Anthony Boccaccio, Wayne Calabrese, Hal Campbell, Royal Chamberlain, Andy Decker, Gary diPalma, Elsa Efran, David C. Efron, Jack Hanna, P. Hawkins, Sandy Hill, Bruce Horwitz, Rosemary Kendrick, Susan Kost, D. Kovnat, Jim Laragy, Francine Larente, P. Nadell, K. Parker, H. V. Rickner, Charles M. Rowe, Judy Sanchez, Wayne Scarberry, Randall Tagg, Dan Verney, Tony Wells, and Werner Wolff.

Where possible, we have included the graduation class year of alumni pictured in this book. If no class year is noted, the person may not have graduated, or we simply were unable to verify that information.

We are grateful to have had access to the collections in Rush Rhees Library, the Sibley Music Library, the Edward G. Miner Medical Library, and the Memorial Art Gallery as well as the George Eastman House International Museum of Photography and Film.

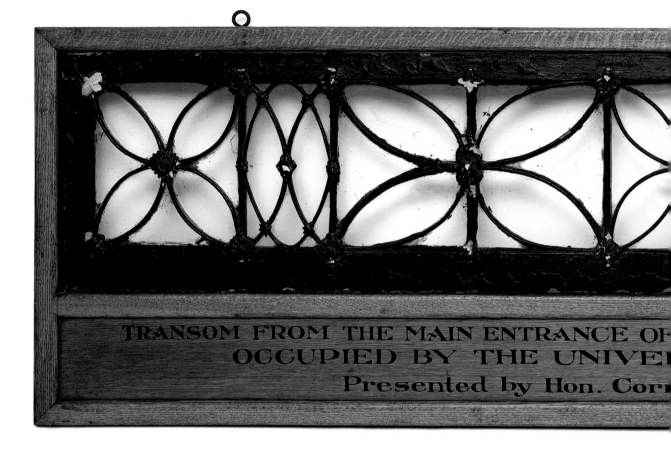

TRANSOM FROM THE MAIN ENTRANCE OF
OCCUPIED BY THE UNIVER
Presented by Hon. Cor

E BUILDING ON WEST MAIN STREET
TY FROM 1850 TO 1861.
us R. Parsons, 1898.

Louis Ouzer (courtesy of the Sibley Music Library): 109

Philip F. Peterson '48 (UA-RBSCP): 68 (center left)

Chris Quillen (UA-RBSCP): 51 (bottom left), 125 (top right, bottom left), 147 (top left), 148, 162, 166

Jim Reed '61 (UA-RBSCP): 111

Stephen Reynolds: 151 (top left)

Susan Bleyler Richardson '58 (UA-RBSCP): 100, 105 (top left, bottom left)

Rochester Photograph Collection (Department of Rare Books, Special Collections and Preservation, River Campus Libraries): 29 (Watson and son)

Rochester City Directory, 1864–65: 3

Department of Rare Books, Special Collections and Preservation, River Campus Libraries: 17 (Corinthian Hall advertisement)

Rochester Review: 64, 152–153 (excluding portraits)

Daniel Schapiro '55 (UA-RBSCP): 105 (tug-of-war)

Joseph Schiff (UA-RBSCP): 24

Scrantom, Wetmore and Co. (Department of Rare Books, Special Collections and Preservation, River Campus Libraries): 26

The Score, 1943 (Eastman School of Music student yearbook): 76

Sibley Music Library: 167

Carol Cronk Stoesen '58 (UA-RBSCP): 98 (top left, bottom left)

Barbara Sutro (UA-RBSCP): 90

Shannon Taggart (UA-RBSCP): 204

Papers of Theta Chi, Alpha Zeta Chapter (UA-RBSCP): 124

Thomas Thackeray Swinburne, 1898 (Department of Rare Books, Special Collections and Preservation, River Campus Libraries): 46

Times Union: 87 (left), 103 (top right)

Unitarian Church Papers (Department of Rare Books, Special Collections and Preservation, River Campus Libraries): 9

University of Rochester Department of Athletics: 19 (men's basketball team)

University of Rochester Medical Center: 194

Brandon Vick (University Communications): 51 (bottom right), 119 (top left, top right, center), 158, 197

The White House: 143

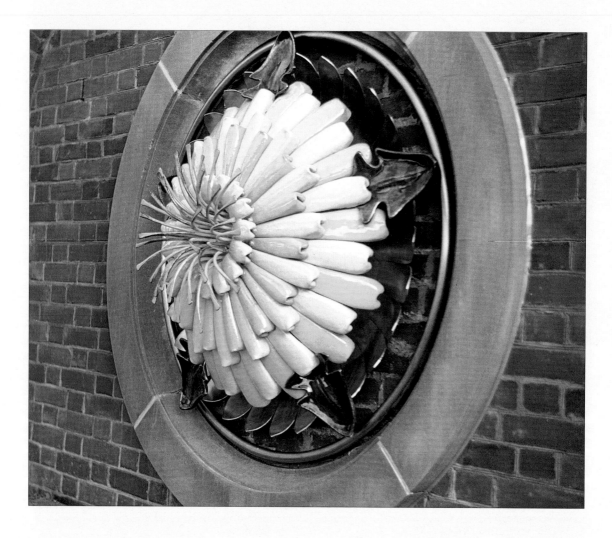

In 1853, Azariah Boody donated eight acres of cow pasture on his East Avenue estate to the University. With an additional 17 acres purchased from Boody, this became the Prince Street Campus. According to legend, the well-fertilized cow pasture produced a profusion of dandelions that distinguished the campus and led to the flower's adoption as the school emblem.

"Dandelion yellow" is one of the University's official colors, and "The Dandelion Yellow" is one of its official songs. The first verse highlights Boody's—and his cows'—contribution:

O, Azariah Boody's cows were sleek and
    noble kine,
They wandered o'er verdant fields where
    grew the dandelion.
And when they drove the cows away
To build a home for knowledge,
They took the color from the flow'r
And gave it to the college.

William Ehrich, assistant professor of fine arts and resident sculptor at the University, was commissioned in 1954 to create an architectural ornament of a stylized dandelion to be mounted on Spurrier Gymnasium facing the Genesee River. Constructed from stainless steel and individual enameled copper petals, the four-foot-diameter flower was later transferred to a more visible location on the façade of the men's gym—now the Goergen Athletic Center—where it looks down on Dandelion Square. Ehrich's other work on campus includes many of the bronze plaques and, most notably, the meridian marker at the center of the Eastman Quadrangle.

Index

University of Rochester. Rochester, N. Y.

Panoramic postcard of the Prince Street Campus showing, from left to right, Sibley Hall, Anderson Hall (with the Anderson statue in front), Reynolds Laboratory, and, far right, the Alumni Gymnasium

Thank You

The staff of Creative Services, a division of University Communications, wishes to thank the following for their assistance with the design and production of this book.

Valerie Alhart
Phyllis Andrews
Mitch Christensen
David Peter Coppen
Rick Crummins
Marie Emmendorfer
Laura Gula
Jenny Hamson
Lucy Harper
Scott Hauser
Christopher Hoolihan
Peter Iglinski
Julia Joshpe
Eugene Kowaluk
Bob Marcotte
Karen McCally
Dennis O'Donnell
Eleanor H. Oi
Lori Packer
Celia Palmer
Stephen Reynolds
Dan Schied
Leonor Sierra
Betsy Slavinskas
John M. Soures
Sophia Tokar
Stephanie Von Bacho
Shirley Zimmer-Kidd

COLOPHON

A NOTE ON THE TYPE

This book was typeset using Garamond Premier Pro, designed by Robert Slimbach, in 10 point on 12 point leading and Myriad Pro in 8 point on 10 point leading. Garamond Premier Pro is a new interpretation of roman typefaces designed by French punchcutter Claude Garamond and italic types by Garamond's contemporary Robert Granjon in the 16th century. Myriad Pro is a 20th-century Adobe original typeface designed by Robert Slimbach and Carol Twombly. Both typefaces were released in the OpenType format, which makes possible large character sets and advanced typographic features as well as consistent encoding, representation, and handling of text.

EDITORIAL STYLE

The University of Rochester's own editorial style guide as well as *The Chicago Manual of Style* informed the editorial decisions herein.

PAPER AND PRESSWORK

The presswork was done at Thomson-Shore, Inc. in Dexter, Michigan, an employee-owned company. The text pages were printed in four-color process on acid-free 80# Huron Gloss Enamel, a Forest Stewardship Council–certified paper.

Owl and *Meliora* on the southwest-facing façade of Dewey Hall